SPARK
NOTES

LIBRARY *of* GREAT AUTHORS

SPARK
NOTES

Library *of* Great Authors

Albert Camus
Lewis Carroll
Fyodor Dostoevsky
Barbara Kingsolver
Gabriel García Márquez
Toni Morrison
Vladimir Nabokov
J.K. Rowling
J.R.R. Tolkien
Virginia Woolf

SPARK
NOTES

LIBRARY *of* GREAT AUTHORS

Fyodor
Dostoevsky

His Life and Works

Stanley P. Baldwin

EDITORIAL DIRECTOR Justin Kestler
EXECUTIVE EDITOR Ben Florman
SERIES EDITOR Emma Chastain

INTERIOR DESIGN Dan Williams

Produced by The Wonderland Press and published by SparkNotes

Spark Publishing
A Division of SparkNotes LLC
120 5th Avenue
New York, NY 10011

10 9 8 7 6 5 4 3 2 1

Please submit comments or questions, or report errors to www.sparknotes.com/errors

Printed and bound in the United States of America

ISBN 1-58663-835-1

Cover photograph copyright © 2003 by Corbis, Inc.

Library of Congress Cataloging-in-Publication Data available on request

Contents

Contents

{
III.
# Crime and Punishment
# 75
}

An Overview 77

Reading *Crime and Punishment* . . . 82

Contents

IV.
{ The Brothers Karamazov } 155

An Overview 153

Reading *The Brothers Karamazov* 111

Contents

{ Topics In Depth }

St. Petersburg, Loved and Hated 22
Immanuel Kant's Beautiful and Sublime 26
Robots in Utopia 36
Russian Nights 40
Denis Diderot and Catherine II 42
Winter Notes on Summer Impressions 46
"The censors are swine" 48
The Overcoat 54
Invisible Man 62
"very strange, very un-Germanic music" 66
The Double 88
Bentham and Mill 92
A Faulty Dialectic 96
Emperor Napoleon, Extraordinary Man 120
Nietzsche's Übermensch 122
Utopia on Earth 124
The Story of Lazarus 128
"Crossing the Irtish Ferry" 148
The Brothers Dostoevsky 164
Schiller and the Ode to Joy 170
The Spanish Inquisition 186
A Quiet Town for a Cruel Retiree 190
The Book of Job 194
The Russian Orthodox Church 196
Oedipus 204
Dostoevsky's Epilepsy 210

SPARK
NOTES

The
LIBRARY *of*
GREAT AUTHORS
series explores the
intimate connection between writing and experience, shedding light on the work of literature's most esteemed authors by examining their lives. The complete LIBRARY *of* GREAT AUTHORS brings an excitingly diverse crowd to your bookshelf, from Fyodor Dostoevsky to J.K. Rowling.

Each book in the LIBRARY *of* GREAT AUTHORS features full-length analysis of the writer's most famous works, including such novels as *Crime and Punishment, Lolita, The Lord of the Rings,* and *Mrs. Dalloway.* Whether you are a reader craving deeper knowledge of your favorite author, a student studying the classics, or a new convert to a celebrated novel, turn to the LIBRARY *of* GREAT AUTHORS for thorough, fascinating, and insightful coverage of literature's best writers.

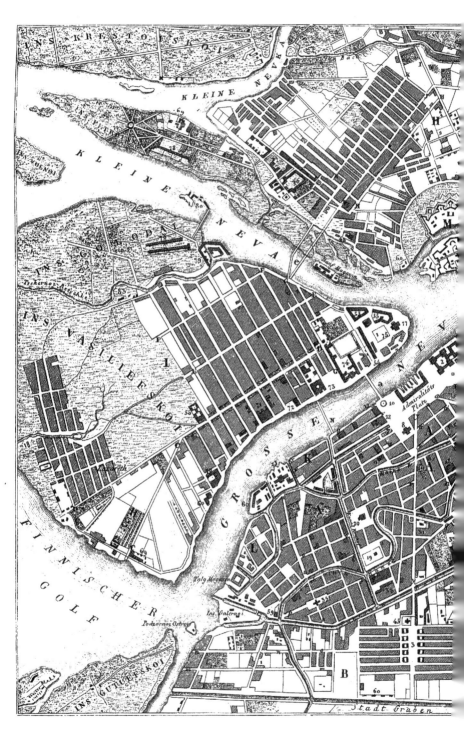

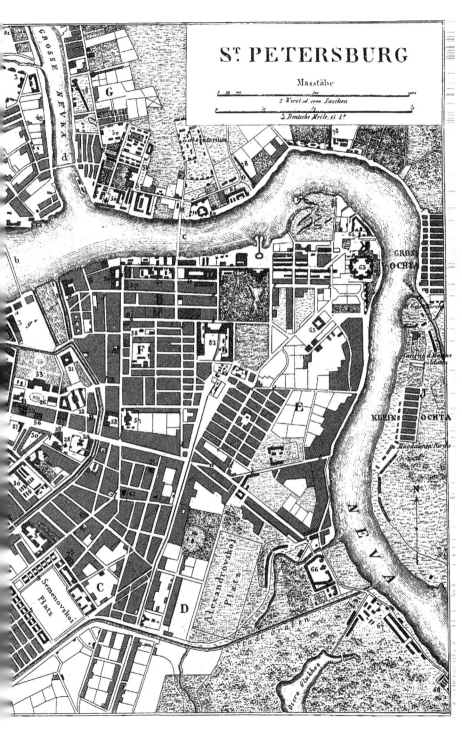

I

THE LIFE OF FYODOR DOSTOEVSKY

Fyodor Mikhailovich Dostoevsky was born in Moscow on October 30, 1821, the second of seven children born to **Maria Fyodorovna** and **Mikhail Andrevich Dostoevsky**. Mikhail Dostoevsky, a physician at a hospital for the poor, was descended from nobility. However, because Dr. Dostoevsky's father and grandfather were Russian Orthodox priests, the Dostoevsky family lived in relative poverty. The doctor taught Latin and literature to his children, but the Bible was the family's favorite book. Maria and Mikhail Dostoevsky fostered an enduring religious devotion in Fyodor and his siblings.

When Fyodor Dostoevsky was ten years old, the family's fortunes improved after his father inherited farming estates in the villages of Daravoe and Cheremoshna in the countryside outside Moscow. There Dostoevsky spent his summers observing his mother's compassionate management of the estates and learning firsthand about peasant life. These experiences strongly influenced Dostoevsky's first novel, *Poor Folk* (1846).

At age twelve, Dostoevsky left home to attend boarding school, where he immersed himself in literature. When Dostoevsky was sixteen, his mother died, and his father grieved inconsolably. Dr. Dostoevsky soon retired to the Daravoe estate and descended into heavy drinking and cruelty toward his servants. He died two years later, murdered—or so the traditional belief holds—at the hands of his ill-treated servants. Officially, apoplexy was identified as the cause of death. It is possible that an ambush brought on Dr. Dostoevsky's apoplectic stroke, or that he died of natural causes. Before his death, Dr. Dostoevsky directed that his two eldest sons—Fyodor and **Mikhail**, who would remain Fyodor's best friend and lifelong correspondent—enter careers in military engineering in St. Petersburg.

During his days in St. Petersburg, Dostoevsky lived the high life, frequenting fine restaurants, theaters, and casinos. With his arrival in St. Petersburg, Dostoevsky fell victim to a compulsive gambling habit that would haunt him for most of his life. Largely because of his gambling, he squandered his military salary as well as the income he received from his father's estate, getting caught in a vicious cycle of spending and debt.

By 1843, Dostoevsky was in dire financial straits. He requested a lump-sum payment of his inheritance and used this money to launch his literary career. His first publication was a translation of **Honore de Balzac**'s (1799–1850) master-piece *Eugenie Grandet*. The modest success of this translation encouraged Dostoevsky to resign his military commission and immediately set to work on *Poor Folk*. This novel, Dostoevsky's first, was serialized in a journal edited by **Nikolay Nekrasov** (1821–1878), a celebrated radical poet of the era who once said of Dostoevsky, "a new Gogol is born to us."

Dostoevsky attended St. Petersburg's progressive literary salons with Nekrasov and became a follower of influential critic **Vissarion Belinsky** (1811–1848) and other Socialist writers. In Moscow's literary salons, he met the novelist **Ivan Turgenev** (1818–1883), who would become another of Russia's great nineteenth-century novelists. Dostoevsky carried on collegial but strained relations with Turgenev throughout his life. Turgenev, along with other members of their social circle, mocked Dostoevsky's first two novels, *Poor Folk* and *The Double*, despite the works' success.

Dostoevsky soon began attending meetings of another radical intellectual salon, the Petrashevsky circle, named for **Mikhail Petrashevsky** (1821–1866), a prominent Socialist radical and a follower of the French utopian Socialist **Charles Fourier** (1772–1837). The Petrashevsky circle was a Socialist group that called for complete transformation of society and belligerently criticized **Tsar Nicholas I** (1796-1855). Meanwhile, to pay off his rising debts, Dostoevsky contributed regularly to a journal called *Notes of the Fatherland*, which published his stories "The Landlady" (1847), "A Novel in Nine Letters" (1847), "White Nights" (1848), "A Weak Heart" (1848), and the serialized novel *Netochnka Nezvanaova* (1848–49).

Dostoevsky's debts became the least of his worries when, in April 1849, he was arrested and imprisoned, partly because of his involvement with the Petrashevsky circle. This catastrophic event silenced Dostoevsky's literary voice for a full decade and radically transformed him and his work. He was sentenced to death for his transgressions. At the eleventh hour, as Dostoevsky stood before a firing squad, Tsar Nicholas commuted the sentence to four years of exile, working in Siberian prison camps.

Dostoevsky's years in Siberia affected him profoundly, leaving marks on both his personal life and his writing. He lived in squalid conditions among petty thieves and murderers. His fellow prisoners and the guards loathed him because he was an educated nobleman. For the entire four years of Dostoevsky's sentence, his only reading material was the New Testament, which became well worn from countless readings. It was during this time that Dostoevsky began to suffer severe attacks of epilepsy, which would plague him the rest of his life.

Still, in Siberia, Dostoevsky maintained his sanity and developed a new understanding of the lives of Russian peasants. He studied the psychology of his fellow prisoners with fascination. They allowed him a first-hand glimpse into the workings of the criminal mind, and he drew on what he learned from them in writing *Crime and Punishment* and his other great post-exile works. Dostoevsky later recounted the horrors of his imprisonment in the fictionalized memoir *House of the Dead* (1860).

By the time of his release from prison in 1854, Dostoevsky was a changed man. The brutalities of his imprisonment had stripped him of much of the idealism of his youth, including his strong belief in radical Socialism. In its place, he developed a more conservative, reactionary outlook on politics and social issues, and he looked for guidance from Christianity.

After the long period of literary deprivation, Dostoevsky read voraciously, focusing on the ancient Greek classics and histories and the German Romantic philosophers **Immanuel Kant** (1724–1804) and **Friedrich Hegel** (1770–1831). These philosophers would shape his newly altered moral, psychological, and aesthetic sensibility.

After leaving prison, Dostoevsky was ordered to serve for five years as a soldier in remote Semipalatansk, now part of Kazakhstan. There he married a widow, **Marya Isaeva** (c. 1824–1864). The two shared a loving but stormy marriage punctuated by Dostoevsky's various infatuations and stunted affairs. After his discharge from military service in 1859, Dostoevsky slowly revived his literary career. In 1861, he moved back to St. Petersburg. There, he and his brother Mikhail launched a new periodical, *Vremya* (*Time*), in which his novel *The Insulted and the Injured* (1861) was published in installments. Dostoevsky also traveled extensively throughout Europe, trips that would become the basis for his memoir *Winter Notes on Summer Impressions* (1863), a scathing indictment of Western rationalism and materialism.

> "**G**od sometimes sends me moments at which I'm absolutely at peace; at those moments I love and find that I am loved by others, and at such moments I composed for myself a credo in which everything is clear and holy for me. That credo is very simple: . . . to believe that there is nothing more beautiful, more profound, more attractive, more wise, more courageous and more perfect than Christ."
>
> **FYODOR DOSTOEVSKY**, IN A LETTER FOLLOWING HIS RELEASE FROM PRISON

Fyodor Dostoevsky

After government censors shut down *Time* in 1863, the brothers Dostoevsky launched another magazine, *Epokha* (*Epoch*). The inaugural issue featured the first half of a new novel by Fyodor Dostoevsky, *Notes from Underground* (1864). This novel is a masterpiece of the psychology of human alienation and a bitter polemic fueled in part by Dostoevsky's long-held resentment toward his former radical intellectual colleagues and the cultural nihilism they fostered during the revolutionary era of post-1860s Russia.

In the early months of 1864, Dostoevsky's wife died of tuberculosis after a long illness. Weeks later, Dostoevsky was devastated by the unexpected death of his brother Mikhail. His life fell into disarray as he struggled to support his brother's family, alternating between keeping *Epoch* afloat and gambling away the remainder of his earnings. In 1865, Dostoevsky signed a contract with a somewhat disreputable book publisher and temporarily escaped his rising debts by moving to Berlin. There he began work on the first few sections of *Crime and Punishment* (1866). After returning to Russia a few months later, he finished *The Gambler* (1865), a novel with which he planned to fulfill his book contract. With his deadline looming, he had no choice but to hire a young woman, **Anna Snitkina**, to transcribe the manuscript from his disorganized pile of notes. Not only did Anna deliver the manuscript on time, she became the new love of Dostoevsky's life.

> "**D**ostoevsky is always perverse, always impure, always an evil thinker and a marvelous seer."
>
> **D.H. LAWRENCE**

After marrying Anna in 1867, Dostoevsky enjoyed renewed stability and entered the most prolific period of his career. The couple traveled through Europe for four years, during which time Dostoevsky completed his novels *The Idiot* (1868) and *The Eternal Husband* (1868). He also began work on an epic project he had long been planning, which eventually became his last three novels: *The Possessed* (1872), a work of political disillusionment about the dangers of radicalism; *A Raw Youth* (1875), a fictionalized account of Dostoevsky's adolescence; and the author's last novel, *The Brothers Karamazov* (1879), a profound masterpiece of family, religion, and moral disintegration.

Dostoevsky's fame expanded in Russia in the 1870s, and he became widely recognized in St. Petersburg and throughout the country. Because his politics were now decidedly reactionary, Dostoevsky was invited to edit a conservative publication, *The Citizen*. As a supplement to the magazine, he published installments of *Diary of a Writer* (1876–1878), filled with political and literary ruminations from his later years.

In 1880, Dostoevsky was asked to deliver the keynote speech at an event honoring the life of Pushkin. His impassioned oration about the fraternity of humankind and Russia's exalted place in European culture cemented Dostoevsky's high standing among the Russian people. The crowd roared with applause and rushed the stage to embrace their compatriot and literary hero.

Six months later, as he began to piece together notes on his next novel, Dostoevsky succumbed to the chronic lung problems from which he suffered in his later years. He died on January 28, 1881. Upon learning of his death, fellow literary giant **Leo Tolstoy** (1828–1910) remarked, "I never saw the man, and never had any direct relations with him, yet suddenly when he died, I understood that he was the nearest and dearest and most necessary of men to me." Dostoevsky's funeral was attended by thousands of mourners, and he was buried with high religious honors in St. Petersburg's venerated Tikhvinsky Cemetery.

Fyodor Dostoevsky

People, Events, and Trends

That Influenced Dostoevsky's Work

Dostoevsky wrote during one of the most important eras in Russia's literary and intellectual history. It was a time of volatile politics that culminated in the Russian Revolution of 1917.

Peter the Great: No Russian tsar had a greater impact on the national character of Russia than Tsar Peter I, also known as **Peter the Great** (1672–1725). It was during his reign in the late seventeenth and early eighteenth centuries that cultural influences from Western Europe in industry, education, and even the calendar were introduced to Russia. Using Western models and architects, Peter the Great designed and built the new Russian capital of St. Petersburg. These westernizing influences stoked tensions among those who wanted cultural inspiration to come solely from Russia's Slavic history and those who wanted to allow the influence of Western culture. These intellectual and political disputes polarized the two groups, which were known as "Slavophiles" and "Westernizers." Dostoevsky was a passionate Slavophile who believed that Western influences on Russian culture and philosophy would weaken the character of his motherland.

Napoleon and a New Europe: The great French conqueror and emperor **Napoleon I** (1769–1821) altered the map of Europe with his many early-nineteenth-century conquests, which extended from Russia to the pyramids of Egypt. But in 1812, Napoleon's vast army was overwhelmed and pushed out by Russian troops. The Russian victory marked the beginning of the end of Napoleon's supremacy and the rebirth of a powerful, nationalistic Russian state. Napoleon died in 1821, the same year Dostoevsky was born.

Nicholas I and His Reign: The reigning tsar during the first half of Dostoevsky's life was **Nicholas I** (1796–1855). On his first day in power in 1825, Nicholas set the tone for his thirty-year reign by crushing an uprising of the liberal Decembrists, who agitated for a constitutional government. Following this inauspicious beginning, Nicholas's minister of culture demanded adherence to the motto "autocracy, orthodoxy, nationality," and the secret police clamped down on radical political activity. During this era, Russia enjoyed a golden age in literature with the ascendance of Nikolay Gogol, Mikhail Lermontov, and Aleksandr Pushkin, whose works together painted a vivid portrait of characters from all walks of Russian life. Intellectual life also thrived during this time, and despite the mandates of the state to promote Russian ideals, German and French literature and philosophy were debated in secret intellectual salons throughout the 1830s and 1840s.

The Feudal System: During Dostoevsky's lifetime, Russia's economy and society were based on the feudal system of nobles and serfs that was established during medieval times. Under the feudal system, all property—land and its accompanying peasant workers (serfs)—was controlled by the tsar (king) and distributed among a hierarchy of noble landowners. With the rise of a new educated middle class in most of Europe during the sixteenth and seventeenth centuries, the feudal system slowly disintegrated. In 1861, Russia officially abolished serfdom. Still, the system's influence lingered into the early twentieth century, ending abruptly with the Russian Revolution in 1917.

Liberalism, Rationalism, and Socialism in Europe: Following the scientific and intellectual advancements of the Age of Enlightenment (also known as the Age of Reason) in the eighteenth century, Russian intellectuals and liberal revolutionaries explored the ideas of natural rights, egalitarianism, and representative democracy that had developed in France, England, and America. The Enlightenment worldview cast humanity in an optimistic light, celebrating the powers of reason and the scope of human knowledge. The hopeful belief that suffering could be eased with a scientific and rational approach to problems was popularized by utopian Socialist thinkers such as **Charles Fourier** (1772–1837) in France and utilitarian philosophers such as **Jeremy Bentham** (1748–1832) and **John Stuart Mill** (1806–1873) in England.

An Age of Revolutions: In mid-nineteenth century Europe, revolutionaries who touted Enlightenment and Socialist values rose up against established monarchies. Ending in France with the February Revolution of 1848, these revolutions generally failed after being forcefully silenced or taken over by political moderates. But these movements sounded an alarm for reigning European monarchs who had vivid memories of the horrors of the French Revolution (1789–1804).

Fyodor Dostoevsky

In Russia, the 1848 uprisings prompted Nicholas I to crack down on radical groups. This crackdown led to Dostoevsky's arrest and imprisonment.

Russian Radicalism and Nihilism: Despite the tsarist counterattack on revolutionaries, radical ferment continued in Russia in the latter half of the nineteenth century. In particular, utilitarian and utopian Socialist philosophy influenced the radical Russian intellectuals and writers of the 1860s. Because radicals rejected liberal ideals in favor of more extreme Socialist beliefs, and because of their scorn of tsarist Russian society in general, their philosophy was similar to anarchism and nihilism, systems of belief that reject all social values. Such radicals became popularly known as the Nihilists after Ivan Turgenev (1818–1883) coined the term in his celebrated novel *Fathers and Sons* (1862). One of the most prominent Nihilists was Nikolay Chernyshevsky, whose novel *What Is To Be Done?* became a handbook for young radicals throughout Russia during the decade. Radical students coordinated their efforts in the 1870s and 1880s, culminating in the assassination of Tsar Alexander II in 1881, just two months after Dostoevsky's death. Later the radicals' beliefs gave way to the revolutionary Communist ideology that triumphed in the Russian Revolution of 1917.

Dostoevsky's Literary Context

His Influences and Impact

Dostoevsky's novels are masterpieces of human psychology. *Notes from Underground* and *Crime and Punishment* investigate the psychology of their tortured main characters. Both novels also explore the nature of mankind through the microcosm of one man. Later, writers such as **Albert Camus** (1913-1960) and **Jean-Paul Sartre** (1905-1980) placed great importance on Dostoevsky's despairing, anxious, self-aware characters as early examples of existential philosophy and literature. *Notes from Underground* can also be read as a parody of the utopian rationalist ideals of Dostoevsky's involvement wtih radicals prior to his term in Siberia. *Crime and Punishment* is not only an existential and psychological novel, but detective fiction as well. In later works, such as *The Brothers Karamazov,* Dostoevsky examines man as he operates within familial and religious contexts.

Dostoevsky studied the works of Russia's foremost Romantic poet, **Mikhail Lermontov** (1814–1841), as well as those of Lermontov's celebrated English predecessor, **Lord Byron** (1788–1824). Dostoevsky's literary material is partly inspired by the fiction of **Nikolay Gogol** (1809–1852), whose tales of provincial and city life influenced Dostoevsky's views of the average Russian. Most prominent among Dostoevsky's influences was **Aleksandr Pushkin** (1799–1837), whose gritty tales of Russian folk life encouraged Dostoevsky's Slavic consciousness and nationalism. Among his other favorites were the French Romantic novelist and poet **Victor Hugo** (1802–1885), Scottish Romantic poet and novelist **Sir**

Walter Scott (1771–1832), and especially the German Romantic dramatist and poet **Friedrich von Schiller** (1759–1805), whose moral and aesthetic idealism influenced many of Dostoevsky's works. Along with his main Russian contemporaries, Leo Tolstoy and Ivan Turgenev, Dostoevsky helped popularize Russian literature internationally.

II

NOTES FROM UNDER-GROUND

An Overview

Key Facts

Genre: Philosophical and psychological novel

Date of First Publication: 1863

Setting: Mid-1800s; St. Petersburg, Russia

Narrator: Nameless, first-person narrator, alienated from society and plagued by extreme consciousness

Plot Overview: A nameless, alienated narrator retreats to the underground to confess, examine his actions, and torture himself with logic and reason.

Style, Technique, & Language

Style—Imagery and Metaphor: Several symbols in *Notes from Underground* help define the paradoxical identity of the Underground Man.

Underground: On a basic level, the underground is the narrator's tiny, stuffy apartment on the fringes of St. Petersburg. On a symbolic level, it is a manifestation of the narrator's highly developed consciousness—the curse of reason that enables him to see the contradictions of the outside world. The underground is the metaphysical universe that imprisons the narrator. He is trapped in the underground of his consciousness, halted by inertia and a circular struggle to shut off the reasoning that trapped him in the first place.

Fyodor Dostoevsky

Crystal Palace: The Palace symbolizes the stifling boredom and un-humanness of utopian society. According to utopian ideals, we could live in a Crystal Palace of happiness if only we would follow the mandates of our innate rationalism. The Underground Man cannot stand the idea of the Crystal Palace. In his view, the Palace destroys life's meaning. To live in it, humans would have to live according to pure rationalism, thereby forfeiting their individual free will. For the Underground Man, the meaning of life consists in living day to day and exercising free will, including the free will to make stupid, irrational decisions.

"How much the mere tone of *Notes from the Underground* is worth!"

LEV SHESTOV

The Mouse and the Fly: These creatures stand for the two different ways in which the Underground Man views himself. In the underground, he sees himself as a mouse—an impotent creature, but one with the will to choose. As he says, "the main thing is that he, he himself, considers himself to be a mouse; nobody asks him to do so, and that's the important point." In the underground in Part I, the narrator defines himself and takes comfort in his ability to choose his identity. But in Part II, the narrator seeks for *others* to define him and assign him an identity. He obsessively imagines how others see him, and all he can do is appear intelligent and morally superior. Regardless of his attempts to make others see him as a superior man worthy of respect, the Underground Man believes that everyone sees him as a fly, an annoying creature with no purpose. The fly symbolizes the identity created for the Underground Man in the outside world.

Technique—Inverse Structure: The novel's two-part structure progresses backward in time. In Part I, the Underground Man reflects on the ideas and characters that we see in Part II. In Part I, "Underground," the narrator philosophically explains his psychology. Part II takes place sixteen years before Part I, examining the experiences that brought the Underground Man to the underground in the first place. In contrast to the cramped, claustrophobic apartment setting of Part I, Part II takes place in the outside world. It also features elements of a traditional novel, such as characters and action, in contrast to the stifling world of paralyzed thought depicted in Part I. As a polemical treatise, Part I takes aim at the rational egoism of Chernyshevsky along with the Enlightenment and utilitarian philosophers who guided Chernyshevsky's thought. Part II is an attack on the Romantic writers of the 1840s who put forth grand ideals, such as the notion of selfless love, but do nothing to act on those ideals.

Language—Parodying Philosophers and Bookworms: The language of the Underground Man's *Notes* enacts one of Dostoevsky's primary intentions, to show how an overdeveloped mind can become trapped in its own cleverness. The Underground Man is paralyzed, suspended between reason and compassion, thought and action, ideal and reality. These contradictions define his character. In Part I, the Underground Man speaks of his thoughts and reason, but we see the limits of this kind of reason when all his thoughts and logic add up to nothing. His philosophical tone duplicates the tone of theorists against whom he argues, mainly the rationalists of the 1860s. Dostoevsky condemns philosophers who spend their time thinking but take no action by making the Underground Man speak in their style: carefully analyzed sentences, an occasional stream-of-consciousness style, passionate rambling packed with contradictions, and a precise, if confused, logic. By achieving nothing with rationalism's devices, the Underground Man exposes the purposelessness of following pure ideology.

In Part II, the Underground Man changes his tone, using one more similar to Romantic literary works of the 1840s. In fact, this new tone resembles that of Dostoevsky's earlier novels. The Underground Man loses himself in fantasies of a literary life. He has no experience of reality and instead bases all of his interactions in the outside world on what he has read in books. Thus, he can describe the events that take place only in literary language. Dostoevsky suggests that, like philosophers crippled by their own logic, readers can be crippled by the anemic knowledge of real life that comes from too extensive a knowledge of literature.

Characters in *Notes from Underground*

Apollon: The only servant of the Underground Man. Apollon is not paid well and does not do much. He has learned his master's weaknesses and dominates the Underground Man. The Underground Man loathes Apollon for his disrespect and recalcitrance.

Army Officer: A haughty, dignified military man. The Underground Man wants to pick a "literary" fight with him at a tavern, but the Officer ignores the Underground Man because he is not worthy of his attention. For two years, the Underground Man devises a plan to grab the Officer's attention by bumping into him while strolling on the grand boulevard of St. Petersburg.

Boy: The only friend of the Underground Man during the "penal servitude" of his school days. The boy learned to worship him, but the Underground Man later despised him for it and rejected him.

Ferfichkin: An arrogant friend of Simonov. The Underground Man twice challenges Ferfichkin to a duel, and Ferfichkin mockingly rises to the challenge.

> " The central concern of all Dostoevsky's work is a series of questions about identity; not only 'who am I?' but 'how can I be?' or 'if I am that, who, then, are others?' "
>
> MICHAEL HOLQUIST

Liza: A young prostitute. The Underground Man dominates Liza and supposedly saves her from her dissolute life but later rejects her after she falls in love with him. Liza symbolizes the Romantic notion of innocence and the redemptive power of love.

Olympia: A favorite prostitute at the brothel visited by the partygoers and the Underground Man. She once laughed at the Underground Man and insulted his appearance.

Anton Antonych Setochkin: An office chief in the civil service and the host of weekly salons. Setochkin lends money to the Underground Man on several occasions.

Simonov: A former schoolmate of the Underground Man. Simonov is the only person the Underground Man considers a friend, although the Underground Man correctly suspects that Simonov despises him. Simonov lends money to the Underground Man so that he can go to the brothel after the dinner party.

Trudolyubov: A friend of Simonov's. Trudolyubov attends the planning session and dinner party for Zverkov. He is a military man and a distant relative of Zverkov, whom he worships for his success. The Underground Man calls Trudolyubov "insignificant" but notes his physical strength.

Underground Man: The nameless, solitary, self-conscious narrator of the novel. He lives hidden away in a run-down apartment in St. Petersburg. The Underground Man resents his readers and society around him but feels unable to change his situation. He is an admitted masochist whose only pleasure comes from knowing that others despise him because he irritates them. His willful acts of spite are the only remnants of his freedom.

Zverkov: A former schoolmate of the Underground Man. The Underground Man remembers despising Zverkov for his arrogance and empty boasting. When they meet again at a dinner, Zverkov seems willing to let bygones be bygones, but the Underground Man is determined either to become friends with him or to humiliate him.

Reading *Notes from Underground*

PART ONE: UNDERGROUND
Chapter I

The narrator, hereafter known as the **Underground Man**, begins his monologue. He is forty years old and describes himself as a sick, spiteful, and generally unpleasant person. He lives in a run-down apartment in St. Petersburg, even though he knows that the city is expensive and bad for his health. He supports himself with a small inheritance he received one year ago, a windfall that enabled him to retire from his job. His liver is diseased but out of spite he refuses to see a doctor, although he respects physicians. His spite, he says, is not necessarily directed toward doctors, although he cannot explain "precisely who will be hurt" by this spite. He has been living under these circumstances for twenty years.

The Underground Man worked as a civil servant until his inheritance enabled him to quit his job. Working for the public, he says, permitted him the amusement of being rude to the petitioners who brought their problems to him.

> "The ellipsis after the opening sentence of *Notes from Underground* is like a window affording us a first glimpse of one of the most remarkable characters in literature, one who has been placed among the bearers of modern consciousness alongside Don Quixote, Hamlet, and Faust."
>
> **RICHARD PEVEAR**

Then the Underground Man quickly reverses himself and says that he was *not* actually rude to his petitioners and that if anyone had shown him a sign of warmth, he might have responded differently. Then he changes his mind again and says he would have continued being spiteful anyway, since, out of shame, he would have rejected any overtures to friendship. He changes positions once again and admits that the descriptions of his nastiness as a bureaucrat were untrue and he has just lied to the reader out of spite. The Underground Man says he once experienced "contradictory elements" within himself that were the opposite of spite. Although these feelings swarmed inside him, he repressed them until there came a time in his life when finally he got "fed up."

The Underground Man realizes that he is intelligent, and says he can be neither bad nor good, since "an intelligent man cannot seriously become anything." His intelligence means he has no character at all. He then argues the opposite case, saying that people of character and action are never intelligent. The Underground Man gives further descriptions of his "nasty," smelly apartment. The chapter concludes with the Underground Man's decision to continue talking about himself, since he says this is what gives a "decent man" the greatest pleasure.

UNDERSTANDING AND INTERPRETING
Part One, Chapter I

An Infuriating Narrator: The mood of the novel is immediately paradoxical. From the opening sentences, we face a vexing first-person narrator who delivers a rambling, sometimes baffling, monologue. We wonder, who is this man, and why does he talk in riddles? Why does he feel such spite? Is he insane? The narrator speaks in contradictions, making opinionated statements and then immediately reversing his position and calling himself a liar. *Notes from Underground* reads like a journal or diary, as though the narrator decided to pick up a pen and write down the thoughts that torment him. (One translation of the title, in fact, is *Diary from Under the Floor.*) Unlike traditional diaries, in which the diarist writes primarily for his own eyes, this diary is addressed directly to an imagined audience, whom the Underground Man sometimes calls "gentlemen." He engages in a mock dialogue with this imagined audience. Later, the Underground Man compares his work to a "confession," a highly personal disclosure of his thoughts and sins. Dostoevsky originally called Part I "Confessions."

The Antihero Invites Our Aversion: The opening sentences of the novel illustrate the Underground Man's compulsion to provoke our disgust. He starts with "I am a sick man," pauses, and then describes himself as not sick but "spiteful" and "unpleasant." By describing himself as "sick," he risks eliciting pity from his audience. By characterizing himself as "spiteful" and "unpleasant," he presents himself in a different light, intentionally warding off a sympathetic reaction. It seems that the Underground Man does not want to be liked—an unusual attitude for a human being and shocking for a fictional character of Dostoevsky's era. The romantic novels of Dostoevsky's early career and of the nineteenth century in general featured protagonists whom readers could sympathize with and applaud. In contrast, the Underground Man is an "antihero" (as he will later call himself) —a man who has few redeeming qualities and does not care if we dislike him.

Insane or Just Tormented?: The Underground Man's reversals, contradictions, and sometimes disorganized narrative make us to wonder whether he is mentally ill. He is angry and spiteful toward his readers as well as people he encountered long ago in his work. He has an unhealthy appetite for pain; his liver is diseased, but he refuses to get treatment since he enjoys the pain it brings him, saying, "Good, let it hurt even more!" He tells a story about his behavior as a civil servant and then immediately says the story is a lie. He sounds passionate and confused, sometimes arguing with himself as if he is two men: "I shall not leave Petersburg! . . . Oh what difference does it make whether or not I leave Petersburg?" The Underground Man is fascinating and grotesque because he is possibly mad. We want to keep watching and listening so we can figure out what ails him.

The Underground, Prison and Refuge: The narrator lives on the outskirts of St. Petersburg, in what is a prison to him, since here he is thoroughly alienated from the outside world. Because his character is an embodiment of his dwelling, he refers to himself as the "Underground Man." He makes his smelly apartment sound like a filthy hole dug into the ground. Although he sees his

ST. PETERSBURG, LOVED AND HATED

The rivers, grand boulevards, and dark alleys of St. Petersburg loom in the background of many of Dostoevsky's greatest works. The author had an ambivalent attitude toward his home city. In 1703, Peter the Great had conceived the city as the new capital of Russia. It was built in the far north of Russia on drained swampland, not far from the border of modern-day Finland. It was fashioned as an efficient model of European progress. Italian and French architects, whom Peter had imported after extensive tours of Western Europe, designed the city. Dostoevsky saw decadence and empty Western materialism in these European influences, and he thought they opposed true Russian values. Nonetheless, the city became the educational and cultural center of Russia. It was home to Pushkin and Tolstoy, as well as to Dostoevsky and, later, Nobel laureate Joseph Brodsky. In 1914, revolutionaries renamed the city Petrograd to purge it of the Germanic root "-burg." After Lenin's death in 1924, the city was again renamed, this time Leningrad. In 1991, the post-Soviet nation of Russia brought back the name originally bestowed by Peter the Great, and the city was once again called St. Petersburg.

apartment as a filthy prison, he also considers it a refuge from the outside world of St. Petersburg—and in another contradiction, although he seeks refuge from St. Petersburg, he also feels loyalty to the city.

Hybrid St. Petersburg: St. Petersburg was (and is) the center of Russian cultural and intellectual life. It makes sense that the Underground Man lives there since he thinks of himself as an intellectual. St. Petersburg was a hybrid, a Russian city constructed to be a model of Western progress and enlightenment. It became the center of cultural exchange between Russia and Europe. The Underground Man is Russian, but he is inextricably attached to the Western influences of the city, which include the philosophies that reflect the contradictions within him. He will, in turn, blame the culture of the city and its philosophies for his predicament in the underground.

Paralyzed by Intelligence: The Underground Man lives in a state of perpetual inertia, which he blames on his intelligence. He says that intelligent people like himself are fated never to become anything. He contrasts the intelligent people to what he calls "men of action," who are limited in intelligence but possess character. The Underground Man, intelligent but characterless, does nothing in his underground corner except think. Even his method of thinking accomplishes little. The Underground Man can barely move forward with his thoughts because they consist of endless reversals and paradoxes. He can hardly articulate a complete thought because of his capriciousness and lack of resolve.

The Battle of Reason and Irrationality: Forces of reason and irrationality do battle in the Underground Man, leaving him in a frenzy. Irrationality consistently triumphs over logic. The Underground Man decides to stay in St. Petersburg, despite the fact that St. Petersburg is expensive and bad for his health. He refuses to see a doctor when he is sick, even though he understands the rationality of doing so, because he rejects medical science as "superstition." He is guided by something other than reason, and he acts illogically. His reasons for acting this way will become clearer in the chapters that follow.

Dostoevsky's Note: Dostoevsky includes a short introductory footnote to the title of Part I. In it, he states that the narrator of these *Notes* is fictional, but "nevertheless, such persons . . . not only may, but must, exist in our society, if we take into consideration the circumstances which led to the formation of our society." He says his intention is to show us "one of the characters of our recent past" who represents "the current generation." Dostoevsky wrote this note in Russia during the 1860s, an era during which the cultural ground in Russia was shifting dramatically. Radical Socialists in Russian political and intellectual circles were sanctifying Western ideas of utopian Socialism and utilitarianism. These intellectuals were popularly known as Nihilists because they rejected society's values—a rejection that would turn to revolutionary violence in decades to follow. "Representative of the current generation," the Underground Man stands for the Nihilists who embrace new Western philosophies and turn their backs on their own society's values. But Dostoevsky also calls the character a representative of the "recent past," which may mean that the Underground Man stands for Nihilists of the more romantic, less rebellious era when Socialist ideals were looked upon as a benevolent force for change.

PART ONE
Chapter II

The Underground Man tells us that he is "overly conscious" and that his consciousness is like a disease that prevents him from doing anything with himself. He argues that modern culture provides too much consciousness and that a fraction of this consciousness would be more than sufficient. He has noticed in his past that whenever he becomes capable of discerning the subtleties of all things "beautiful and sublime," he simultaneously commits the most horrific and depraved acts (acts which he does not describe). The more conscious he becomes of beauty, the more incapacitated he feels by it.

This inhibition soon becomes his everyday condition, and he gives up struggling against it. His consciousness shows him the irrationality of seeing good but feeling compelled toward malevolence. This irrationality tortures the Underground Man with shame, but from that shame he derives a secret pleasure. The Underground Man reveals that he began writing these *Notes* to discover whether these feelings of incongruity are unique to him or shared by others. Consciousness, he maintains, allows us to recognize that we cannot fundamentally change ourselves. Unchangeable laws of nature make it impossible to deviate from our true character. But awareness of this impossibility offers us no consolation.

The Underground Man considers himself "guilty" because he is more clever than everyone around him, but he also calls himself an "innocent victim" of the laws of nature that have given him one unchangeable character and prevented him from being able to change that character. The Underground Man returns to the idea of shame. He tells us that he is capable of deriving pleasure from despair and humiliation, and that, in fact, "the most intense pleasures occur in despair, especially when you're very acutely aware of the hopelessness of your own predicament." If he were slapped in the face, he says, it would be enjoyable for him, even though he is a proud and vain man. However, he would not forgive a person who slapped him in the face, since the person's actions were prescribed by the laws of nature. Because the person acted in accordance with these laws, forgiveness would be unwarranted. By that rationale, he says, it would not make sense to seek revenge on the face-slapper.

UNDERSTANDING AND INTERPRETING
Part One, Chapter II

A Surfeit of Consciousness: The Underground Man is trapped in the maze of his own consciousness. He repeatedly calls himself "overly conscious." He thinks and rethinks his arguments and his situation. The weight of his thoughts overwhelms him and leaves him paralyzed. He blames this situation partially on St. Petersburg. He says that because he is a "cultured man" living in this "enlightened" city, his consciousness has spun out of control. Later in the chapter, the Underground Man says that an excessive degree of consciousness is a "disease."

The Unenlightened Enlightenment Man: The Underground Man argues that too much consciousness is a disease, which contradicts the philosophies of the Age of Enlightenment (a.k.a. the Age of Reason). The Age of Enlightenment placed ultimate importance on consciousness, which led to the greatest proliferation of philosophical inquiry and culture in European history. Enlightenment philosophers argued that human beings are inclined toward moral action and can achieve perfection through enlightened self-interest. This belief took an extreme form in the ideology of Russian radicals of the 1860s. In the Underground Man's opinion, this culture of enlightenment infects people with a "disease" of consciousness. Despite the fact that the Underground Man sees himself as a product of Enlightenment thinking, he actually represents the *inverse* of the enlightened human being. According to Enlightenment thinkers, humans live by a social contract and feel pleasure in doing good. The Underground Man, in contrast, is inclined toward immoral behavior. Instead of seeing people as essentially good, he sees only baseness and shame. Instead of reacting with virtue to the "beautiful and sublime" of nature, he reacts by committing depraved acts. The Underground Man argues that the Enlightenment had too rosy a view of basic human nature. If people are not essentially decent, enlightenment in the form of too much consciousness may do more harm than good.

IMMANUEL KANT'S
BEAUTIFUL AND SUBLIME

The Underground Man's conception of the "beautiful and sublime" relates most importantly to Kant's *Observations on the Feeling of the Beautiful and Sublime* (1756) and to his later *Groundwork of the Metaphysics of Morals* (1785). In these texts, Kant argues that a person's moral principles are not the result of individual identity, but rather, are universal and based on nature's limitless beauty. The "sublime" is pain or anxiety associated with our failure to understand this limitless beauty. This feeling of the "sublime" is internal and subjective. When a person experiences the sublime, he chooses to act morally, according to the ways of nature. Upon feeling the sublime, the Underground Man demonstrates anxiety of the sort Kant describes. In contrast to Kant's theory, however, the anxiety causes the Underground Man to act immorally.

Beautiful and Sublime: The phrase "beautiful and sublime" is often repeated in *Notes from Underground* and is mocked by the Underground Man, who puts the phrase in quotation marks. Enlightenment thinker Edmund Burke first used the phrase "beautiful and sublime," and German Romantic philosopher Immanuel Kant suggested that "beautiful and sublime" means that an appreciation of beauty leads to greater morality. The Underground Man mocks of Kant's interpretation. Beauty inspires the Underground Man not to behave morally, but to behave badly.

A Slave to Natural Law: The Underground Man puts forth an extreme interpretation of natural law in this chapter. Enlightenment philosophers said that human behavior ought to be dictated by immutable laws of nature. Through the Underground Man's extreme extension of this idea, a person is a slave to his own individual nature. One's personality has been prescribed and cannot change, and therefore one cannot be blamed for one's actions. The Underground Man uses the example of a slap in the face to prove this point. He says it would be useless for him to forgive the person who slapped him, because the slap was prescribed by nature. It would be equally futile to take revenge against that person for slapping him, because by his own nature, he cannot take action. The Underground Man has decided that his nature is to be paralyzed by his overactive consciousness.

> "From *Notes from the Underground* and on, Dostoevsky is no longer content to rehash his old certainties and to justify himself in his own eyes . . . He exorcises his demons, one after the other, by embodying them in his novels."
>
> **RENÉ GIRARD**

Superiority, Humiliation, and Pride: Dostoevsky demonstrates how a man can both enjoy humiliation and maintain pride. The Underground Man is prideful, but he likes being humiliated, and the marriage of these contradictory pleasures leads to his superiority complex. Because the Underground Man considers himself intelligent and cultured, he feels superior to those around him. When he is insulted, he feels humiliated. Paradoxically, this humiliation only increases his pride because he interprets the insult as proof that he is morally superior to the person who humiliates him. The Underground Man undergoes this masochistic cycle over and over again.

PART ONE
Chapter III

The Underground Man examines "spontaneous men and men of action" who are capable of taking revenge. He says these men rush forward into action like charging bulls. They can only be stopped by a wall. The wall soothes them because it means nothing more can be done. These "men of action" are different from the thinking person, like the Underground Man, who sees the wall and uses it as an excuse not to act in the first place. The Underground Man respects and envies spontaneous people, and he thinks that although they are stupid, they are "normal."

The Underground Man suggests that a thinking person like himself, one with an acute sense of consciousness, would consider himself as a mouse when surrounded by men of action. The Underground Man says of the mouse that "the main thing is that he, he himself, considers himself to be a mouse; nobody asks him to do so, and that's the important point." Even though the mouse can choose to be a mouse, he is an impotent creature compared to these charging bulls. If the mouse wanted to take revenge against someone, he would surround himself with so many doubts and questions that he would make it impossible to carry his revenge to fruition. Instead, he would stand by and do nothing while men of action laughed at him. Then he would feign contempt for them and crawl back into his mouse hole in the underground.

There, the humiliated mouse would stay, recalling all the insults he suffered during the previous forty years and developing malice for those around him. The mouse's revenge comes only in trivial acts, and the mouse is aware that he himself is suffering more than the targets of his revenge. Despite this misery, the mouse can find a strange pleasure in being slapped in the face. The Underground Man argues that no one will understand what he has just said unless they have been slapped in the face, although he admits that he himself has never been slapped in the face.

The Underground Man then returns to the idea of the wall. People of action will always submit to a wall. A wall stands for the limits that the laws of nature, science, and mathematics impose. These laws clarify our descent from monkeys, that "a drop of your fat is dearer to you than the lives of one hundred thousand of your fellow creatures," and that "two times two is a fact of mathematics." When confronted with these laws, says the Underground Man, there is "no reason to make faces. Just accept it as it is." He dislikes the wall, and although he will not break through it, he will not reconcile himself to it just because it is there. While other people, such as men of action, may be consoled by the impossibility of the laws of nature, the Underground Man takes pleasure in his consciousness that the wall exists and in refusing to reconcile himself with that fact. He refuses to accept the futility of his own existence in the face of these walls by convincing himself that *he* is to blame for them. But it becomes clear that no one is to blame for the walls. In spite of the difficulty of finding someone to blame, "it hurts you just the same, and the more you don't know, the more it hurts!"

UNDERSTANDING AND INTERPRETING
Part One, Chapter III

The Freedom to Be Ridiculous: The Underground Man finds pleasure and freedom in refusing to accept the laws of nature. He revolts against convention and against those who would accuse him of silliness. When the Underground Man confronts impossibility, he does not give up immediately, as does the theoretical man of action. But he does not break through the wall of impossibility either. He takes pleasure in knowing that the wall—in this case, the laws of nature—exists. He takes pleasure in being unconcerned by the wall, saying, "Good Lord, what do I care about the laws of nature and arithmetic when for some reason I dislike all these laws and I dislike the fact that two times two makes four?" He refuses to reconcile himself to the laws of nature even if people claim that his refusal itself is an impossibility: "'For goodness sake!' they'll shout at you, 'it's impossible to protest: it's two times two makes four! Nature doesn't ask your opinion.'" With underground freedom, the Underground Man can refute the truths of the world. He can take the blame for everything in the universe, if it makes him feel happy. He does not actually believe his own silliness, as would an insane man; he knows that he is fooling himself. He consciously and stubbornly chooses to believe in impossibilities, however frivolous, ridiculous, and painful this belief may be to him.

Bull and Mouse: The Underground Man likens "spontaneous people and men of action" to bulls who act without thinking. He says he respects and envies these bulls because they have the capacity to act. The Underground Man compares himself to a mouse who, unlike the bull, scurries away to the underground instead of acting. In comparing himself to a mouse, the Underground Man defines himself for the first time. He sees himself from his own perspective, not filtered through the eyes of others. The mouse's most important ability, he says, is the ability to define himself. The Underground Man's isolation has granted him an identity uncorrupted by the outside world. This self-definition has its limits, however, and outside of the underground, it is almost impossible to hold on to an identity unaffected by others. The Underground Man's story of the mouse's humiliations is actually his own life story, a narrative of "spontaneous men of action" laughing at him, judging him, and driving him underground.

PART ONE
Chapter IV

The Underground Man argues that it is possible to find pleasure in a horrible toothache, since the pain is a reminder that one cannot beat the laws of nature. Your tooth will hurt until nature decides to let it stop hurting. Your tooth hurts even though there is no reason for the pain, and no one to blame for it. The consciousness of your inability to stop the pain humiliates you. The Underground Man calls the moans of a cultured man with a toothache nasty and spiteful. The cultured man moans louder and louder, knowing that moaning will not help cure his toothache and that no one will have sympathy for him. Moaning does nothing but irritate everyone, so it is an act of spite. In this spite, the cultured man finds pleasure in the fact that others despise him.

The Underground Man voices his worry that his readers are not following his arguments, since they do not have as much consciousness as he does. He adds that his arguments lack "self-assurance," since he has no respect for himself. He insists that a man who possesses a consciousness like his own can never respect himself. He seems pleased to think that we might not be following his logic.

UNDERSTANDING AND INTERPRETING
Part One, Chapter IV

The Pleasure of a Toothache: The Underground Man describes a toothache, further developing his previous point about feeling shame when failing to defeat the laws of nature. Since a toothache is not a form of pain or offense inflicted by another person, as is a slap in the face, the laws of nature create the pain. Since you cannot take an action like revenge in response to getting a toothache, the spite that builds from this offense is a pure kind of pleasure uncomplicated by revenge. The toothache allows the sufferer to enjoy masochistic pain.

Moaning and Groaning: Someone who suffers a toothache spitefully enjoys annoying others with his moans and groans. He admits he is a "nasty little man, a rogue," but says, "So be it!" He is proud to be labeled this way and takes pleasure in drawing contempt. The Underground Man resembles the toothache sufferer, for his *Notes* thus far have been an amplified version of the moans and groans of an exposed consciousness. The Underground Man knows he is provoking our annoyance and takes pleasure in the idea that we might not understand him.

PART ONE

Chapter V

The Underground Man says it is impossible for someone who takes pleasure in his own humiliation to have any self-respect. As a child, he says, he was bored and often got into trouble. He would apologize and repent sincerely, even apologizing for things when he was not at fault. Twice the Underground Man tried to fall in love and feel the suffering that accompanies love, but he always knew deep inside that his love affairs were exercises in self-deception, acted out in the name of conquering boredom.

As a result of this unending boredom, inertia finally overtook the Underground Man. He calls inertia the "direct, legitimate, immediate" consequence of consciousness. Now, instead of attempting any action, he sits with his arms folded. The Underground Man maintains that spontaneous men act only because they are stupid, striking at "secondary causes" of problems because they cannot identify and comprehend the "primary causes." Men of action have confidence that their actions are the only right ones. But the Underground Man knows no such confidence. Every primary cause leads to another cause, and then another, and on and on into infinity.

> "Every important cultural development of the past half-century—Nietzscheanism, Freudianism, Expressionism, Surrealism, Crisis Theology, Existentialism—has claimed the underground man as its own; and when he has not been adopted as a prophetic anticipation, he has been held up to exhibition as a luridly repulsive warning."
>
> **JOSEPH FRANK**

In the case of revenge, a spontaneous man acts in pursuit of justice. He feels satisfied with his actions because he believes that justice is a true cause. But the Underground Man acts only out of spite, not because he believes in justice. His spite outweighs all other causes of action because it is the only thing that brings him pleasure. He also cannot act out of a sense of justice because he scorns the nobility of justice. He thinks the laws of nature prove that justice is a hollow concept. The determinism of natural laws mean that no one is to blame for anything, for everyone acts as his nature dictates he must. This eliminates the possibility of true justice, for how can justice be achieved if no one is to blame? When you examine justice, says the Underground Man, you find that it is brought about by other causes and that those in turn result from other causes. In the end, every cause can be boiled down to the laws of nature, for which no one can be blamed. Thus there is no one against whom revenge is warranted.

> "They call me a psychologist. It is not true. I'm only a realist in the higher sense; that is, I portray all the depths of the human soul."
>
> **FYODOR DOSTOEVSKY**, FROM HIS NOTEBOOKS

The Underground Man suggests that spite could replace justice as a primary cause. But this cannot be right, either, because the laws of nature are the only primary cause. There is no cause for anything, so there is never any reason to act at all, even out of spite. Consequently, you can do nothing but beat your head against a wall harder and harder. If you try to act blindly, carried away by emotion, you will soon begin to despise yourself for being deceived about the causes of your own actions. The Underground Man tells us he considers himself intelligent because he has always followed his own precepts and thus has never started or finished anything in his life. In the final sentence of the chapter, the Underground Man makes a direct allusion to the novel *What is to Be Done?*, claiming that even if he is babbling, "talking in endless circles" is the only option open to an intelligent person.

UNDERSTANDING AND INTERPRETING
Part One, Chapter V

Luxuriant Boredom: The Underground Man says that the actions he attempted in the past were not tried in pursuit of a goal, but rather, as a deterrent to boredom. Now, in the underground, he believes that to attempt an action would be to betray his strongly held philosophy that all action is futile. In his past, he fought boredom by cultivating suffering, carrying on empty love affairs, getting into trouble, and forcing himself to repent. Now he lets boredom consume him. He sits and does nothing because he has become a conscious man. The "direct, legitimate, immediate result of consciousness" is inertia.

The Futility of Action: Most people identify reasons that motivate their actions, reasons such as revenge, love, or the pursuit of justice. The Underground Man says that such things as revenge and justice are not primary causes, but secondary causes, because they are derived from the one true primary cause—the laws of nature. For example, natural laws predetermine how we will behave, so no one is responsible for his or her own actions. Therefore, justice is an empty concept. The Underground Man, with his overdeveloped consciousness, deduces the following syllogism: if he can trace the primary cause of everything to natural laws, and if he cannot fight those laws, then he cannot act. Action is defensible only if you deceive yourself into thinking that secondary causes, like justice and revenge, are really primary causes. This is how the spontaneous men of action operate. But the Underground Man refuses to deceive himself.

What is to Be Done?: *Notes* can be read in its entirety as a direct parody of Nikolay Chernyshevsky's novel *What is to Be Done?*. This novel was the handbook of Russian radical intellectuals of the era. In the final sentence of Chapter V, Dostoevsky makes a direct reference to the novel by Chernyshevsky, who was one of the Nihilists of the 1860s and Dostoevsky's primary target of satire in *Notes from Underground*. The Underground Man is a parody of the cultured and intelligent protagonist in *What Is to Be Done?*. In Chernyshevsky's novel, pure reason and "enlightened self-interest" guide humans to a perfect, utopian, predetermined world of social virtue based on the pseudoscientific principles of mathematics and nature. The Underground Man understands Chernyshevsky's theories and the laws of nature, but far from finding a utopian world, he finds he is paralyzed and characterless. Dostoevsky argues, in the plight of his Underground Man, that following Chernyshevsky's principles would lead to profound unhappiness.

A Revolt Against Reason: Intellectually, the Underground Man has decided to prostrate himself to his rational side. Emotionally, however, he finds this decision difficult to swallow. He wants to live according to his principles, which demand inaction, but doing so makes him unhappy. This contradiction sets him on his "endless circles" of thought. His conscience tells him that guilt and pain are irrational and unjustified according to the laws of nature, but he still feels guilt and pain. It is possible that the Underground Man delights in his own pain because his pain is the most human part of him. His masochism, which in most people would indicate a degree of abnormality, represents, for him, moral and spiritual health.

PART ONE
Chapter VI

The Underground Man says that laziness is not to blame for his inertia. He would welcome the label "sluggard," because laziness would then be his "vocation." The Underground Man wishes he had chosen such a vocation, whether it had been laziness, gluttony, or something else by which he could define himself. He would not have been an ordinary glutton or sluggard, but an extraordinary man who sympathized with everything "beautiful and sublime." In his real life, the so-called "beautiful and sublime" has annoyed him for forty years. But had he been a glutton and drunk, it would have been different. Every day he would have shed tears and drunk a glass to the "beautiful and sublime." Eventually, he himself would have been transformed into something "beautiful and sublime."

The Underground Man cites examples of contemporary art and writing that he would have toasted in his alternate life because they would have seemed "beautiful and sublime." He imagines himself as a tear-soaked sponge, growing old and fat, living peacefully and dying triumphantly.

UNDERSTANDING AND INTERPRETING
Part One, Chapter VI

Longing to be a Sluggard: The Underground Man reiterates that he cannot have an identity since his consciousness prevents it. He might appear to be a sluggard, but that would mean his inertia is caused by laziness, and he would be able to blame it on laziness. But it is his understanding of the laws of nature, not laziness, that makes him unable to act. According to the Underground Man, he cannot become a drunk or a sluggard or a connoisseur of wine, much as he wants to, because he would have to deceive himself into thinking that some primary cause has urged him to be a drunk or a sluggard. Too smart for that, the Underground Man knows that the laws of nature are the only true primary causes.

"Just As You Please": Dostoevsky puts the phrase "just as you please" in quotation marks in order to mock it, making a direct attack on two other intellectuals of the era: M.E. Saltykov-Shchedrin, a liberal writer, and N.N. Ge, a Romantic painter whom Saltykov-Shchedrin praised in an essay titled "Just As You Please." The title brings to mind the enlightened self-interest of Chernyshevsky's rational egoism, by which people pursue their individual needs to create a utopia. Dostoevsky suggests that if everyone did just as they pleased, the result would certainly not be utopia. Not surprisingly, Saltykov-Schedrin attacked *Notes from Underground* after its publication.

PART ONE
Chapter VII

The Underground Man summarizes a popular social theory of his age which holds that people commit bad acts only because they do not know that their true interest lies in doing good. The theory asserts that if people's true interests were disclosed to them, they would understand that it is always in their best interest to do good. Consequently, they would do only good because people act only in their own self-interest. The Underground Man derides these ideas as hopelessly naïve. He argues that history has disproved the assumption that human beings always act to their greatest advantage. Many people take great risks even though their advantage lies in doing otherwise. In some cases, people may perceive an advantage to doing harm to themselves.

Fallacious theories like the one he attacks were based only on statistics and scientific and economic formulas that count things like "prosperity, wealth, freedom, peace" among the advantages that people seek. In the Underground Man's opinion, there is a "more advantageous advantage" that these formulas ignore. This advantage, he later says, is free will, or "independent desire." Humans will abandon reason and break laws and rules of honor in order to exercise their free will.

Any theory that does not factor in the existence of independent desire is naïve. Such theories are just "logical exercises" as absurd as the theory put forth by **Henry Thomas Buckle** (1821–1862), the English historian and philosopher who posited that greater civilization leads to peace. This theory is obviously false. The Underground Man observes that bloody wars are taking place between civilized

> " In [*Notes from Underground*], Dostoevsky is not yearning for some ineffable and inexhaustible *je ne sais quoi* [of character]. He seeks to convey a much starker reality, a psychological life so impoverished that it generates an incredible amount of repetitive and mechanical behavior."
>
> **RENÉ GIRARD**

societies, from Napoleon's conquests to the Civil War in America. Civilization, according to the Underground Man, has only expanded the range of human sensation, including the pleasure that comes from killing. In fact, war has become more barbaric than it was in the past. Human beings have not learned how to act according to reason and science, as optimistic theorists proposed they would.

ROBOTS IN UTOPIA

Russian radical and ideologue **Nikolay Chernyshevsky** (1828–1889) is one of Dostoevsky's primary targets in *Notes from Underground*. Chernyshevsky was a disciple of the radical Socialist **Vissarion Belinsky** (1811–1848) in the 1850s, just as Dostoevsky was in the 1840s. Chernyshevsky's works, *The Anthropological Principle in Philosophy* (1860) and his novel *What Is To Be Done?* (1863), argue that if people lived according to rational egoism and followed their own true interests, they would find themselves in a harmonious utopia. His characters are like robots, manipulated into perfect examples of his theories on marriage, collective industry and farming, extreme egalitarianism, and enlightened self-interest. Although *What Is To Be Done?* was widely considered one of the worst novels of its time, it was incredibly popular, not for its contributions to literature, but for its ideas — it became a handbook for young radicals throughout Russia during the 1860s. Chernyshevsky's revolutionary ideas remained popular for another fifty years and became part of the ideological basis for the Russian Revolution in 1917. **V.I. Lenin** (1870–1924) mentioned the novel as one of the books that guided his principles.

The Underground Man imagines a futuristic world in which human beings are taught reason. In this world, science shows people that they act according to natural laws, not according to their own free will or desire. Because they accept the dominance of natural laws, they become simple piano keys or organ stops. Once people act strictly according to natural laws, their actions are calculated mathematically and classified according to logarithmic tables. Since all actions are reduced to laws of nature, there are no longer any actions, and life is terribly easy . The answers to all questions are known, and there are no more adventures. At this point, the "Crystal Palace" can be built and man will enjoy " halcyon days."

The Underground Man thinks that this imagined world would be very rational and boring. Human beings, he says, are stupid and ungrateful. Even in this utopian future, someone would probably propose to destroy the world, even if the world provided unending happiness. Human beings, he continues, often act irrationally because of their desires. They occasionally oppose their own interests and advantages, and sometimes they *must* do so. Human beings do not have "virtuous" or "rational desire," but "independent desire," which is not always a moral or rational force. Because the will of the individual is the ultimate advantage we pursue, theories aimed at improving human existence are always "smashed to smithereens."

Part One, Chapter VII

To Behave Badly Is Human: Without naming Chernyshevsky, the Underground Man lays out the central tenets of his theories and then exposes their fallacies. He rips apart the idea that "if [man] were to be enlightened . . . he would stop doing nasty things at once and would immediately become good and noble." He shows that even if we were all enlightened, we would not automatically follow only the logical course or only the good course. Rational behavior is incompatible with basic human nature. The Underground Man argues that humans do not always follow the path to the greatest advantage, and that sometimes they willfully choose to hurt themselves or do something stupid. He destroys the assumptions that underlie rational egoism.

Tables and Encyclopedias: The Underground Man says that if all humans acted in accordance with natural law, all human behavior could be classified in tables and mathematical equations. This is a direct reference to works by thinkers such as utopian Socialist **Charles Fourier** (1772–1837), who created a table of all human drives that are necessary and sufficient for rational behavior. Fourier argued that if people acted according to the drives prescribed by these tables, they would act rationally and produce a better society. The Underground Man also refers to an encyclopedia, **Denis Diderot**'s (1713–1784) massive *Encyclopédie* (1751–1765), a compendium of human knowledge assembled with contributions by some of the most prominent *philosophes* of the Enlightenment to demonstrate the vast extent of human knowledge. The tables and encyclopedia demonstrate the Enlightenment's celebration of the progress of humanity and faith that science and mathematics will create a better society.

> " It says much for Dostoevsky's extraordinary powers that we not only accept the Underground Man's presentation of himself but also most instinctively come to have a positive respect for him, even a fellow-feeling."
>
> **JOHN BAYLEY**

Piano Keys and Organ Stops: The Underground Man believes that if people always acted rationally, they would be living without free will. We could then classify all human behavior, filing it under a logarithm or table of behavior. In this imaginary world of constant rational behavior, people would be like piano keys or organ stops, pushed and pulled according to the laws of nature. The image of piano keys arises directly from Diderot's essay " Conversation Between D'Alembert and Diderot," in which he argues that human beings are like "instruments" controlled in harmony by the laws of nature. Diderot presents this image as desirable, but the Underground Man considers it sinister.

Choosing Irrationality: Kant's theories again come under attack when the Underground Man argues that irrationality is the path to freedom. Kant says humans are the only animals with the capacity for rational thought and this allows them to rise above nature. He claims the only way for a person to free himself from the laws of nature is to exercise reason. But the Underground Man argues the opposite, saying that by exercising reason, we enslave ourselves to the laws of nature. The laws of nature are immutable and rational, and only by acting *irrationally* can we shake ourselves free of them. Humans need the feeling of choice, need to feel that they can choose not to live by natural laws.

Cleopatra's Golden Pins: The Underground Man briefly mentions Cleopatra's golden pins in this chapter. Cleopatra tortured her servants by sticking them with golden pins. The Underground Man views this torture as an example of the barbarism that still plagues the world, as evidenced by the barbarism of the Civil War in America. He also sees the golden pins as evidence of our perverse, irrational, independent will. People do not do things because they are reasonable things to do, but because they want to conquer boredom and establish individuality. Thus, Cleopatra sticks pins into people, and some people might desire to be stuck with pins.

The Crystal Palace: The Crystal Palace, an imagined utopia, is a significant metaphor that will be important throughout the rest of Part I. A physical Crystal Palace appears in *What Is to Be Done?*. It is a theoretical place where people live and work in harmony, modeled on the "phalansteries," or ideal communities, imagined in Fourier's theory of utopian Socialism. (It is also an actual structure in England that Dostoevsky visited during his travels in Europe and judged a defining symbol of the excesses of rationalism and materialism and of the decadence of the West.) The Underground Man sees the imagined Crystal Palace not as a wonderful ideal, however, but as a supreme bore. He explains that in order to live in the Palace, people would have to surrender their free will. They would never make such a sacrifice. People, he argues, would rather kick over the Crystal Palace and live with their free will than submit to the unrelenting rationalism that the Crystal Palace requires. The "independent desire" that man seeks is greater than any advantage found in the Crystal Palace.

PART ONE
Chapter VIII

The Underground Man says he knows critics will tell him that desire and free will do not exist and that these concepts are simply constructs of our biology. These critics will argue that science will find all the formulas for our desires, so that, like anything else, free will can be charted on tables and graphs. The concept of free will becomes unnecessary, because people's choices are the same thing as nature's choices for them. For instance, his critics would argue, if someone makes a rude gesture, science and mathematics will prove that it was impossible *not* to make that rude gesture. The rude gesture was a predetermined action. Ultimately, by this method of quantifying desires and choices, it becomes possible to calculate your future.

Refuting his imagined critics, the Underground Man says that reason can only satisfy one small part of human life, whereas desire is a "manifestation of all life." A man may do something stupid, irrational, or contrary to his advantage, just to "have the right" to do something stupid. These acts of stupidity and irrationality are expressions of individuality and personality and cannot be predicted. Even if human beings are in part rational, they are still prone to

RUSSIAN NIGHTS

The mention of human "advantage" is in part a reference to *Russian Nights* (1844), a collection of prose-poems by Vladimir F. Odoevsky (1804–1869). Like Dostoevsky, Odoevsky parodies utilitarian theories and their reverence for advantage. In *Russian Nights*, Odoevsky, a Romantic poet who fused philosophical inquiry with fiction, depicts a futuristic world in which the West has perished and only Russia and China remain. Sections of the work are a prototype of modern science fiction. In the fictional new world order that Odoevsky imagines, the sublime love of humanity is so great that tragedy is rendered obsolete in literature. A notable section of *Russian Nights* contains this parody of utilitarianism: "What can force [humankind] to execute his obligations as if they were sacred? One thing only—his own advantage! In vain would you attempt to diminish the rights of man, if his own advantage leads him to preserve them . . . . Yes, *advantage* is the essential motivator for all men's actions! Whatever is useless is harmful, whatever is useful is permitted. That is the only solid foundation for society! Advantage and advantage alone—may that be your first and last law!"

misbehavior and they are still ungrateful and imprudent. The Underground Man argues that history is majestic, colorful, and monotonous, but decidedly not rational. Even those people who preach reason and enlightened action always betray their own ideals in the end.

The Underground Man imagines a utopian world in which humans enjoy prosperity and peace and have nothing to do but eat and sleep. Even in that world, he says, human beings will do stupid, ungrateful, and repulsive things. They will cause chaos and destruction. We will always do these things to prove that we have free will, so that we can realize dreams and fantasies even at the cost of losing a perfect existence. Ultimately, even if we did discover that all of our actions are governed by scientific reason, we would go insane in order to lose that reason and be free of that system.

At the end of the chapter, the Underground Man again imagines his critics' response to his ideas. They will claim that no one is destroying free will. Instead, they will argue, the goal of life is to arrange things so that people will freely choose in accordance with reason, arithmetic, and the laws of nature. In response to this, the Underground Man reasserts his original idea: when everything is reduced to reason and arithmetic, there is nothing left besides mathematical tables, and free will vanishes.

UNDERSTANDING AND INTERPRETING

Part One, Chapter VIII

Choosing Madness: The Underground Man stresses how dearly we cherish our right to act rationally. He says that, in a rational utopian world, we would commit acts of destruction and chaos in order to exercise free will. Beyond that, he says that, in an imagined rational world where the tables and logarithms of natural law predetermine that human behavior would not include irrational, destructive acts, people would choose to go insane rather than give up their right to choose their own actions. Our human inclination toward irrationality is so deep-rooted that we would choose madness over the sacrifice of free will.

Using Rationality to Argue for Irrationality: The Underground Man defines a human being as essentially irrational, "a creature who walks on two legs and is ungrateful." He disagrees with those philosophers who define humans as rational animals. To the Underground Man, reason constitutes only one aspect of human nature, existing side by side with irrational whims and desires. For instance, spite—one of the defining features of the Underground Man—is a wholly irrational drive. The Underground Man flaunts his irrational spitefulness, as if proving his irrationality to us.

DENIS DIDEROT AND CATHERINE II

Denis Diderot (1713–1784) was one of the most influential of all Enlightenment thinkers. His life's work, the *Encyclopédie*, epitomized the spirit of the age in which knowledge and human invention were the most highly regarded achievements. In his essay *Conversation Between D'Alembert and Diderot* (1769), Diderot writes that human beings are "instruments endowed with feeling and memory; our senses are so many piano keys that are struck by surrounding nature, and that often strike themselves." Diderot may have incurred Dostoevsky's wrath because Diderot's patron later in life was Catherine II, an heir to Peter the Great's westernizing reforms and a true subscriber to Enlightenment thought. Catherine II also admired Voltaire and other French Enlightenment writers, whose work Dostoevsky considered a corrupting Western influence on Russia.

Yet, while the Underground Man lashes out at reason, he continuously uses reason and logic in his arguments. He speaks from within the framework of philosophical arguments and seems, at times, more rational than the philosophers he criticizes. Therein lies the contradiction of his character: the Underground Man is a model of pure reasoning ability who thinks only in rational terms, but he uses his rationality to argue that humans are irrational beings.

In another way, the Underground Man uses himself to prove philosophers wrong. They theorize that the perfect rational human will be happy, but in many ways, the Underground Man is the perfect rational human, yet he is spiteful, unpleasant, and unhappy. He is a tormented man who can do nothing and be nothing, and reason has put him in that position. The character of the Underground Man is Dostoevsky's ultimate attack on his rationalist contemporaries. With this character, Dostoevsky suggests that the "rational man" born of their theories will be compelled to revolt against them.

PART ONE
Chapter IX

The Underground Man tells his readers he is joking but then quickly reveals a few questions that are tormenting him. For example, even if it is possible for humans to shed their desire and embrace pure reason, is this necessary? Why must desire be "improved" by reason? How are reason and the laws of nature ultimately advantageous for humans? He thinks the theory of rationalism is a law of *logic*, but not necessarily a law of *humanity*.

The Underground Man then offers a new metaphor about roads. He says that human beings are creative and love to build roads, but also have an urge to destroy, to drive off of these roads. This urge to swerve is manifested in our act of building structures that we do not like to inhabit. After building such structures, we sometimes abandon them to domestic animals like sheep, or to creatures, like ants, that always build the same structure. Unlike ants, human beings enjoy striving for a goal more than they enjoy achieving it. The goal of human existence, therefore, may lie not in the act of attaining one's goal, but in striving for this goal.

The Underground Man wonders if the goal we strive for is "two times two equals four." While we search for it, we find the beginning of death. We take risks—go to war, sail across oceans—to reach "two times two," but we are afraid of reaching it because afterward there is nowhere further to go. The

Underground Man insists, though, that there is nothing special about "two times two is four." He says "two times two is five" can be charming, too. He wonders why the believers in "two times two is four" are so convinced that only the "normal and positive" is advantageous for human beings. What if people love suffering just as much as they love well-being? He argues that we need not consult history books for an answer; if we are alive, we know that sometimes, suffering is a desirable thing.

> "Dostoevsky wrote of the unconscious as if it were conscious; that is in reality the reason why his characters seem 'pathological,' while they are only visualized more clearly than any other figures in imaginative literature…He was in the rank in which we set Dante, Shakespeare, and Goethe."
>
> **EDWIN MUIR**

The Underground Man says he advocates neither suffering nor well-being, but simply argues for "[his] own whim and for its being guaranteed to me whenever necessary." In other words, he stands for free will. Suffering, he says, is not permitted in the proverbial "Crystal Palace." But people will never renounce real suffering—that is, suffering that comes from destruction and chaos—because "suffering is the sole cause of consciousness," and consciousness is the thing that humans will never trade for any other type of satisfaction.

In the Crystal Palace, there is nothing to do and nothing to learn. We would have to "plug up [our] five senses and plunge into contemplation" to live there. Consciousness might lead to similar inertia, but at least, says the Underground Man, consciousness allows us to avoid boredom by flogging ourselves every so often.

UNDERSTANDING AND INTERPRETING
Part One, Chapter IX

2 x 2 = 5: The Underground Man imagines a world in which the equation 2 x 2 = 5 is valid. This equation is inherently irrational, and it is charming precisely because irrationality does have a place alongside rationality. The Underground Man does not reject rationality, but he doesn't see why we should reject a world where 2 x 2 = 5 can peacefully coexist with 2 x 2 = 4.

Suffering = Consciousness: In explaining our desire to suffer, the Underground Man makes one of his most convincing arguments against rational behavior. He says that anyone who has experienced life should know that sometimes, we desire suffering and that at times we desire it passionately. To be sure, it is irrational to desire suffering, and the Underground Man does not claim that suffering is just as rational as well-being. Rather, he says we crave the choice between the two, the ability to decide according to whim. The Underground Man objects to the metaphorical Crystal Palace partly because in the Palace, there is no suffering, and without suffering, there is no consciousness. It is suffering that produces and nurtures consciousness. In fact, the Underground Man says, suffering is the "sole cause of consciousness." He realizes that his much touted consciousness leads to a state of paralysis and inaction similar to the state of people living in a Crystal Palace. There is one crucial difference, however: even if consciousness leaves you catatonic, you can "liven things up a bit" by flogging yourself from time to time, reminding yourself you are alive by inflicting suffering on yourself. In the Crystal Palace, you do not have consciousness, so you do not even have that option.

PART ONE
Chapter X

The Underground Man suggests that his critics believe in the Crystal Palace—the utopian society in which humans live rationally—because it is indestructible. The Underground Man fears the Palace. He notices that in the Crystal Palace, it is impossible to stick out one's tongue or to make an obscene gesture. The natural laws will not allow such a choice. He compares the Crystal Palace to a chicken coop. He says that if it were raining and he saw only a chicken coop, he would crawl into it to get out of the rain. Despite this, he would rather seek shelter in a mansion. Only if the sole purpose of life were to stay dry would he prefer a chicken coop to a mansion. The coop fulfills the immediate need, but the mansion fulfills other needs and desires.

The Underground Man desires more from life than dryness, so he would rather live in a mansion. To convince him otherwise, you would have to destroy or change his desire. He states that it does not matter whether or not the mansion is only a figment of his imagination. He will not accept a compromise. He will follow someone elsewhere only if his desires are destroyed, his ideals are eradicated, and something better is placed in front of him. But as long as he is

WINTER NOTES ON SUMMER IMPRESSIONS

Dostoevsky traveled extensively throughout Western Europe in 1862, including a month in Paris and a week in London. He chronicled these travels in his diary, *Winter Notes on Summer Impressions*. The diary entries are a series of essays on morality and economics that unfold like a dialogue between the author and the readers. He addresses these imagined readers as "gentlemen," just as the Underground Man does. Before setting out on his travels, Dostoevsky already held a number of anti-European prejudices about Europe's supposed worship of materialism and rationalism. His visits only strengthened these prejudices. Dostoevsky equated Paris with Baal, the ancient pagan civilization that demanded human sacrifice, and he mocked London for its simultaneous great wealth and extreme poverty. In London, Dostoevsky came upon the Crystal Palace, which was a prefabricated structure of steel and glass built to house the Great Exhibition of 1851. The edifice symbolized for him all that is artificial and pointless: "the full triumph of Baal, the ultimate organization of the anthill."

alive and keeps his desires intact, he will never contribute "one little brick" to the Crystal Palace/chicken coop because he will not be able to tease it by sticking out his tongue at it. He does not particularly like sticking out his tongue, but he would rather have it cut off than live in a world where he no longer desired to stick it out at anything.

Why, asks the Underground Man, does he desire this mansion of his imagination? He refuses to believe that he was granted consciousness and desires only so he could realize that his way of life is a fraud and the mansion does not

> "**D**ostoevsky is chaos and fecundity. Humanity, with him, is but a vortex in the bubbling maelstrom."
>
> **HENRY MILLER**

exist. To conclude the chapter, the Underground Man states that all underground men should be controlled, because once they start speaking after forty years of silence, they cannot be stopped.

UNDERSTANDING AND INTERPRETING
Part One, Chapter X

Another Option: By the end of this chapter, it seems that the Underground Man is getting fed up. He hates to think that reason is right and his revolt against reason is wrong. He cannot believe that the dilemma itself will be his unending solution. He asks, "Can it be that I was made this way only in order to reach the conclusion that my entire way of being is merely a fraud? Can this be the whole purpose? I don't believe it." The Underground Man seems to be searching for another option, one that is neither the Crystal Palace nor his underground home of revolt.

The Crystal Palace and the Chicken Coop: In real life, we need more than simple logic, and therefore, the Crystal Palace/chicken coop is not the ideal place of the Underground Man. He rejects the Crystal Palace because "you can never stick out your tongue" at it. The Underground Man uses sticking out his tongue as an example of asserting will, revolting, and acting out of pure spite and capriciousness, and the Crystal Palace is so odious to him because it does not allow such capricious gestures. The Underground Man compares the Crystal Palace to a chicken coop. If you have only very basic needs, and the coop/Palace is the only thing available to fulfill those needs, you might choose it. But the coop/Palace is useless for people who have more than basic needs.

"THE CENSORS ARE SWINE"

In his original text, Dostoevsky makes it clear that the mansion the Underground Man longs for represents Christianity as humankind's salvation. The Russian government removed references to religion in *Notes from Underground*, including references in the section that discusses the mansion. Dostoevsky could not understand why these sections were censored, because, he claimed, they were not blasphemous in any way. He wrote in frustration, "The censors are swine. Those places where I mocked everything and sometimes blasphemed *for appearance's sake*, they let pass. But where I deduced from all this the necessity of faith and Christ, they deleted it." Meanwhile, the proofreaders of the book did not reconstruct the chapter in a coherent way after the deletions, so the jumbled state of the chapter remained in print. The deleted sections have never been recovered, and for reasons unknown, Dostoevsky never reinserted them in later printings of the novel.

The Mansion and the Underground: The Underground Man envisions a third place, neither underground nor chicken coop/Palace, but a mansion where his desires and free will are valued. If he cannot have the mansion and his only other option is the Crystal Palace, the Underground Man would still choose the underground as his dwelling place. If he accepted the Crystal Palace, it would be a compromise that would not betray his desires. In the underground, all he can do is revolt against the Crystal Palace, determinism, and the laws of nature while in a state of inertia. The Underground Man believes this life to be better than a life in which he has compromised himself.

Censorship and Confusion: There is some confusion within the text of this chapter that merits explanation. The mansion, the third structure the Underground Man mentions, is also referred to as a "Crystal Palace" in some sentences, and in places it is difficult to tell which structure he is talking about. This is not intentional. This chapter was heavily censored by the Russian government before publication, and large chunks of the text were removed. In places where the Underground Man seems disorganized or the discussion of buildings seems confused, it is likely the fault of the censors.

PART ONE
Chapter XI

The Underground Man concludes that he likes his state of conscious inertia in the underground, saying "long live the underground!" Although he still envies the normal man, he would not trade his current way of life to change places with him. However, he says, he is lying again. It is not the underground that is better than normal life. There is something altogether different from either life that he will never be able to find.

The Underground Man says that life would be better if he believed even a fraction of what he has written thus far, but he does not believe it, not one single word. He then reverses himself again, announcing that he *does* believe it but simultaneously suspects that he has been lying throughout his entire monologue. He imagines once again what his critics would say about him. Speaking for them, he points out all the problems with his ideas and method of argument: he is persistent but shies away before drawing conclusions; he is angry and spiteful but still tries to be funny; his jokes are not funny but he hopes they will be well received because of their literary merit; he is desperate to say something after forty years of silence but conceals his ultimate conclusions because he lacks resolve; his mind is working, but his heart is black and depraved.

The Underground Man replies that he invented all these words, and for forty years he has been listening to others speak through a crack in his underground corner. He invented the only words that occurred to him. He says he will not let anyone read what he has written. He wonders why he keeps addressing his readers as "gentlemen" when he has no true intention of having any readers. Confessions like his are not written for others to read. All people, he argues, have certain secrets they will not reveal to anyone, and decent men have more secrets than others.

Recently, he says, he decided to write down some of his secrets and "earlier adventures." A completely honest retelling of his life is impossible; even the eighteenth-century philosopher Jean-Jacques Rousseau's *Confessions* was full of untruths. Rousseau created these untruths out of vanity because vanity allows you to invent the worst crimes for yourself. In short, the Underground Man maintains, he is writing for himself, not for the public. Since he does not expect readers, he does not worry about editing himself. He will write down whatever comes to mind, in no particular order.

He understands that it is strange, if he does not anticipate an audience, that he would go to such lengths to justify himself, clarifying and reclarifying his arguments, and continually apologizing. The Underground Man realizes that he cannot answer this question. He wonders if perhaps he does these things because he is a coward or because he tries to behave better when there is an audience watching.

The Underground Man asks himself some final questions: if he has no audience, why write at all? Why not confine his thoughts to his own mind? He says he writes because his style will be more "impressive" and "dignified" if recorded on paper. Moreover, he has memories that he cannot escape, and writing them down may be the only way to get them out of his system. Lastly, he writes because he is bored and idle. Writing feels like work, and work is supposed to make a person good and honest. The Underground Man opens the door to Part II of his *Notes* by mentioning that it is snowing outside—a wet, yellow, thick snow. It has been snowing for a few days, in fact, and the snow reminds him of a particular incident from his past.

UNDERSTANDING AND INTERPRETING
Part One, Chapter XI

Hurt and Bluffing: The Underground Man suffers, and we see the pain of his dilemma: he longs for something entirely different, not the underground, not the Crystal Palace. He claims he prefers staying in the underground to being normal, but it becomes clear that this claim is partly a bluff like the cry of a hurt child.

Actually, the Underground Man cannot decide whether he truly prefers his plight to normality. He writes, "I said that I envy the normal man to the point of exasperation, I still wouldn't want to be him under the circumstances in which I see him (although I still won't keep from envying him. No, no, in any case the underground is more advantageous!) At least there one can . . . Hey, but I'm lying once again!" He longs for change, but decides "it's better to do nothing."

A Romantic Mode: The end of Part I makes a transition to Part II, marked by the Underground Man's mention of his own writing. He says he is not writing his confession for a readership and justifies writing it down by saying that his monologue "somehow . . . appears more dignified on paper. There's something more impressive about it." Part II is the more literary section of the book, more typically novelistic in plot and tone, so it is fitting that Part I ends with the Underground Man investigating the motives of the man who writes. Just as Part I examines the rationalism of the 1860s, Part II will appraise the sentimental Romantic literature of the 1840s. The Underground Man begins the shift into a romantic mode in the last paragraph when he describes the snow that falls outside.

Wet Snow: When the Underground Man describes the wet snow falling, he raises the curtain on his past in the Romantic 1840s. A critic of the 1840s once wrote that "wet snow" is an essential element in Russian Romantic writing of the 1840s, and by mentioning it, Dostoevsky situates the narrative to come in that Romantic period. The wet snow instantly conjures an image of St. Petersburg streets, and it reflects the instability of the narration. Wet snow is heavy, slushy, and not quite frozen. It is neither here nor there, as if it cannot decide whether it wants to be snow or rain. In its indecisiveness, it matches the stasis of the Underground Man and the vacillating tone of the novel.

PART TWO: APROPOS OF WET SNOW

Chapter I

Part II opens with an excerpt from a poem written in 1845 by Nikolai Nekrasov. Then the Underground Man begins to recount an episode in his life that occurred when he was twenty-four years old. At this stage in his life, he is not very different from what he will become later in life. He is gloomy, spiteful, and "solitary to the point of savagery." He loathes his colleagues at work, and they loathe him. He knows he is not handsome, but he still tries to look intelligent and noble. He thinks of himself as a "coward" and a "slave" and believes that every "decent" man is a coward and a slave. Above all, he feels that he is not like anyone else, writing, "I'm alone . . . and they are *everyone.*"

At times he believes just the opposite, laughing at his intolerance for everyone else, recognizing that his attitudes feel "borrowed from books" and considering befriending his colleagues. But when the Underground Man tries to cozy up to them, he soon starts arguing again and then stops talking altogether. So he spends most of his time alone, reading books that "agitated, delighted, and tormented" him. Isolated, he sinks into a "dark, subterranean, loathsome depravity," accompanied by irritability and hysterical fits of depression.

In a digression, the Underground Man indicts the Russian Romantics, calling them dreamers and not men of action. The Romantics want to safeguard the "beautiful and sublime" and be "wrapped up" in lyrical verse and pretty stories. By doing so, he says, they wrap up themselves "like precious jewelry," as if their ideas are too precious for the real world. Russian Romantics are full of "contradictory sensations," says the Underground Man—they seek material security in apartments or pensions or jobs, while writing poetry that scorns materialism. Though they are honest at heart, the Underground Man considers them rascals.

One night, the Underground Man walks by a tavern, where he witnesses a fight. A man is thrown out a window. He feels envy for the man and decides to enter the tavern in hope of starting a literary quarrel in which he too might be thrown out the window. When he tries to pick a fight with an **Army Officer**, the Officer ignores him and pushes him aside like a piece of furniture. Instead of further instigating a fight, the Underground Man withdraws and goes home dejected, thinking that no one will understand him because he only speaks "literary Russian."

After that night, the Underground Man sees the same Army Officer all over the city. He begins to despise the Officer and secretly follows him to learn more about his life. He writes a brief sketch of the Officer. Two years later, the Underground

Man writes a letter to the Officer, challenging him to a duel. He never sends the letter, hoping that the Officer might someday embrace him and that they will become friends. The Underground Man begins seeing the Officer on periodic strolls along the city's grand boulevards.

The Underground Man feels he is "a fly in the eyes of society, a disgusting, obscene fly" compared with finely attired citizens of St. Petersburg like the Officer. The Underground Man knows he is smarter and more cultured than these people, but he also knows that they look down on him despite his education.

Each time the Underground Man sees the Officer on the boulevard, the Underground Man steps aside to let the Officer pass. Each time he steps aside, he regrets it. One day, he resolves *not* to step aside the next time they meet and to jostle the Officer in hopes that the Officer will stumble and finally notice the Underground Man. The Underground Man borrows money from his boss, **Anton Antonych Setochkin**, to purchase fine clothing so that he can look respectable while carrying out his plan. He even buys a beaver collar for his shabby winter coat. In many subsequent meetings on the boulevard, the Underground Man cannot work up the nerve to bump into the Officer. One day, the Underground Man steels himself and finally jostles the Officer. The Officer continues walking, unperturbed by the incident, but the Underground Man is ecstatic at having attained his goal. He was sure then, and he is sure now, fourteen years after the incident, that the Officer was only pretending to be unruffled by the incident.

> "The *Notes* are a fable of consciousness and choice, and of absolute contradiction—duality or doubling in a new guise…. The book in its overall mood is an indecent exposure of consciousness, not a confession, not an unburdening on troubled conscience."
>
> **JOHN JONES**

UNDERSTANDING AND INTERPRETING

Part Two, Chapter I

A New Style: In contrast to the metaphysical and philosophical analysis of Part I, Part II consists of a more traditional narrative with characters, action, and a plot. The writing in Part II features vivid descriptions of characters and places. It is in the style of naturalism, also known as Romantic realism, with which Dostoevsky first made his name as a novelist. If Part I is the Underground Man as philosopher, Part II is the Underground Man as author.

THE OVERCOAT

The Underground Man's pursuit of the Army Officer is a grotesque parody of **Nikolay Gogol**'s most famous short story, "The Overcoat." Nikolay Gogol (1809–1852) is one of the pillars of Russian literature, and his novels and stories of everyday people are a major influence on Dostoevsky. In "The Overcoat," a hapless but sympathetic bureaucrat saves money to buy a new coat with a fur collar to replace his old, tattered garment. His new prized possession is soon stolen, and he dies of a delusional madness a few days later. No one notices his death, since he was a person "who was not dear to anyone, whom no one thought of taking any interest in, *who did not attract the attention even of a naturalist who never fails to stick a pin through an ordinary fly.*" The bureaucrat gets revenge when his ghost returns and strips overcoats from the fine people on the boulevards of St. Petersburg. The Underground Man attaches great importance to a similar fur-collared overcoat, but he has no such luck in wreaking vengeance. Like Gogol, Dostoevsky describes his hero as a pesky, insignificant fly.

Longing for a Literary Life: The excerpted poem that begins Part II points to the Underground Man's preoccupation with literature. The poem is by **Nikolai Nekrasov** (1821–1871), a distinguished Russian Romantic poet of the mid-nineteenth century whose work focuses on poverty and social change. The poem is about a man who saves a fallen woman, a popular theme in Romantic poetry and fiction of the era. The Underground Man cuts off the poem with a bored "etc. etc.," which suggests he has heard the poem before, or thinks it cliché and predictable and so not worth finishing. Yet despite his evident scorn for the poem, he uses it to lend a literary tone to the beginning of Part II.

Escaping into Fiction: The Underground Man uses literature to quiet his overactive self-awareness. To escape his own mind, he uses books. The Underground Man lives in the romantic fantasy of his own consciousness and of fiction, and he wishes the world outside of those refuges were more like his literary fantasies. Venturing outside only disappoints him, and reality confuses him because it does not match the fictional world in his books.

The Underground Man as Author: The Underground Man craves literary experiences. He wants to get thrown out a window after a literary fight, for example, because such an incident would resemble an episode from a novel. He believes that a fight in a bar, especially one between a domineering Army Officer and himself—the underdog—has all the ingredients of great fiction. He also rejects anything nonliterary, such as the conversations and card games at his coworkers' apartments, because they lack the beauty and magnificence of books. When the Underground Man cannot find the fiction he craves in his real life, he invents it. The Officer shoves aside the Underground Man at the tavern, which is not literary enough for the Underground Man. Being ignored is not something that happens in books. In response, he plots a literary revenge on the Army Officer, writing a brief sketch of him, composing a letter challenging him to a duel, and finally behaving rudely to him on the boulevard. This course of action is cribbed from the Underground Man's books. It is a melodramatic scheme complete with letters, duels, and honor. Even when the whole plan fails, the Underground Man constructs a fantasy that it was successful.

Condemning the Romantics: Dostoevsky takes aim at the Russian Romantic authors, with whom he associated in the 1840s before he was sent to Siberia. In part, then, when he indicts the Romantics, he indicts the man he used to be. Dostoevsky sees the 1840s as a time of liberal idealism in which he and his literary cohorts suffered from an "egoism of principle." They created great ideals for themselves and for the world, but they did not live by these ideals in their own lives. The Underground Man calls the Russian Romantics dreamers and not men of action. They want to coddle the "beautiful and sublime," swathing it in lyrical verse and pretty stories and holding it out of reach of the real world. Russian Romantics, says the Underground Man, are hypocrites who condemn materialism in their poems, but crave posh things for themselves. The main difference between the Underground Man of the 1840s and the Underground Man of the 1860s is the younger man's overwhelming Romanticism. He brims with the ideas of the Romantics and remembers, "I could not speak except as though I was reading from a book." Dostoevsky uses the Underground Man's social difficulties to show how harmful it is to take the Romantics' dictates to heart. The Underground Man, a believer in Romanticism, admits to his own vanity, feels morally superior to everyone, and wants to make everyone see how wonderful he is. He is obsessed with how people perceive him and feels terrifyingly different from other people ("I'm alone, and they are *everyone*").

> "In the world of Dostoevsky, no one is spared, but there is a supreme consolation: no one is excluded."
>
> **IRVING HOWE**

Pride, Superiority, Humiliation: Because of his damaged pride, his natural arrogance, and the indifference he encounters, the Underground Man suffers from a massive superiority complex. In order to feed and nurture this superiority, the Underground Man craves humiliation. By inflicting abuse on himself and putting himself in embarrassing situations, he can stoke the flames of his hatred for others and increase his own self-regard and sense of moral superiority.

PART TWO
Chapter II

After his success in bumping into the Officer, the Underground Man says he felt nauseated and remorseful. He comes to endure these feelings as part of everyday life but imagines an escape in which the world expands and becomes beneficent and beautiful. In this dream world, he is a hero, even though, in his regular life, he usually sees himself as dirt. He says, "[e]ither a hero or dirt—there was no middle ground." These flights of imagination spice up his usual depravity. He fantasizes about a world in which he is rich and superior to everyone else but also possesses the humility to forgive all the slights made to him during his life. He might march across Europe and give away a grand fortune to do good for humanity. He might confess to all his sins like Lord Byron's *Manfred*. He might preach ideas and defeat all reactionaries, even forcing the Pope to resign.

These dreams, which can last for three months at a time, fill the Underground Man with such urgency that he wants to "embrace all humanity." He feels the need to go into society, so he visits his boss, Anton Antonych, the only lasting acquaintance in his life. He goes to Setochkin's house, where he listens to other guests talk about money, taxes, and matters of state. These discussions bore the Underground Man, and he never takes part in them. After returning home from these visits, he postpones his desire to embrace humanity. The Underground Man has another acquaintance, **Simonov**, a former schoolmate, in whom he detects a hint of honesty and independence of thought. He wonders if Simonov secretly finds him repulsive. Having not seen Simonov for a year, the Underground Man goes to visit him.

UNDERSTANDING AND INTERPRETING
Part Two, Chapter II

The Danger of Idealized Love: Dostoevsky uses the Underground Man's fantasies to criticize the Romantic poets, mentioning Lord Byron by name. In the Underground Man's dreams, which are so powerful they practically replace his real life, he lives in the "beautiful and sublime" world of the Romantic poets. This world features a complicated, abstract version of love that is not directed at other people, but exists only as an idealized concept, like the idealized love in the poems of Byron. The Underground Man, a literature fanatic, naturally believes in a literary form of love. To direct his love at someone else is "an unnecessary luxury," since it is the idea of love that is important, not the feeling itself. Dostoevsky points out, by showing us the Underground Man's fantasy, that the Romantics propagate a dangerous form of love that inspires readers to withdraw into themselves. Idealized love might exist harmlessly in poetry, Dostoevsky suggests, but it has no place in real life. Idealized love can actually exist in real life only if the would-be lover becomes nearly mad, retreating into his own head and shutting out other humans.

Dreams of Napoleon: In the Underground Man's fantasy, his exaggerated pride causes dreams of benevolent world domination. He imagines marching across Europe like Napoleon and giving away a grand fortune to do good for humanity. These dreams of being a supremely willful superman counter the Underground Man's actual existence as a small, sneering, prideful person, unable to overcome inertia and impotence. In real life, he expresses his will only for "petty vices." In his dreams, he expresses his will to conquer the world.

PART TWO
Chapter III

When the Underground Man arrives at Simonov's apartment, he finds Simonov with two other former schoolmates, **Ferfichkin** and **Trudolyubov**. The Underground Man describes them and again compares himself to a fly. When the Underground Man came in, the three men were discussing a farewell party for **Zverkov**, another former classmate. Zverkov is now an Army Officer and has just been assigned a post in a distant province. The Underground Man remembers that he despised Zverkov in their school days because Zverkov had good manners, charisma, and self-confidence. Zverkov was full of wit and vigor, and everyone loved him even though he was an arrogant braggart.

Simonov and his two friends decide to pool their money and buy dinner for Zverkov. They exclude the Underground Man from their conversation, but when he pipes up, they grudgingly decide to let him accompany them. On his way out the door, the Underground Man curses himself for intruding on their plans, wondering why he would bother going to a dinner for an enemy like Zverkov. He is more furious at the realization that he would attend the dinner even if it was only to enjoy their scorn.

That night, the Underground Man has a dream about his years of "penal servitude" during his school days, when he was endlessly picked on by the other boys. His schoolmates blindly worshipped success and ridiculed the lowly and oppressed. The Underground Man's only friend was another **boy** who was picked on more than he was. Soon he got bored with the other boy and started to dominate him. He says, "I began to despise and reject him immediately—as if I only needed to achieve a victory over him, merely to subjugate him." Seeing his former schoolmates, the Underground Man realizes that his life now is much the same as it was when he was young.

The Underground Man wakes from his dream with a feeling that something important will happen to him that day. He decides to attend the dinner for Zverkov, if only to prove he is not a coward. Hoping to present himself as a man worthy of respect, he obsesses over his clothing and the polish on his boots and hires a carriage to take him to the hotel restaurant. He plans either to "conquer" Zverkov and the others or to make them love him. Just as he leaves, he realizes that he does not want to see them at all. Filled with anxiety again, he decides to meet them anyway.

UNDERSTANDING AND INTERPRETING
Part Two, Chapter III

Better a Mouse than a Fly: The Underground Man has two identities. The first takes hold when he is alone in the underground, and the second emerges when he is living in the world and interacting with people. In the underground, he thinks of himself as a mouse—an insignificant creature, but one who chooses his own identity by deciding to run away and hide underground. Outside, he feels like a fly, something people ignore or swat away. In the Underground Man's conception, the mouse creates himself, while the fly is created by the perceptions of others. People see the Underground Man as an annoying, fly-like creature, so that is how he sees himself. In order to think of himself as worthwhile, even something as worthwhile as a mouse, he must stay isolated in the underground. Outside, stripped of his fantasies, he is merely an irritating fly.

Equating Beauty with Worth: Despite his reservations, the Underground Man succumbs to the world's opinion that beauty and fine appearances equal respectability. He himself believes that physical appearance is petty, meaningless, and a bad basis on which to judge a person, but he is keenly aware of every defect in himself, especially in his clothes. He says he wishes he could trade his ugly but intelligent face for the handsome but stupid face of Zverkov because then the outside world would consider him respectable. Just as he worried about his coat when plotting against the Officer, he now worries that the clothes he wears to dinner are too ratty and will not earn him any respect. He polishes his boots twice and hires a nice carriage to take him to the hotel restaurant, all in the name of appearances.

The Pleasures of Domination: The Underground Man thinks of himself as a "despot at heart," and his memories of school show that he had an easier time dominating people when he was young than he does as a man. Although the Underground Man was isolated from most of the other boys in school, he made a companion of a boy who was abused even more than he was. This boy became submissive to the Underground Man, who enjoyed dominating him for a time. He developed a taste for the pleasures of domination, but as an adult, he has a nearly impossible time finding anyone to dominate. He now has to deal with men, not boys, and he is not up to the challenge. Only petty and spiteful kinds of domination are within his grasp. He uses a toothache, for example, to dominate those around him by making them suffer through his moaning and groaning.

Fyodor Dostoevsky

PART TWO
Chapter IV

The Underground Man arrives for dinner at five o'clock only to learn that the dinner plans have been changed to six o'clock, although no one told him of the change. He is further ignored by the waiters as he awaits his former classmates. He sits and waits for the rest of the party. When the others arrive, he is so happy his waiting is over that he forgets his anger at the change of plans. Zverkov enters first and is surprised to see the Underground Man. Zverkov says he hopes they will be friends, but the Underground Man feels he is being patronized. When Zverkov asks him about his job, the Underground Man detects scorn and sarcasm in his questions.

The Underground Man soon gets drunk and argues violently with the others. Trudolyubov accuses him of attending the dinner just to "settle old scores." Zverkov soothes the sudden tension by steering the conversation to lighter topics. The Underground Man is soon relegated to the background. He sits back and listens to the conversation around him and realizes he is being humiliated again. Despite resolving to get up and leave the restaurant, he stays in his seat. He thinks about somehow offending them all and finally interrupts one of Zverkov's stories with a rude remark. The others scornfully shush him and raise a toast to Zverkov.

The Underground Man says he wishes to make his own speech, and when the others mockingly quiet down to listen, he delivers a ridiculous, pompous toast. The others shout him down, and Zverkov taunts him. The Underground Man then challenges Ferfichkin to a duel. Ferfichkin sarcastically accepts and joins the others in a roar of laughter. Picking up a bottle to throw at them, the Underground Man instead pours himself another drink. As the night goes on, he gets increasingly drunk, and they continue to ignore him.

He begins to pace up and down alongside the table, getting dizzy and sweaty and stomping his feet, but they still ignore him. He keeps pacing and pacing, grunting and moaning at the others' conversation. He feels it is the most humiliating episode of his life. He "mentally addresses" the others, wishing they could hear his internal thoughts so they would know how cultured he is.

At eleven o'clock, the others decide to leave for a brothel. The Underground Man clumsily begs their forgiveness for his rudeness, but they brush him aside. When he blocks their way, Zverkov finally asks him, "Well, what is it you want?" The Underground Man says he only wants Zverkov's friendship and forgiveness for insulting him. Zverkov laughs him off, "My dear sir, I want you to know that never, under any circumstances, could you possibly insult *me!*" The others leave for the brothel, and the Underground Man begs some money from Simonov so that he can take a separate cab and meet them there. He hopes that by the end of the night the others will beg him for friendship. He resolves to slap Zverkov in the face if they do not.

UNDERSTANDING AND INTERPRETING
Part Two, Chapter IV

A Painful Night: The night out confirms two distressing facts for the Underground Man: that he can neither befriend or humiliate his schoolmates as he longs to do, and that others see him as a fly-like man, irritating and persistent. His schoolmates ignore him by neglecting to tell him of the change in plans, and the waiters ignore him as he awaits the partygoers. His fantasies of dominating Zverkov dissolve as soon as Zverkov opens his mouth and asks the Underground Man dreary, everyday questions about his job. This is not the conversation that the Underground Man wanted, since it lacks the depth of literary conversation. He cannot dominate Zverkov or the others because he cannot carry on a simple dinner conversation. Instead, he immediately jumps into a more "literary" tone of impassioned self-righteousness and conflict. Instead of answering the questions, he injects drama into the proceedings by trying to prove his intelligence. His erratic, aggressive behavior irritates his former schoolmates, and they shoo him away and try to ignore him, just as if he were a fly.

A Failed Revenge Plot: When the Underground Man fails in his attempts at domination, he plots revenge. He frantically paces back and forth, trying to distract them, and grunts during their conversation. This kind of revenge is similar to the behavior of the man with the toothache, discussed in Part I, who forces others to suffer by making them listen to his groans of pain. The Underground Man wants to take revenge against his companions by making them embarrassed at having to watch him pace the room. As usual, though, his revenge fails. The attempted revenge hurts the Underground Man far more than it hurts his companions, for its failure makes him realize that his companions can easily ignore his existence and pretend he is not present in the room.

An Absurd Duel: At a loss in normal conversation and unable to dominate through linguistic prowess, the Underground Man resorts to a more physical and Romantic manifestation of conflict: he challenges Ferfichkin to a duel. Not only is the duel dramatic and literary—duels are usually fought over a point of honor or courtly love, both highly Romantic concepts—but duels are the

INVISIBLE MAN

Of the many literary descendents of *Notes from Underground*, **Ralph Ellison**'s *Invisible Man* (1952) stands out as an American successor to the novel. In the novel, Ellison (1914–1994), an African-American, tells the cautionary tale of a nameless narrator — a black man in Depression-era Harlem — and of the destruction of his identity at the hands of ideological and racial forces. In the prologue, the invisible narrator ("I am invisible . . . because people refused to see me") is speaking from his underground home, which he calls a hole. He lives there outside of society, his only apparent power the electricity he has filched from the electric company. Through the lens of the racial politics of the era, Ellison portrays a narrator whose forays into the outside world lead only to subjugation and alienation, just like the ventures of the Underground Man.

most extreme, and lethal, form of a civilized argument. This is appropriate for the Underground Man, since he almost always operates at extremes. The schoolmates react with laughter to the idea of a duel, because a normal person would never propose fighting to the death over a non-argument such as Ferfichkin and the Underground Man have been having. That the schoolmates can laugh at the suggestion shows that they consider the Underground Man absurd, not threatening.

Appearances Make the Man: The Underground Man, for all his undeniable intelligence, has great difficulty reading basic social cues. He desperately wants his companions to consider him superior. He silently thinks, "Oh, if you only knew what thoughts and feelings I'm capable of, and how cultured I really am!" Despite this longing, he has little understanding of what causes people to seem superior and admirable to their friends. He wonders why the others are so drawn to Zverkov. He does not understand that Zverkov's charisma and success make him a desirable friend, because he cannot see these traits as important. The Underground Man sees only Zverkov's good looks, nice clothes, and stupid behavior—behavior that others see as charismatic—and decides that handsomeness gives Zverkov his appeal. Thus, the Underground Man's bid for superiority consists of copying the appearance of superiority. All he must do to seem admirable, he thinks, is present an attractive front.

PART TWO
Chapter V

During the cab ride to the brothel, the Underground Man fantasizes about slapping Zverkov in the face and humiliating Zverkov's prostitute, **Olympia**, who is a favorite at the brothel and once insulted the Underground Man's looks. He dreams of being dragged out of the brothel by the others. He begins to feel anxious at the prospect of meeting them all at the brothel and considers how else he might dishonor Zverkov. In an elaborate fantasy, he imagines going to Siberia, returning years later and confronting Zverkov, explaining all he has sacrificed for that slap in the face. He also dreams of tracking down Zverkov years in the future, challenging him to a duel, and simply firing a shot into the air to prove he is the more honorable man. But after devising these plans, the Underground Man concludes he must confront Zverkov at the brothel to wipe out his earlier disgrace at the restaurant. He is in such a pitch of emotion that he slaps his driver.

Fyodor Dostoevsky

When he arrives at the brothel, the others have already left. A young prostitute is sent into the room with him. When he approaches her, the Underground
Man catches sight of himself in a mirror and notices how disgusting he looks. He
feels delighted that he will repulse her when he has his way with her.

UNDERSTANDING AND INTERPRETING

Part Two, Chapter V

Finding Passion in a Dream World: Only the Underground Man's fantasies allow
him to feel sensation. When dreaming, he can feel despair, shame, rage, and
elation. Reality, on the other hand, leaves him cold and blank. During the carriage ride to the brothel, as the Underground Man fantasizes about dominating
Zverkov, he feels impassioned. He tells himself that he will at last have the "con-
frontation with reality" for which he has longed. By now, we know that the
Underground Man is unable to act and that the slap in the face will never happen .
He should probably realize, as we do, that he is incapable of carrying out what he
imagines. As he thinks of the escape to Siberia, the waiting, and the triumphant
return, he utterly convinces himself of the merit of his revenge plot. His untena-
ble fantasies bring him to great heights of emotion. He feels the need to cry and
thinks of himself as a character from a Pushkin or Mikhail Lermontov story.

PART TWO
Chapter VI

After he has sex with the prostitute, the Underground Man lies with her in a
half-conscious state. He opens his eyes and notices her staring at him. Her gaze
is "oppressive" to him. The "dismal thought" of dominating her spreads through
the Underground Man. To break the silence, he asks her name, which she tells
him is **Liza**, and asks about her family. Then he tells her the story of a funeral
procession he saw that day.

The procession was for the funeral of a poor woman who was a prostitute
and died of tuberculosis. The Underground Man tells Liza that after a year as a
prostitute, she will be worn out and will eventually end up like the poor woman
who died, living a destitute life and dying in squalor. Liza seems not to worry
about death and tells the Underground Man not to feel sorry for her. He tells
Liza that she still has time to live a happy life with a husband, but she says married life is not for her. When the Underground Man says she would be happier
back in her father's house, safe and sound, Liza insinuates that it was her father
who sold her into prostitution. The Underground Man says that such things hap-

pen in families where there is "neither God nor love." He then delivers a long speech in which he describes the joy and bliss of marriage. After hearing his harangue, Liza says sarcastically that he sounds "just like a book."

UNDERSTANDING AND INTERPRETING
Part Two, Chapter VI

A New Domination: In Liza, the Underground Man finds a new victim to dominate. After physically dominating Liza by sleeping with her, the Underground Man taunts Liza as a way of dominating her psyche. Her oppressive gaze gets under his skin, and the idea of controlling her spreads through him virulently. The Underground Man likens it to the feeling you get "upon entering a damp, moldy underground cellar." All of his bitterness and pettiness well up, "seeking an outlet." Liza is the unfortunate outlet that comes to hand.

A Grotesque Parody of Compassion: The Underground Man's speech to Liza is not sincere, but more like an academic exercise. When he sees Liza, he sees a chance to apply something literary to the outside world, to use the "cherished little ideas" from his life of books. The speech arouses emotion in him, but not because he feels compassion for Liza. Instead, he feels excited about the words coming out of his mouth. He knows his speech is false, but he concludes that "artifice goes along so easily with feeling." Love comes up frequently in this speech, but it is the sort of love we saw in Part I: an idealized, romantic notion that has nothing to do with real life. The only variety of love the Underground Man does feel is based on domination and humiliation. Love is not something he knows about from personal experience, and Liza suspects that his rhetoric is just hot air. At the end of the speech, Liza tells the Underground Man that he sounds "just like a book." This is perhaps the most damning insult she could utter. The Underground Man thought he had at last successfully incorporated his fiction into real life, but in fact his speech struck his listener not as realistic, but as strange and scripted, like something read from a book.

PART TWO
Chapter VII

The Underground Man brushes off Liza's remark that he sounds like a book. He notes that the sarcasm in her voice suggests she is repressing the true effect of his words on her. He continues his speech, forecasting her future, claiming she will get used to living in the brothel if she does not attempt to find a better life.

"VERY STRANGE, VERY UN-GERMANIC MUSIC"

The great German philosopher Friedrich Nietzsche (1844–1900) read *Notes from Underground* and said it had "music, very strange, very un-Germanic music." Although Nietzsche found fault in Dostoevsky's conclusions about the nature of humanity and took exception to his veneration of Christianity, he called Dostoevsky "the only psychologist from whom I had anything to learn." Nietzsche's theory of "master and slave morality" is greatly influenced by Dostoevsky's conception of domination and submission in the Underground Man. The Underground Man is also similar to Nietzsche's *Übermensch*, or superman, a little man with grand fantasies, longing to be a conqueror.

He likens her plight to that of a serf, pointing out that her servitude is unending while at least a serf's existence has a limit. He tells her she is "enslaving [her] soul" and doling out her love to any drunk who walks through the door. Even if she has a regular lover, he says, the man would never marry her because she will get no respect from him or anyone else.

He warns that when she gets older, she will be kicked out of the brothel and will have no friends. She will end up living on the streets, being abused, suffering from tuberculosis, and regretting her whole life. The Underground Man's emotion begins to overcome him, and he gazes at Liza, who is now sobbing in despair. His arguments have convinced her that she needs to change her life and find love. Her reaction surprises the Underground Man, and he loses his nerve. Although he feels he must get away from her as soon as possible, he takes her hands and gives him his address. Liza jumps up and shows him a love letter from a man she recently met at a party. The Underground Man senses that the letter is the one prize she keeps to remind herself that she is worthy of being loved. He leaves and walks home through the wet snow, pondering an "ugly truth" that he has just realized.

UNDERSTANDING AND INTERPRETING
Part Two, Chapter VII

The Ugliness of Love: The ugly truth that the Underground Man suddenly understands is the truth of what actual love might feel like. While he tries to dominate Liza, compassion creeps up on the Underground Man. "It was the sport, the sport that attracted me; but it wasn't only the sport," he thinks to himself. Expecting to enjoy the game of talking in a literary manner to Liza, the Underground Man takes himself by surprise. He did not expect to be so convincing, and now he seems to have convinced himself. His own feeling of love—vague and anemic as it may be—is brought on by Liza's intense suffering, another sensation he did not expect.

Sudden, Unexpected Success: To the Underground Man's surprise, he not only succeeds in dominating Liza, he succeeds in making a positive impression on her with his long-winded speech. Instead of recoiling from his obvious spite, Liza takes his arguments as an honest appeal to her sense of self-worth, a heartfelt reaction for which he is wholly unprepared. Liza sees him as a man with a certain power, someone who has moral superiority over her. She sees the Underground Man as he longs to appear, and the success of his playacting catches the Underground Man off guard.

PART TWO
Chapter VIII

The Underground Man wakes the next morning, astonished at his sentimental reaction toward Liza the previous night. He immediately puts the episode aside in his mind and begins trying to save his reputation with Simonov and Zverkov. He borrows more money from his boss, bragging that he spent the night carousing at rich clubs. He then writes a note to Simonov and encloses the money he owes, apologizing for his behavior at the restaurant.

As the Underground Man goes out for a stroll, he has the nagging feeling that something is wrong, as if "some crime were weighing on [his] soul." He replays the previous night in his mind, thinking that he did a noble thing for Liza, but this thought does not appease him. He vividly remembers Liza's pale face and tormented expression. Liza might come to see him, he thinks. He is terrified that if she comes, she will see the poverty he lives in. The night passes, and Liza does not visit the Underground Man. The next day, he dismisses the episode with Liza as nonsense. Still, he is sure that the prostitute will visit him. He devises a plan to insult her and spit on her if she comes to his apartment.

Three days pass, and still she does not come. He imagines another plan in which he will decline the love that she will offer him. In this plan, the Underground Man will reject her love and spout "some European, George-Sandian, inexplicably lofty subtleties," then reverse his position, accept her, and live happily with her for years. The Underground Man dispels these thoughts and then ponders them again. Meanwhile, he wrangles with his servant, **Apollon**, who he says gets paid just enough to "do nothing." For years, the Underground Man tried to punish Apollon by withholding his pay, but Apollon would always defeat him with severe stares and the silent treatment.

Now, the Underground Man resolves to conquer Apollon once and for all. He confronts his servant and shows him the unpaid wages sitting in a drawer. The Underground Man announces he will not pay Apollon until he is treated with respect. Apollon laughs. As they argue, the door opens. It is Liza. Her entrance causes the Underground Man to flee the room, disgraced at his appearance.

UNDERSTANDING AND INTERPRETING
Part Two, Chapter VIII

Liza, Lifeless Doll: Although the Underground Man seems to think about Liza obsessively, he is actually obsessed with himself. He thinks about Liza only insofar as she relates to him. It terrifies him to think that Liza will come to see him, because if she does, she will realize that he is not as superior as he pretends to be. If she does come, he plans to put on his "dishonest, deceitful mask" and behave cruelly to her to compensate for the squalor of his apartment and his cowardice in the face of Apollon. Never considering her actual character or her difficult plight, he moves her around in his fantasy land as if she is a lifeless doll. Despite the Underground Man's self-obsession, empathy stirs just perceptibly within him. He feels slightly uncomfortable and upset when he thinks about Liza, although he does not yet understand why.

Liza, Clichéd Waif: Dostoevsky continues to mock the Romantics by painting Liza as the clichéd helpless waif, the typical symbol of the redeemable woman easily shaped and molded by ideas. Liza could have stepped out of a Nekrasov poem. In the Underground Man's daydream, Liza offers her love to him, and he rejects it using sophisticated, "George-Sandian" language. With the mention of **George Sand** (1804–1876), Dostoevsky again emphasizes the danger of idealizing love. Sand was a French Romantic novelist whose novels featured the same kind of romantic love and reform that the Underground Man admires in Nekrasov's poetry. Taking Sand and Nekrasov to heart, the Underground Man suggests, will encourage people to become delusional and controlling. The Romantic Underground Man takes Liza, an ideal of innocence and selfless love, and imagines molding her, creepily musing on "how little idyllic sentiment . . . was necessary to turn a whole human soul according to my wishes at once."

Apollon, Dominator: As usual, the Underground Man's attempts at domination fail and put him in a submissive position. When he attempts to boss Apollon around, Apollon easily intimidates his master. Despite the fact that Apollon is the social inferior of the Underground Man, he bests him with his superior ability to intimidate. Apollon wins a staring contest and then utilizes the same spiteful techniques of the man with the toothache mentioned in Part I: he sighs and sighs, dominating the Underground Man by forcing him to listen to his expressions of pain, until finally the Underground Man relents and pays him.

PART TWO
Chapter IX

The Underground Man stands ashamed before Liza. She sits down obediently, staring at him wide-eyed. He tells her he is not ashamed of his poverty since he still feels noble, and dispatches Apollon for tea. Suddenly, he bursts into tears, which amazes and confuses Liza. Thinking about how angry he is at her, the Underground Man asks Liza if she despises him. He stops weeping, and they sit in silence for five minutes. Liza looks perplexed, and the Underground Man thinks to himself that he is suffering more than she is because he knows his own stupidity and meanness.

Finally, Liza speaks. She wants to get herself away from the brothel for good. The Underground Man becomes angrier with her but still says nothing. After some time, he embarks on another long speech, saying that he knows she came to hear more words of pity. He abruptly tells her that he only meant to humiliate her at the brothel, because he did not get to humiliate Zverkov earlier that night. His speeches to her—lies, he calls them now—were made only to dominate her.

Liza, listening to him in disbelief, turns white. The Underground Man says he wishes that everyone would stop bothering him. He calls himself an "egoist" and cries out to Liza that he wants to be left alone. He says his fate is to endure insults from everyone because he is really nasty, petty, and vain, an "envious worm." Finishing his rant, the Underground Man perceives that Liza is insulted and crushed by what he says but that she has also understood the deep unhappiness in his admissions. The Underground Man writes, "[s]he understood out of all of this what a woman always understands first of all, if she sincerely loves—namely, that I myself was unhappy." Liza throws herself at the Underground Man, embracing him and bursting into tears. He bursts into tears too, and finally says, "They won't let me . . . I can't be . . . good!"

As they embrace, the Underground Man feels shame when he realizes that Liza is now the heroine of the situation, and he is being humiliated. He feels a twinge of envy because Liza is the one dominating him. The Underground Man realizes he can't live without tyrannizing others. When he finally stops crying, he feels even more intent on domination and possession. His hatred for Liza rises again within him. He looks at her and sees fear and bewilderment cross her face, but then she embraces him again, "warmly and rapturously," and he takes her to bed once more.

UNDERSTANDING AND INTERPRETING
Part Two, Chapter IX

Romantic Ideal vs. Self-Absorbed Reality: In his behavior toward Liza, the Underground Man touts the behavior advocated by the Romantic poem that began Part II. In a few lines from the same poem, lines that precede this chapter, the redeeming man invites the fallen woman into his house to become his wife, allowing her to cast off her shame. In contrast, the Underground Man cannot suppress his own concerns long enough to think about how he could help Liza.

He is reluctant to let Liza inside, for shame about his poverty obscures his ability to imagine Liza's shame. In the poem, the woman's face is "full of shame and horror" when she comes to terms with her own corruption, but in life, the Underground Man refuses to let Liza take emotional center stage. Instead of allowing her to unburden her soul, he burdens it more by turning the conversation to his feelings. "Liza, do you despise me?" he asks.

The Rejection of Love: Compassionate Liza demonstrates the selfless love of the Underground Man's Romantic dreams and fantasies, yet the Underground Man cannot accept it. If he could shed his spitefulness, he could find salvation through Liza's love. But in true Romantic form, the Underground Man sees love as a beautiful idea, not as something that exists in real life. When given the chance to find actual love, he recoils. To the Underground Man, humiliating others is more pleasurable than loving them. Liza embarrasses him by trying to redeem him, when, according to the Underground Man, it should be *him* trying to redeem *her*. In anger and humiliation, the Underground Man dominates her by stealth, embracing her as if out of love, then dominating her sexually out of hatred. Liza believes they are consummating a newfound love for each other, but actually, the Underground Man is taking revenge against her for humiliating him.

PART TWO
Chapter X

After sleeping with Liza, the Underground Man paces the room and watches her weep. He perceives that she now understands everything—that he only wanted to humiliate her, that he hates her, and that he is a despicable person. The Underground Man realizes he cannot love anyone. Love, he tells us, means exercising power over another person and demonstrating moral superiority over him or her. Love begins with hatred and ends with moral subjugation, and then the other person becomes useless. The Underground Man has no idea that Liza has come to his apartment to love him, not to hear "words of pity." With this love, she seeks salvation and resurrection.

The Underground Man wants Liza to leave so he can be alone in his underground. He says "real life" oppresses him because it is so unfamiliar. Liza hurries to collect her coat and hat. When she looks at him sadly, he smiles at her spitefully. Before she leaves, the Underground Man forces a five-ruble note into her hand as a final insult, then bolts away to avoid seeing her face. Out of shame and despair, he rushes after her into the hallway, but she is gone. He returns to his room and finds the ruble note crumpled on the floor. After quickly dressing, he rushes out the door to catch her but loses her tracks in the freshly fallen snow.

He asks himself why he is running after her. He knows that if he begs her forgiveness and she returns to his apartment, he will grow to hate and torment her. He decides it is better for her to leave and that his insulting offer of money will be good for her character. He poses a final question: "Which is better: cheap happiness or sublime suffering?" Although during that night he has experienced more suffering and remorse than ever before, he says that for a long time, he held onto his theory that insults and hatred, which please him, are better than love and acceptance.

The Underground Man concludes with an explanation of what he has written. He calls his work a form of "corrective punishment," not literature. He has ruined his life, losing his morals and isolating himself from the rest of society with useless ill will. He is not the hero of the book, he says, but the antihero. He has shown, he says, that everyone is estranged from life and that when real life becomes a chore, we realize that life is better as it exists in books.

It would be worse if all our desires were fulfilled. If we were given more freedom, he says, we would give some of it back. The Underground Man believes he will be criticized for generalizing about humanity, but says all he has done is take to the extreme what his critics "haven't even dared to take halfway." He concludes that all people are "stillborn," and soon we will all be conceived by ideas, not in living flesh. When the Underground Man's writing stops, an unnamed narrator writes a final note, explaining that the Underground Man's *Notes* do not end here, but it seems a good place to stop.

> "All Dostoevsky's novels were written for the sake of the catastrophe . . . . Only upon arriving at the finale do we understand the composition's perfection and the inexhaustible depth of its design."
>
> **KONSTANTIN MOCHULSKY**

UNDERSTANDING AND INTERPRETING
Part Two, Chapter X

The Underground Triumphs Over Love: The Underground Man dooms himself with his pride, his need to dominate, and his inability to accept love as it actually exists in the real world. He fantasizes about an ideal love that exists in books. Real love is impossible for him. As he consciously admits, he rejects Liza's love because it does not fit into his own ideas of what love should be. He says, "'Real life' oppressed me—so unfamiliar was it—that I even found it hard to breathe." The Underground Man lives in a world of his own ideas and fantasies. He knows that his fantasies doom him, but his lack of experience in the real world and his overactive consciousness confine him to inaction. Although the Underground Man experiences a frantic pang of feeling, causing him to run after Liza, it comes too late. For the first time in the course of the novel, he acts impulsively, in response to his feelings, but his cruelty has already driven Liza away.

"Cheap Happiness or Lofty Suffering?": The Underground Man chooses suffering—both lofty and petty—and suffering, paradoxically, brings him a perverse happiness. Liza offers him something better than his claustrophobic underground existence and the creepy utopian Crystal Palace he abhors, but he cannot accept her offer. His own world of suffering consumes him, and everything outside it seems like "cheap happiness."

Real and Imagined Life: We discover that the Underground Man does not view his *Notes* as literature, but as a form of "corrective punishment." In them, he shows how his isolation and moral decay in the underground have ruined his life. He calls us cripples, worrying that, like him, we are "estranged from life" because we retreat into the pure ideas of books, where fictional life is better than reality. The Underground Man has written a cautionary story in order to show his readers what dire consequences result when "rational egoism" meets real-life experience. The pure reason of rational egoism can lead only to life underground, a life of spitefulness, humiliation, and skepticism. By thinking only of his self-interest, the Underground Man has become a Nihilist, believing in nothing, alienated from everyone. The final note by the new narrator implies that the Underground Man is still at work, scribbling paradoxes, alone.

Conclusions

The Underground Man is the first true "antihero" of modern literature, a character with whom the reader does not necessarily identify or sympathize, and one who is defined by what he *does not* believe and what he *does not* do. *The Underground Man* can also be read as a parody of the utopian rationalist ideals of Dostoevsky's ideological past prior to his term in Siberia, and as a preface to the great psychological novels of his later years.

III

CRIME AND PUNISHMENT

An Overview

Key Facts

Genre: Psychological novel

Date of First Publication: 1866

Setting: 1860s. Parts I–VI take place over a week or so in the Haymarket slums of St. Petersburg, Russia; the epilogue takes place eighteen months later in Siberia

Narrator: Third-person omniscient

Plot Overview: An emotionally conflicted, alienated young man murders a corrupt pawnbroker and her sister and then pays for his crime, suffering intense psychological torment.

Style, Technique, & Language

Style—A Stuffy Apartment and a Lazarus Figure: Dostoevsky uses the color yellow to symbolize disorientation, paint and painters to symbolize redemption, and Lizaveta's crosses to symbolize salvation. In addition, he uses extended metaphors, one of which is Raskolnikov's apartment. The apartment stands for Raskolnikov's isolation and separation from his friends, family, and humanity. The cramped, stuffy apartment is compared to a "corner" and a "coffin" where Raskolnikov hides from the rest of the world. In his room, the solitary Raskolnikov is left to his own intellectual reasoning, which increases his alienation. The apartment seems eerily complicit in Raskolnikov's crime, for Raskolnikov plots his murder while alone in the apartment, and it is the apartment's stale air that aggravates his illness and delirium.

Dostoevsky mentions the biblical story of Lazarus three times in the novel, using it to suggest a parallel to the salvation of Raskolnikov's soul. Porfiry mentions the story of Lazarus, foreshadowing Raskolnikov's search for a way to achieve salvation. Like Lazarus, who is raised from death by Jesus, Raskolnikov yearns to be given new life by his own savior, Sonya.

Technique—Third-person Narrator and Cliffhangers: A detached, omniscient (all-knowing) man narrates the novel, providing an objective view of the actions and thoughts of the characters. He does not take part in the events of the novel, but observes them. For much of the book, the third-person narrator closely follows Raskolnikov, allowing us to witness the horror of Raskolnikov's internal struggle. At other times, the narrator provides us with the internal monologues of other characters, using a style known as free indirect narration. The thoughts of these characters give us a new perspective on Raskolnikov.

Crime and Punishment is divided into six parts and an Epilogue. Part I deals with the crime, and Parts II through VI focus on the punishment. Part I can be considered a prologue to the events of Parts II through VI, because it recounts the single act that sets the rest of the novel's action in motion. The Epilogue is about Raskolnikov's prison term and gradual regeneration. Perhaps in order to create suspense, Dostoevsky ends many chapters with a surprise development or the introduction of a new character. Before it was published as a book, *Crime and Punishment* was serialized (published chapter by chapter) in magazines and newspapers, and its structure reflects its serial publication. Cliffhangers and self-contained chapters appealed to the novel's initial audience.

Language—Revealing Character through Dialogue and Dreams: Dostoevsky paints a vivid portrait of the characters, allowing their way of speaking to reveal their personalities. The pretentious, devious Peter Luzhin expresses himself in lawyerly speeches and letters. Sonya speaks gently and carefully, frequently invoking her faith in God. Raskolnikov, Dostoevsky's greatest achievement, either keeps almost silent or rants and raves. Dostoevsky gives us detailed glimpses into the characters' inner lives, including their psychology, their subconscious impulses, and their dreams. The dreams shed light on the characters' personalities and reveal their hidden fears. In fact, some critics argue that *Crime and Punishment* is one long nightmare taking place entirely in Raskolnikov's mind.

Characters in *Crime and Punishment*

Alena Ivanovna: An old, malicious pawnbroker and moneylender. Most of the poor residents of St. Petersburg hate her because she charges high interest rates on loans. Alena is said to beat her kindly sister, Lizaveta. Raskolnikov thinks of her as a "louse." He murders Alena with an axe.

Lizaveta Ivanovna: Alena's half-sister, Lizaveta cooks and cleans for Alena and helps the family business by visiting the homes of poor people who need to sell their possessions. She is kind, gentle, devoutly religious, and a friend of Sonya Marmeladov. Lizaveta is the innocent victim of Raskolnikov's crime.

> "The best of all murder stories, *Crime and Punishment* seems to me beyond praise and beyond affection."
>
> **HAROLD BLOOM**

Andrey Semenovich Lebezyatnikov: The friend and roommate of Peter Luzhin. Andrey is a devoted Socialist who loves to expound on the popular liberal and intellectual theories of the day. Andrey exposes Luzhin's false accusation against Sonya.

Amalia Ivanovna Lippewechsel: The irritable and argumentative German landlord of the Marmeladovs. She calls herself Ivanovna, but Katerina Marmeladov maliciously calls her "Ludwigovna" to draw attention to her German ancestry. She evicts Katerina and her three children.

Peter Petrovich Luzhin: The wealthy fiancé of Dunya Raskolnikov, he is sneaky, duplicitous, arrogant, and vain. He sees Dunya as the ideally virtuous bride who will be unceasingly grateful to him. After losing Dunya's hand, he tries to win her back by framing Sonya.

Semen Marmeladov: The husband of Katerina Ivanovna and father of Sonya. He is an ex-government clerk and an alcoholic. Raskolnikov meets him at a bar. He steals money from his family to fund his drinking habit and later dies after throwing himself in front of a moving carriage.

Katerina Ivanovna Marmeladov: Semen Marmeladov's wife. She is proud, violent, and ill-tempered, but she seeks justice and goodness for her family at any cost. She slowly descends into madness after her husband dies. In the end, she is evicted from her apartment.

Fyodor Dostoevsky

Sonya (Sophia) Semenovna Marmeladov: The eighteen-year-old daughter of Semen Marmeladov and stepdaughter of Katerina Ivanovna. Sonya works as a prostitute to earn money for her family, although she knows her father steals everything she earns. She is kind and endlessly compassionate toward others. Raskolnikov sees in Sonya the totality of human suffering. She proves to be the person who will help him find redemption.

Porfiry Petrovich: The brilliant examining magistrate who battles wits with Raskolnikov. He approaches crime from a psychological viewpoint. Rather than arrest his suspects, he subtly forces them to see their own guilt and confess. He respects Raskolnikov's great intellect and his theory of crime.

Dmitri Prokofich Razumikhin: The charismatic, self-assured best friend of Raskolnikov. He is usually rational and even-tempered, but occasionally he has fits of hot-headedness and impulsiveness. He drinks heavily on occasions, likes socializing, and seems to know everyone in St. Petersburg as a result. He falls in love with Dunya. Porfiry Petrovich is his distant relative.

Avdotya (Dunya or Dunechka) Romanovna Raskolnikov: The smart, compassionate sister of Rodya Raskolnikov. She consents to marrying Peter Luzhin to help her family, but is self-assured enough to reject him when she discovers his true nature. Her former employer is Svidrigaylov, who is infatuated with her. She falls in love with Razumikhin.

Rodion (Rodya) Romanovitch Raskolnikov: The protagonist of the novel, he is a former student who lives in abject poverty in a tiny apartment, where he is isolated and alienated from the rest of society. He is intelligent, but he is also haunted by conflicting emotions. The root of Raskolnikov's name (*raskol*) means "split" in Russian, which accurately reflects the clash between his compassion and his intellect. Raskolnikov puts forth a rational theory of crime about "extraordinary men" for whom "everything is permitted," including murder, if murder will lead to good. He tries to prove that he is an extraordinary man by murdering Alena Ivanovna, which he thinks will bring about a greater good for society. With Raskolnikov, Dostoevsky warns of the dangers of alienation and the worthlessness of utilitarian theory.

Pulkheria Raskolnikov: The kind mother of Raskolnikov and Dunya. She borrows money to send to her son so he can continue his university studies. When Raskolnikov abandons the family, she goes mad.

Arkady Ivanovich Svidrigaylov: Dunya's wealthy former employer and unsuccessful suitor. An admitted sensualist and libertine who takes pleasure in women and wine, he falls in love with Dunya because of her chastity and sympathy for him. When Dunya rejects him, he gives much of his fortune to Sonya and the Marmeladov orphans and then commits suicide.

Marfa Petrovna Svidrigaylov: The kind wife of Svidrigaylov. She plays matchmaker to Peter Luzhin, a distant cousin of hers, and Dunya. Soon after Dunya leaves the Svidrigaylov estate, Marfa dies under suspicious circumstances. Dunya suspects that she was poisoned by her husband. Marfa's ghost haunts Svidrigaylov.

Alexander Grigorevich Zametov: The chief police clerk. In a delirious state, Raskolnikov mockingly confesses to him.

Dr. Zosimov: A medical doctor and a friend of Razumikhin. He treats Raskolnikov during his illness and fears his patient may be slightly mad.

Reading *Crime and Punishment*

PART ONE
Chapter I

On a stiflingly hot July afternoon, a young student, **Rodion Romanovitch Raskolnikov**, slips past his landlady and leaves his miserable apartment in the Haymarket slums of St. Petersburg. Raskolnikov is tall and "strikingly handsome." He lives in a tiny room, he owes many weeks' rent, his clothes are ragged, and he has not eaten for two days. His abject poverty has made him depressed, and he has cut himself off from his friends and family. Raskolnikov tries to go unnoticed as he moves through the Haymarket. He mutters to himself as he walks, constantly repeating certain phrases. The most insignificant gestures of other people attract his notice, especially when people make an effort to talk to him. A drunken man walks by and yells something about Raskolnikov's hat, and Raskolnikov immediately berates himself for wearing an article of clothing that draws attention. Raskolnikov has memorized the number of paces it takes to get to the pawnbroker's house. As he walks there, he repeats to himself the phrase "trifles are important." He contemplates the details of a crime he is planning.

Raskolnikov makes his way to the shop of **Alena Ivanovna**, an old pawnbroker and moneylender whom he has visited before and from whom he has borrowed money. When he arrives, Alena lets him in cautiously. She wears a yellow strip of flannel around her neck. Her fur is "yellow with age," her furniture is painted yellow, and even the light in the room is an orange shade of yellow because the sun is setting. While haggling over the price of a watch he is pawning, Raskolnikov takes mental notes of the layout of the shop. Alena offers him a paltry amount for the watch, and for lack of other options, he reluctantly accepts. She reminds him that he is late paying back money he already owes her. She discounts the value of the watch, insulting it as "trash" even though it is obviously an item of great sentimental value to Raskolnikov. He leaves in a state of confusion, telling her he will return soon with something else to sell. Raskolnikov loathes the old pawnbroker. He stops in at a bar and drinks a cold beer, which clears his mind.

UNDERSTANDING AND INTERPRETING
Part One, Chapter I

Dirt and Stench in the Haymarket: A master of realism, Dostoevsky renders the St. Petersburg slums in the Haymarket district immediate and tangible. The places, bridges, and streets are named after actual locations in St. Petersburg. The apartment buildings of Raskolnikov and the pawnbroker are actual addresses. Raskolnikov's wanderings can be accurately traced on a map. We get a gritty picture of city life in the poorer quarters from Dostoevsky's descriptions of the dirt and the sounds of the street and the smells of the taverns and the sewage. The dirty neighborhood reflects Raskolnikov's mind, which is claustrophobic, isolated, and dark. His movements reflect his mind too; he goes from his cramped room, down the "narrow and dark" streets filled with noise, to the dark, dingy apartment house of Alena Ivanovna.

Intentional Isolation: The cramped condition of Raskolnikov's apartment suggests his isolation from society and his withdrawal "completely into himself." The room is like a jail cell and it is later described as a "coffin." Raskolnikov moves through the Haymarket, trying to remain unnoticed by sticking to the shadows and avoiding conversation. He has intentionally cut himself off from the society around him.

Obsessive Behavior: Raskolnikov behaves obsessively as he walks the streets. He is full of self-loathing and self-consciousness. He mutters to himself as he walks, and constantly repeats certain phrases. He also notices the most insignificant gestures of other people, especially when they make an effort to talk to him. For instance, when a drunken man walks by and yells something about Raskolnikov's hat, Raskolnikov is upset that he wore a noticeable article of clothing. Perhaps most strikingly, Raskolnikov's obsessive behavior has led him to memorize the number of paces it takes to get to the pawnbroker's house.

Irresolute but Determined, Handsome but Dirty: Raskolnikov is a study in contradiction. He is not really afraid of his landlady—he just wants to avoid conversing with her—but when he gets to the street, he feels overwhelming fear of the landlady. He walks "irresolutely" to the pawnbroker's, but at the same time, he seems determined to get there. He reproaches himself for his weaknesses, but he appears firm in his purpose. He is tall and "strikingly handsome," but he is dressed shabbily and surrounded by filth.

The Annoying Alena Ivanovna: Dostoevsky shows us why Raskolnikov might dislike Alena Ivanovna as he does. She opens the door distrustfully, at first showing only her eyes. Before Raskolnikov can get down to the business of pawning his watch, Alena Ivanovna reminds him that he is late in paying back money he owes. She scoffs at the watch, calling it "trash," even though Raskolnikov treasures it. Her ridiculously low offer for the watch is another insult to her client. Alena Ivanovna is brusque and snippy and thinks only of her own business and safety.

Yellow Turbulence: The color yellow crops up repeatedly in *Crime and Punishment* to denote the turbulence in Raskolnikov's consciousness. In this chapter, yellow suffuses the pawnbroker's apartment, from Alena Ivanovna's yellow strip of flannel to her yellowed fur to her yellow furniture to the sunlight in the room. Confronted with so much of the color, Raskolnikov leaves the meeting confused, hateful, and irresolute.

PART ONE
Chapter II

In the bar, Raskolnikov meets a ranting drunk named **Semen Marmeladov**, a former civil clerk. Marmeladov was recently reinstated at his job after being fired because of his drinking, but he is now on a binge and has not worked for days. Marmeladov is filthy and admits that he has spent the last five nights sleeping on a hay barge in the river. As he continues drinking, Marmeladov recounts the recent events in his life, including his marriage to **Katerina Ivanovna**, a woman of higher social standing than him who has three children from her previous marriage.

Marmeladov also has a daughter of his own, **Sonya**, who has become a prostitute to help support the family. Marmeladov steals all of her money to pay for his drinking. He mentions that one of his neighbors, a man named **Lebezyatnikov**, once tried to proposition Sonya. When she refused to sleep with him, Lebezyatnikov tried to have the family evicted from the building. On another occasion, Lebezyatnikov beat up Katerina for being impertinent to him.

Marmeladov says he is afraid to go back to his home where Katerina and the children await him after his extended absence. Katerina will certainly beat him, and he knows

"Anyone writing about the alienation of modern man from his fellows, anyone writing about philosophically motivated crime, the validation of the self through action, the relation of thought to action, and the justification of criminal means by utopian ends, anyone writing about any of these very contemporary topics cannot ignore the groundwork provided by Dostoevsky in *Crime and Punishment*."

GARY COX

he deserves it. At one point, Marmeladov asks Raskolnikov, "Do you understand what it means to have nowhere left to turn to?" Raskolnikov decides to guide Marmeladov back to his home. After seeing the terrible poverty of the family and watching a violent spat between Marmeladov and his wife, Raskolnikov leaves them a small amount of money as he exits.

UNDERSTANDING AND INTERPRETING
Part One, Chapter II

Marmeladov, Despicable but Sympathetic: Marmeladov could easily be one of the drunks Raskolnikov saw earlier on the streets of the Haymarket. The old man fits perfectly into the filthiness of the area. A depraved person, he drinks, skips work, steals from his family, and allows his only daughter to prostitute herself to pay for his drinking. Even so, Dostoevsky makes us see something warm and human about him. Marmeladov wins sympathy with his utter helplessness to overcome his drinking and his defeated desire to be a better human. We cannot entirely dislike him, because he seems such a hapless, unfortunate man. Marmeladov is a portrait of great suffering, one of many in the novel.

Raskolnikov, Alienated and Kind: When Raskolnikov feels pity toward Marmeladov, we see that compassion exists in him alongside obsessive behavior and alienation. In contrast to the repugnance and loathing that Raskolnikov exhibits toward the pawnbroker, here he deals kindly with Marmeladov, listening to his ravings, helping him home, and giving money to his family after seeing their desperate situation. Raskolnikov has a dual nature. He loathes humanity and isolates himself, yet he can be kind and empathetic. The two sides of his character are constantly in conflict throughout *Crime and Punishment*.

A Growing Cast of Characters: The second chapter introduces a number of characters who remain offstage until later in the novel. Among them are Sonya (Marmeladov's daughter), Katerina Ivanovna (Marmeladov's long-suffering wife), and a man named Lebezyatnikov, who initially seems violent and vile. Dostoevsky will continue to introduce characters in this fashion, and each will make an appearance later in the novel.

Nowhere to Turn: Marmeladov's comment about having "nowhere left to turn" will haunt Raskolnikov after he commits his crime. During the tormented suffering that follows the crime, Raskolnikov will feel he has nowhere to turn. Marmeladov's words echo through Raskolnikov's consciousness later in the novel, when Raskolnikov comes to a crossroads and must choose one direction or another.

PART ONE
Chapter III

The next day, Raskolnikov awakens in his apartment, feeling dejected and "bilious." Peeling yellowish wallpaper covers the walls of his tiny apartment, and books and papers sit in a corner, covered with dust. The cluttered and unpleasant state of the room matches Raskolnikov's mood. He has retreated from human contact "like a tortoise retreating into its shell." His maidservant rouses him from bed and tells him that the landlady is going to report him to the police if he does not pay his rent. Raskolnikov is repulsed. His servant leaves him a letter that has arrived from his mother, **Pulkheria**.

Pulkheria's letter is heartfelt and informative. She writes that she is sad Raskolnikov has been forced to quit the university for lack of funds. She says she will soon send money to her son, even though she has been forced to go into debt to obtain it. The letter also notes that Raskolnikov's sister, **Dunya**, has been working as a governess for the Svidrigaylov family. Pulkheria describes Dunya as "wise," "resolute," and "capable of bearing a great deal." The man of the house, **Arkady Svidrigaylov**, has made a number of unrequited passes at Dunya while drunk. Dunya rejects Svidrigaylov, not because she cannot conceive of being with him, but because she feels loyalty to Svidrigaylov's kind wife, Marfa, and she does not want to cause a public scandal. At one point, Svidrigaylov's wife, **Marfa**, overheard her husband asking Dunya to run off with him and immediately jumped to the conclusion that Dunya was to blame. Later, Svidrigaylov came clean, and Dunya was let off the hook.

One of Marfa's kinsmen, **Peter Petrovich Luzhin**, has been visiting the household. Pulkheria describes Luzhin as practical and decent, if opinionated. The only faults she perceives in him are vanity and a tendency to be overbearing. Luzhin is wife-hunting, and he specifically aims to find a poor woman to be his bride. Luzhin wants his wife to feel undying loyalty and gratitude toward him. According to these qualifications, Dunya is the ideal woman for him. Luzhin proposed to Dunya, and she accepted. Pulkheria writes that she and Dunya will soon move to St. Petersburg to be with Luzhin. Raskolnikov cries in reaction to his mother's letter.

UNDERSTANDING AND INTERPRETING
Part One, Chapter III

Peeling Wallpaper, Cluttered Room: Dostoevsky continues to use the color yellow as a symbol. In this chapter, its presence signals Raskolnikov's isolation. Yellow peels off the walls, and Raskolnikov wakes up feeling "bilious" (bitter, or literally full of bile, which is the yellow, caustic substance produced by the liver). Like yellow, his stuffy, cramped apartment points to his alienation. Its physical clutter suggests the mental clutter in Raskolnikov's mind.

An Obsessive Focus on One Crime: Raskolnikov's obsessive behavior is described as the kind "found among monomaniacs when they have concentrated all their energies on one point." The one point on which he focuses his energy is his planned crime. Contemplation of this crime has sapped all his energy, leaving nothing left over for the pursuit of basic human necessities. He is so desperately poor he cannot afford food, clothing, or shelter. He has eaten almost nothing for two days. His apartment is in a shambles, and his clothing is ragged. If he does not have any energy for survival, he certainly does not have the vigor to think of school. From his mother's letter and his dust-covered books and papers, we learn that he has dropped out of the university.

THE DOUBLE

Raskolnikov has a literary predecessor in the protagonist of *The Double* (1846), one of Dostoevsky's early novellas. *The Double* is the story of Yakov Petrovich Golyadkin, an ambitious but ambivalent bureaucrat overcome with delusions of grandeur. As Golyadkin's mental state deteriorates and he feels guilty, ashamed, and powerless, he begins to imagine that he has become two separate people. His phantom twin follows him everywhere. At times, the reader cannot tell if the double is real or hallucinated. The double eventually becomes Golyadkin's rival, behaving even more outlandishly than Golyadkin does. The double takes over Golyadkin's job and elopes with his girlfriend, ultimately supplanting the original man. Only when Golyadkin sinks into complete madness does the double disappear. *The Double* is one of Dostoevsky's strongest early novels and is incidentally a favorite of another Russian writer, **Vladimir Nabokov** (1899–1977).

In the Letter, a Lesson on the Raskolnikovs: Letters play an important role throughout the novel. Dostoevsky uses them to introduce characters and create conflicts. In this chapter, Pulkheria's letter reveals much about Pulkheria, Dunya, Raskolnikov, and the background of the Raskolnikov family. We see that the Raskolnikovs are not a family of means, but they are proud. We get to know Pulkheria as the classic figure of the self-sacrificing mother. Her letter to Raskolnikov offers affection and support, and she reveals her unselfish nature when she writes of going into debt so she can send money to Raskolnikov. We see that Dunya is the family's savior and a portrait of chastity and goodness. She casts away the lecherous Svidrigaylov and agrees to marry the wealthy Peter Luzhin as a means of helping her mother and brother. Dunya is modest, virtuous, and dutiful. Meanwhile, Raskolnikov's reaction to the letter shows that pride and desire to provide for his family still exist underneath his obsession with his crime. The letter pulls him back to his everyday existence and upsets him. He is horrified by the thought that his sister must support him through a hasty marriage of convenience.

A Conscientious Libertine and Drunk: Our information about Svidrigaylov comes from Pulkheria, who is not a completely objective source. Even from a subjective point of view, however, Svidrigaylov seems to deserve his reputation as a libertine and a drunk. His intense passion for Dunya seems real, if idealistic. Svidrigaylov is naturally attracted to sensuality, not virtue, which is what Dunya possesses. Svidrigaylov tries to take advantage of people, but he demonstrates conscientiousness by confessing to his wife that he, not Dunya, schemed for them to run away together.

A Generous Tyrant: Luzhin is not a libertine or a drunk, like Svidrigaylov, but he seems more odious than Svidrigaylov. Although the faults Pulkheria identifies in him are not too offensive—he is vain and a bit overbearing—his attitude toward Dunya is distressing. Luzhin sees Dunya as the ideal woman, not just because she is chaste and proper, but because she is poor. Luzhin wants to marry a poor woman in order to feel power over her for the rest of his life. He longs to save a young woman and then luxuriate in her undying loyalty and gratitude.

PART ONE
Chapter IV

Raskolnikov is angered by the news of his sister's impending marriage. He believes that Dunya plans to sacrifice herself to help him. He knows she would not marry a man who only "*seems* good and kind." Once married, Dunya would be servile, and Luzhin would be stingy. Raskolnikov compares Dunya to the young prostitute Sonya Marmeladov, thinking that Sonya having sex with a paying customer is no different than Dunya marrying Luzhin. Impassioned, Raskolnikov resolves to prevent the marriage, although he cannot think of a way to do so. He thinks obsessively about his failures as a son and brother and reproaches himself for his inadequacies. Perhaps, thinks Raskolnikov, Dunya might be better off married.

Later Raskolnikov comes upon a drunken teenage girl staggering down the street, followed by a dandyish middle-aged man who is trying to solicit her. The scene offends Raskolnikov, and he brawls with the man until a policeman arrives. Raskolnikov gives the policeman some money to pay for a cab to send the girl home. But at the last minute he changes his mind and says to the policeman, "What is it to you? Drop it! Let him amuse himself!" After the scene breaks up, Raskolnikov remembers that he was on his way to the apartment of his best friend, **Razumikhin**.

UNDERSTANDING AND INTERPRETING
Part One, Chapter IV

Zigzagging Emotions: Raskolnikov veers wildly between different emotions and convictions as he thinks about Dunya's impending marriage. He catalogues his flaws as a son and brother and dwells on all his inadequacies. Thinking about his failings accentuates his feelings of shame and twists his passion into a contorted conviction. A fierce resolve comes over him for a while, but that falls away, and he reverts to uncertainty and complacency. At the beginning of the chapter, he is furious at himself for letting Dunya sacrifice herself to help him, but after a short while, he rationalizes that Dunya might be better off married.

First Conviction, Then Carelessness: Raskolnikov's encounter with the drunken girl and her would-be customer again shows how warring elements of Raskolnikov's personality clash. At one moment he is passionately determined and at the next, he is cynical and careless. At first, he sticks up for the girl and tries to protect her from the predatory advances of the man. Then, without warning, Raskolnikov changes course and decides he does not care what they do. At first, he is disgusted with the man and eager to intercede on the girl's behalf, but eventually he wonders what right he has to interfere.

"A Wild, Fantastic, and Terrible Question": Raskolnikov feels powerless to protect his family from the Svidrigaylovs and Luzhins of the world, and he suffers for it. This feeling of powerlessness has plagued him for years and has recently reached a peak. The narrator says, "Long, long ago his present anguish had first stirred within him, and it had grown and . . . concentrated itself into the form of a wild, fantastic, and terrible question, that tortured his emotions and his reason with its irresistible demands to be answered." Raskolnikov feels a nagging need to answer his own question, and his mother's letter spurs him to action. Raskolnikov feels an intense urge to act, thinking to himself, "the time had come . . . to act at once and with speed . . . or renounce life altogether." Raskolnikov, who has trouble taking even the smallest action, yearns not just to be a man of action, but to be a godlike man. He feels that he must act or be reduced to the status of a mere mortal—a man who needs help from his mother and sister.

> "*Crime and Punishment* was a work almost in the nature of double jeopardy: as if Fyodor Dostoevsky in middle age—a defender of the Czar, the enemy of revolutionary socialism—were convincing and punishing his younger self yet again for the theories the mature novelist had come to abhor."
>
> **CYNTHIA OZICK**

Squelching Natural Compassion: Raskolnikov's inner monologue shows the influences of utilitarian theory, which was popularized by the English philosopher **John Stuart Mill** (1806–1873). The philosophy of utilitarianism understands human beings as reasonable creatures who do good by following their rational self-interest. By submitting to reason, humanity can find its salvation and create utopian societies that feature "the greatest happiness of the greatest number," in the words of English philosopher **Jeremy Bentham**, 1748–1832. In *Crime and Punishment*, Raskolnikov—an intellectual who, no doubt, learned the tenets of utilitarianism in his university studies—strays from his resolve to save the young girl in the street after pondering utilitarian theories. Raskolnikov tries to account for the wasted life of the young girl by ascribing her downfall to utilitarian theories that argue a certain percent of people must die so that others

BENTHAM AND MILL

English philosopher **Jeremy Bentham** (1748–1832) is considered the founder of utilitarianism. He believed he could scientifically analyze morality and concluded that the common good is a mathematical sum of individual happiness. Therefore, he argued, the greatest good is achieved when the greatest possible number of people enjoy happiness. Essentially, this theory says, the rule of majority is the only important rule, and the individual does not matter. Bentham's friend and fellow Englishman **John Stuart Mill** (1806–1873) further developed this theory to consider the concerns of unrecognized minorities, leading to advances in human rights and proportional representation in government.

may live. Raskolnikov uses reason and science to ease his torment. Utilitarianism, Dostoevsky suggests, suppresses natural human compassion. Furthermore, too much reason is a dangerous thing. The clever Raskolnikov finds it fairly easy to reason his way out of uncomfortable sensations of compassion and guilt.

PART ONE
Chapter V

On the way to Razumikhin's apartment, Raskolnikov decides to put off visiting his friend, even though he has not seen him in months and had planned to ask him for much needed money. He resolves to see Razumikhin "the day after, when *that* is over and done with and everything is different." By "that," Raskolnikov means the crime against Alena Ivanovna. Then Raskolnikov vacillates, wondering if he will ever be able to commit the crime. To ease his nerves, he drinks a glass of vodka at a nearby bar and then falls into a deep sleep behind some bushes.

While sleeping, he dreams vividly of his childhood. In the dream, Raskolnikov is back in his hometown with his father. The two of them watch as a drunken peasant whips his horse, which is pulling a wagon full of other peasants. The drunken peasant says he has every right to beat his horse since it is his property. When the horse disobeys, the man beats it with an iron bar, and then others join him with sticks and whips until the horse falls down and dies. Raskolnikov rushes over to the horse and kisses its muzzle as it lies dead on the ground.

When Raskolnikov wakes from his dream, he is panting and sweating. He writes off the dream as meaningless, but then thinks to himself, "Is it possible, is it possible, that I really shall take an axe and strike her on the head, smash open her skull . . . God, is it possible?" Later, as he walks through the Haymarket, he overhears Alena's half-sister, **Lizaveta**, mention that she will be away from Alena's shop the next evening at seven o'clock. We learn that Lizaveta is as an "absolute slave to her sister . . . trembling before her and even submitting to her blows." Raskolnikov realizes that he now has an opportunity to find Alena alone, and takes this opportunity as a sign that the time has come for his crime. Raskolnikov feels that a greater force, like nature, has allowed him this perfect opportunity to commit the crime.

Fyodor Dostoevsky

Part One, Chapter V

Money Can't Buy Happiness: Raskolnikov thinks that his problem does not stem entirely from lack of funds. He decides not to visit his friend, Razumikhin, even though he feels Razumikhin will be able to help him out of his financial hole. Money is Raskolnikov's immediate need, since it would ease the torment he feels over his powerlessness to help his family's financial situation. But Raskolnikov suggests that even with an infusion of money, nothing would improve. He asks, "did I really think I could settle everything with no more than some help from Razumikhin?" He decides to visit his friend after the crime, since the crime is the important act that will resolve his deeper problem.

The Sympathizer and the Evildoer: Raskolnikov's dream shows how he perceives himself. In the dream, young Raskolnikov is horrified when the crowd viciously beats the horse. He feels sympathy for the horse, which is physically a helpless old creature and symbolically a suffering innocent. Raskolnikov wakes up, terrified at the idea that he could deliver a vicious beating to the old pawnbroker. He sees himself both as the compassionate child who sympathizes with the innocent sufferer, and as the base, immoral man who inflicts violence on a helpless old creature.

Seeing Signs: Raskolnikov decides to go through with the crime only after receiving what he interprets as a sign. Overhearing Lizaveta say she will be away from her sister, Raskolnikov decides that this perfect opportunity to get at Alena means that scientific truth has ordered him to commit the murder: "He did not reason about anything, he was quite incapable of reasoning, but he felt with his whole being that his mind and will were no longer free, and that everything was settled, quite finally." Raskolnikov feels that some greater force, not his own free will, demands that he commit the crime. His actions have been decided for him, he believes, and his submission to the supposed powers of science and nature gives him the strength to act.

Cowering before Alena: Just as Raskolnikov feels helpless in the face of the supposed sign he sees, Lizaveta feels helpless before her sister. She is an "absolute slave" to Alena, who dominates her and even physically abuses her. The timid, submissive, dim Lizaveta is incapable of standing up to her sister's overbearing, intimidating personality. Lizaveta's acquaintances compare her to a "little child."

PART ONE
Chapter VI

Raskolnikov despised Alena Ivanovna even before he met her. They had their first business transaction six weeks earlier, at which time Raskolnikov pawned a ring and then took the money and went to a bar. He could not get the loathsome image of Alena out of his head. At another table in the bar, a student and a young military officer were discussing Alena Ivanovna. The student said Alena is notorious for her spite and bad moods. Many hate her, he said, because she charges a high rate on loans and forecloses if borrowers are even one day late with payment. She is even known to beat her half-sister Lizaveta. Raskolnikov thinks hearing this conversation was "fateful and fore-ordained."

The student in the bar swore he would kill and rob Alena "without a single twinge of conscience." He said her murder would bring plenty of good to the world, especially if her money was used to serve humanity and the common good. He mused, "For one life taken, thousands saved from corruption and decay!" After the student and officer debated a little longer, they both agreed that they would not actually commit the murder.

> "In supplying Bentham with an axe, Dostoevsky thought to carry out the intoxications of the utilitarian doctrine as far as its principles would go: brutality and bloodletting would reveal the poisonous fruit of a political philosophy based on reason alone."
>
> **CYNTHIA OZICK**

Recalling their conversation, Raskolnikov plots the final details of the murder "as if there were indeed something fateful and fore-ordained about it." He goes home and falls into a fitful sleep full of strange dreams. On waking, he sews a loop into the lining of his jacket so he can hide a stolen axe. He reasons that most criminals are discovered not because they leave a trail behind them, but because their reason collapses and recklessness replaces it. Raskolnikov wraps a cigarette case into a tightly secured bundle to bring with him, as if to pawn it. After sneaking away from his apartment, he moves unnoticed through the streets of St. Petersburg. He climbs the stairs to the fourth floor of Alena Ivanovna's building and rings the bell a few times. After a long pause, she opens the door suspiciously.

A FAULTY DIALECTIC

The ideas of the German philosopher **Friedrich Hegel** (1770–1831) pervade the conversation between the student and the officer. Hegel envisions an ideal world in which a universal guiding spirit puts all things in motion, including human will and reason. Hegel posits that the world changes according to a theory known as the *dialectic*. According to the dialectic, a concept (or thesis) generates its exact opposite (antithesis) until the two interact to produce a synthesis. The synthesis in turn becomes a new thesis, and the process continues infinitely. In *Crime and Punishment*, Raskolnikov demonstrates what Dostoevsky identifies as a flaw in Hegel's theory. Within Raskolnikov are reason and its opposite, compassion, but the two never interact and synthesize. His human compassion cannot be reconciled with the reason that pushes him on. His salvation comes from embracing suffering and atonement, a process that does not involve reason.

UNDERSTANDING AND INTERPRETING
Part One, Chapter VI

Raskolnikov's Utilitarianism: The conversation between the student and officer in the bar again reveals Dostoevsky's scorn for utilitarianism. The student says, "Kill her, take her money, on condition that you dedicated yourself with its help to the service of humanity and the common good. . . . One death, and a hundred lives in exchange—why, it's simple arithmetic!" The student is expressing one of the central tenets of utilitarian theory, which holds that individual unhappiness or pain is unimportant if it leads to the happiness of many. The student's expression of these ideas seems revolting and coldhearted. Dostoevsky shows us how odious it is to speak of human life as though it were "simple arithmetic," as is the habit of proponents of utilitarianism.

> "The great preoccupation of Dostoevsky's writing is the war he waged against what could well be called the political correctness of his time—the doctrines of utilitarianism."
>
> **JOHN BAYLEY**

Seeing More Signs: Raskolnikov agrees with the theories outlined by the student, and as a result, he ascribes the coincidence of hearing this conversation to fate. He believes he was ordained to hear the student's conversation and that hearing his own theories in the mouth of another is a sign that he must act. Again, he decides that his decisions are made not by him, but by fate.

Sick with Recklessness: Part of Raskolnikov's preparation for the crime is careful consideration of the psychology of crime. He assumes that most criminals are discovered not because they are careless, but because they become reckless. He thinks "every criminal, at the moment of the crime, was subject to a collapse of will-power and reason, exchanging them for an extraordinarily childish heedlessness." The collapse of reason begins before the crime and continues after it, like an illness. Raskolnikov does not resolve the question of whether this illness causes the crime or results from the crime. Raskolnikov prepares himself for the crime, but he does not realize that the illness of recklessness could descend on him too.

PART ONE
Chapter VII

Alena Ivanovna opens the door a crack to see what Raskolnikov wants, and he quickly pushes his way into her apartment. He explains his abruptness by saying that he is eager to sell the cigarette case. As Alena tries to unwrap the tightly wrapped case, Raskolnikov hits her on the head with the butt of the axe, then hits her again and again until she topples over on her back, blood streaming from her head.

Raskolnikov searches her pockets for the keys to the cabinets in the room. He finally finds the keys around her neck on a string that also holds two crosses and a religious medallion. Raskolnikov searches the bedroom and finds valuables everywhere. Suddenly, he hears a faint cry from the other room. He creeps back and discovers **Lizaveta**, pale and frozen with fear. Without pausing, Raskolnikov strikes her once with the blade of the axe, and she falls down dead. He realizes that he has committed a second, unpremeditated murder, and it fills him with horror and repulsion.

Raskolnikov decides he must leave right away. However, a "growing distraction" creeps up on him and he starts obsessing about the trivial details of his situation, ignoring the bigger picture. He washes his hands in a bucket of water and then spends three minutes cleaning the axe. He spends another few minutes carefully drying the axe and examining it for any trace of blood. A "dark and tormenting idea" strikes him: maybe he is losing his mind, and his panicking is "not at all what ought to be done." Finally Raskolnikov snaps out of his trance and realizes, "My God, I must run, I must run!"

Raskolnikov then notices that when Lizaveta entered the apartment, she left the front door wide open. He starts to flee through the open door, but he hears voices and footsteps below on the landing. He rushes back into the apartment and bolts the door. Two men climb the stairs and knock on the door. They become suspicious when there is no answer and then realize that it is bolted from the inside. The men go back downstairs to find a porter, and Raskolnikov slips out, escaping to an empty apartment on the third floor where painters have just been working. As the two men and the porter go upstairs, Raskolnikov escapes unnoticed and flees to his own apartment. There, he returns the axe and falls into a deep sleep.

UNDERSTANDING AND INTERPRETING
Part One, Chapter VII

Theories, Wrong and Right: Dostoevsky suggests that even the most well-reasoned theories can fall flat when applied to the mess of real life. It is possible to argue that the premeditated murder of Alena was committed in the name of conquering Raskolnikov's internal powerlessness and in the belief that one death can help many people. But Raskolnikov fails to put his theories perfectly into practice when he murders Lizaveta. Alena is a "louse," a corrupt and horrible person who preys on the poor, but Lizaveta is a kind, meek, childlike person. When Raskolnikov's theories prove unequal to real life, he falters and freezes. Another of Raskolnikov's theories ironically turns out to be more powerful than he imagined. Before committing the crime, he theorized that murderers get caught when they lose their reason. Figuring this out does not prevent Raskolnikov himself from losing his reason once he commits the murders. He foolishly wastes time cleaning up and standing around, thus only narrowly evading capture.

Cleansing, Redemptive Water: Water traditionally symbolizes redemption and cleansing in literature, and Raskolnikov uses water to wash off the blood from his hands. He spends long minutes cleaning himself and the axe, as though trying to scrub away his misdeeds. The water also suggests a spiritual cleansing. Although Raskolnikov does not comprehend it at the time, the washing of his soul—the atonement for his evil deeds through suffering—will afford him relief.

Why Did Raskolnikov Commit Murder? This is a central question of *Crime and Punishment*, and one that can be answered in a variety of ways: Raskolnikov killed because he is alienated and feels the impulse to break out of his isolation. He killed because he is desperately poor and wants to steal her money and prevent his sister's marriage of convenience. He killed because he considers Alena Ivanovna a "louse" and believes that the world will be better without her. He killed because he is insane. He never killed at all; the entire novel is a fevered dream taking place in Raskolnikov's diseased mind. Raskolnikov himself justifies the crime in different ways at different times. The question plagues him and the readers throughout the course of the novel.

PART TWO
Chapter I

As Raskolnikov sleeps on the night of the murder, a terrible shivering seizes him. He worries that he is going mad and realizes that he has not locked his door. All the stolen items from the pawnbroker's are still in his pockets. He quickly hides the items in a hole behind the peeling wallpaper. For a moment, he thinks he is completely covered in blood. When he wakes up after sleeping, he realizes he is still clutching a bloody sock and a few other small bloody items. He repeatedly removes the sock and then puts it on again, alternately convinced that the sock will give him away and that it will go unnoticed. He checks his clothes for blood.

Raskolnikov's maidservant arrives and chides him for sleeping so much. The porter is with her, and Raskolnikov fears he has been discovered, since he stole the axe from the porter. The porter apparently knows nothing of the murder, but he brings Raskolnikov a summons to appear before the police. The prospect of seeing the police terrifies Raskolnikov. He worries about leaving his apartment wearing the bloody sock, but since he has no other socks, he goes to the police without changing them. On the way to the station, he contemplates confessing to them.

He arrives and finds the station crowded and noisy. The police clerks are involved with a number of other cases and barely pay attention to him. He feels alienated from everyone. The stuffiness of the office is compounded by the thick smell of fresh paint. After being forced to listen to a number of squabbles, Raskolnikov finds that he has been summoned to the police station because of his late rent. He signs an IOU slip, but he is so feverish and disoriented that he can hardly write.

The police tell him he is free to go, but Raskolnikov nonetheless launches into a long explanation of his debt and his problems with the landlady. He again contemplates confessing, but the police have already moved on to other business. The clerks' discussion turns to the murder of the pawnbroker. Raskolnikov makes his way to the door but faints before he can get out of the station. When Raskolnikov awakens from his fainting spell, he is given a glass of dirty water. He recovers and hurries home, worried that the police are suspicious of him.

UNDERSTANDING AND INTERPRETING
Part Two, Chapter I

A State of Delirium: Raskolnikov embodies his own theory that illness accompanies a criminal's acts. He did not know whether such illness exists before the crime or only infects the criminal afterward, but we can see that in Raskolnikov's case, the state of delirium began well before the crime was committed. Now, after the crime, the illness worsens and overwhelms Raskolnikov's consciousness. We see the "collapse of reason" he theorized previously. After he remembers to hide the stolen goods, he continues to think about them obsessively.

Blood Fixation: Raskolnikov's obsession with blood symbolizes his deteriorating mental state. He fixates on his sock, the toe of which is soaked in blood. He takes the sock off and puts it back on, as if wavering between madness and sanity. He becomes frantic for a moment, convinced that he is coated in blood. Eventually, he falls asleep holding a few bloody things, and it appears as though his panic dogs him even in his sleep.

The Self-destructive Urge: Raskolnikov's pangs of conscience spring from a fear that he will be caught and from a fascination with destroying himself. He considers confessing as he walks to the police station and again just before he leaves. To alleviate his urge to confess, Raskolnikov stumbles through a quasi-confession of something else that causes him guilt: his troubled relationship with his landlady and her daughter, whom he once intended to marry.

Feeling Alienated: Raskolnikov endures a dark moment in the police station when he feels suddenly alienated from everyone around him. "He did not so much understand with his mind as feel instinctively with the full force of his emotions that he could never again communicate with these people." This passage shows that, once again, Raskolnikov's emotion, not his reason, has dictated his behavior. He thinks of his alienation as a feeling, "an immediate sensation," not as "knowledge or intellectual understanding." He feels detached from the world around him, and this impulse causes him pain.

The Sickening Smell of Paint: When paint or painters appear in the novel, it signals that something will soon change or be covered up. After the crime, Raskolnikov escapes to an apartment below that has been freshly painted. In the police station, he is overcome by the "sickly odor" of paint, which stands out from the other smells of the room. Paint suggests renewal—a room is renewed after being freshly painted—and the smell of it makes Raskolnikov dizzy because at this point, he is a long way from seeking redemption or renewal.

PART TWO
Chapter II

Raskolnikov worries that someone will find the goods he stole from Alena Ivanovna's, so he sets out to hide them somewhere in the city. At first he thinks of throwing them in a river, but instead he decides to hide them under a large stone in a park. After hiding them, he laughs to himself in triumph. When he passes by the park bench where he found the drunken girl the night before, he stops laughing, suddenly moved by her plight. Immediately after this moment of compassion, he feels a "boundless, almost physical repulsion for everything around him."

> "The whole novel is built around the unique process of disintegration in the hero's soul: his intellectual life is split off from the life of feeling. . . . this inner split in Raskolnikov is the content of *Crime and Punishment*."
>
> **JOHN BAYLEY**

Raskolnikov remembers that he has promised to visit his friend **Razumikhin**, and while he is walking, he suddenly realizes that he has arrived at Razumikhin's apartment. Razumikhin lets him in, sees that Raskolnikov is a mess, and worries that his friend is ill and delirious. Razumikhin assumes that Raskolnikov is broke, so he mentions that he might earn some money translating the eighteenth-century philosopher Jean-Jacques Rousseau's *Confessions*. Raskolnikov takes the manuscripts and the money and exits. A few minutes later, he returns and puts the papers and money back on the table. He quickly exits again without a word.

Outside, Raskolnikov wanders the streets, and a carriage nearly hits him. The carriage driver whips him in the face, and someone slips money into his hand, thinking that he jumped in front of the carriage intentionally. Raskolnikov returns home and falls into a deep sleep. He dreams that one of the police clerks he met that day is viciously beating his landlady in the hallway outside. When Raskolnikov's maidservant wakes him, he feverishly tells her about the incident, believing it was real. The maidservant realizes Raskolnikov is delirious and gives him some water. She blames his condition on "blood," which she claims can cause visions when given no other outlet. Raskolnikov immediately falls unconscious again.

UNDERSTANDING AND INTERPRETING
Part Two, Chapter II

Confessions: A confession of a different kind appears in this chapter with the mention of the eighteenth-century French philosopher Jean-Jacques Rousseau's *Confessions*, a work in which Rousseau lays bare his sordid thoughts and actions. It is ironic that Razumikhin mentions *Confessions* right after Raskolnikov has nearly confessed to a crime.

Squashing the Twinge of Compassion: Raskolnikov's compassion again intrudes on his reason. His compassion is just a brief twinge this time, and almost immediately after soberly remembering the drunken girl, he wonders why he bothers to worry about other people. Although he momentarily loathes himself for failing to prevent the man from picking up the girl, Raskolnikov then tells himself to be strong and rise above his worries. He blames his "collapse of reason" on his illness—an illness worsened by this kind of compassionate impulse. He represses his compassion and keeps walking, feeling repulsed by everyone.

Ordinary Man, Extraordinary Man: Raskolnikov believes that some men are extraordinary, perceptive enough to commit evil actions if those actions will lead to an ultimate good, and independent. He wants to be one of these extraordinary men, which is why he changes his mind about seeking help from Razumikhin. Raskolnikov wants to believe that he does not need help from anyone. He committed his crime partly to prove to himself that he is one of the extraordinary men, and now he feels ashamed by his lapse into helplessness. His conviction of his own power is again tested when the carriage driver whips him and a passerby tries to help him. Such charity embarrasses and shames him, because as a powerful man he should not be mistaken for a pathetic, suicidal person. To comfort himself, Raskolnikov lashes out. For example, he rejects Razumikhin's offer of charity, returning his money. With this gesture, he feels his pride recharged as if he had "in that moment cut himself from everybody and everything." He chooses alienation because his rational theories of crime and the extraordinary man dictate it. By clinging to reason, he drifts away from normal society, because in his mind, an extraordinary man must be isolated and need help from no one.

Blood Needs an Outlet: Raskolnikov mistakes his dream for reality, as if his life has become an endless nightmare. His maidservant blames his hallucinations on blood, which she says "makes a noise. It's when it hasn't got any outlet . . . then you begin to get visions." Raskolnikov has not yet found an outlet for his own blood, his own life, and so he is stuck in his delirium.

PART TWO
Chapter III

Raskolnikov remains half-conscious and delirious for a few days. His maid-servant and Razumikhin tend to him. Razumikhin tries to befriend everyone, even Raskolnikov's unfriendly landlady, whom he calls by her first name. Raskolnikov seems to have erased the murder from his mind, although he is plagued with the strange feeling that he has forgotten something he should not forget. A stranger arrives and gives him the money his mother borrowed for him. Raskolnikov protests, but Razumikhin persuades him to take it, adding that **Dr. Zosimov** has been checking in on him from time to time. Razumikhin also says he has visited the police station and learned about Raskolnikov's I.O.U. and his fainting episode. Razumikhin mentions that Raskolnikov has been talking deliriously for the past few days, often about how no one should touch his socks. Razumikhin dresses Raskolnikov in new clothes, despite Raskolnikov's protests.

UNDERSTANDING AND INTERPRETING
Part Two, Chapter III

Illness and Isolation: Illness and delirium overtake Raskolnikov, and he can no longer distinguish between dreams and reality. He proves his own theory about the psychology of crime correct to an exaggerated extent: his reason disappears completely, and the illness of recklessness to which he thought himself immune overtakes him. He no longer even recalls the crime, although he has a gnawing sensation that he has forgotten something important. His tiny apartment fills with people trying to help him, which is exactly what he wants to avoid. He is now at the mercy of the very people he tried to put off—his maidservant and Razumikhin. His illness has made him dependent on others, and his isolation has ended.

Razumikhin's Generosity: Raskolnikov's only true friend, Razumikhin shows his generous and outgoing nature throughout this chapter. The root of his name in Russian—*razum*—means "good sense." We learn that he has visited Raskolnikov since his illness first set in and has arranged for a doctor, Zosimov, to check on Raskolnikov. Razumikhin is cheerful and buoyant even when Raskolnikov is gloomy and incapacitated. He is a "magnetic personality" and tries to befriend everyone, even Raskolnikov's unfriendly landlady, whom Raskolnikov could not stand to see.

PART TWO
Chapter IV

Dr. Zosimov checks on Raskolnikov and finds him improved. Razumikhin invites the doctor to a party he is throwing at his apartment that night. He has also invited his distant relative, **Porfiry Petrovich**, the examining magistrate of St. Petersburg, as well as **Zametov**, the police clerk. The conversation turns to the unsolved murder of the pawnbroker and her sister, a crime that is now the talk of St. Petersburg. As Zosimov and Razumikhin debate whether two house painters are guilty of the crime, Raskolnikov suddenly chimes in and becomes passionately involved in their discussion. Zosimov says that Raskolnikov's enthusiasm is a sign of his recovery.

Raskolnikov argues that the painters are innocent and provides an elaborate explanation to prove it. He describes a sequence of events identical to what actually happened, without naming himself as the real murderer. Raskolnikov's rant fills him with pride again, and he suddenly realizes that he is surrounded by people who are helping him. Their debate is interrupted by the sudden appearance of Peter Luzhin at Raskolnikov's door.

> " For the deepest essence of tragedy . . . for the evocation, that is to say, of the profoundest feelings of pity and of terror which can purge the reader's heart — there is, I believe, no work of literary fiction that can take its place by the side of Dostoevsky's *Crime and Punishment*."
>
> **LAURENCE IRVING**

UNDERSTANDING AND INTERPRETING
Part Two, Chapter IV

A Dubious Recovery: The mention of the murder snaps Raskolnikov out of his inactivity and delirium, but he still seems irrational. He participates in the conversation only to rant, spewing forth convoluted arguments and opinions.

Defending the Painters: It makes symbolic sense that the two painters are considered suspects in the murder. Dostoevsky uses painting to symbolize redemption, and as symbols of redemption, their implication in the crime "absolves" Raskolnikov of guilt by drawing attention away from him. Raskolnikov does not appreciate the opportunity to pass the guilt to another party. Instead he is consumed with the idea that the painters have been implicated. He goes so far as to demonstrate how they might be innocent. His guilty conscience is catching up to him and bringing him closer to a crisis.

PART TWO
Chapter V

Peter Petrovich Luzhin introduces himself as the fiancé of Raskolnikov's sister, Dunya. Upon meeting Luzhin, Raskolnikov remembers his resolve to stop the marriage, so he acts rude toward the man. Luzhin mentions an apartment he has obtained for Raskolnikov's sister and mother, and Razumikhin calls it a cheap and dirty place. Luzhin says that since he is a newcomer, he did not know about the apartments, but that the rooms he has rented were absolutely clean. He mentions that he is staying with a friend named Lebezyatnikov. Raskolnikov remembers that Lebezyatnikov was described unfavorably by Marmeladov, the drunk in the bar.

The discussion turns back to the murder, and Razumikhin theorizes that the murderer is a bumbling amateur. The increase in crime in St. Petersburg disturbs Luzhin. Luzhin voices Rationalist theories, and Raskolnikov says that if those theories were true, you could murder at will. Raskolnikov then accuses Luzhin of marrying his sister only to dominate her. Raskolnikov even threatens to throw Luzhin down the stairs. Luzhin finally leaves in a huff. Raskolnikov kicks Razumikhin and Zosimov out. Once out of Raskolnikov's hearing, Zosimov comments that Raskolnikov seems to have a fervent interest in the murder. Raskolnikov turns toward the wall.

UNDERSTANDING AND INTERPRETING
Part Two, Chapter V

Arrogant Peter Luzhin: Luzhin's arrival occurs just as Raskolnikov is coming out of his incapacitation and into his prideful pose as an "extraordinary man." In every way, Luzhin missteps and proves himself to be contemptible, which stokes Raskolnikov's self-righteousness. Luzhin is arrogant and condescending toward Raskolnikov and the others. To Raskolnikov, Luzhin's choice of lodgings for Raskolnikov's mother and sister confirms that Dunya will be condemned to a life of stinginess and servitude.

The Perils of Rationalism: Luzhin voices the idealistic theories popularized by the Russian writer N.G. Chernyshevsky, one of Dostoevsky's contemporaries and ideological nemeses (see page 36). Chernyshevsky's *What is to be Done?* (1863), a novel of an ideal world where human rationality and perfection have been achieved, comes under fire in both *Notes from Underground* and *Crime and Punishment*. Dostoevsky shows the danger of taking Chernyshevsky's rational theories to an extreme. When we hear Luzhin mouthing Rationalist theories, we know he is a buffoon.

A Dangerous Game: Raskolnikov's snippy dismissal of Luzhin's vague philosophical arguments is breathtakingly boldfaced. He tells Luzhin, "Carry to its logical conclusion what you were preaching just now, and it emerges that you can cut people's throats," when Raskolnikov has indeed carried the theory to its logical conclusion and murdered the pawnbroker. Raskolnikov diverts his friends from thinking he might have anything to do with the crime by objecting so strongly to Luzhin's point, although he does betray his passionate interest in the topic. When Raskolnikov ejects everyone from his apartment, he again achieves total isolation. Turning his face to the wall, he feels he has returned to the ideal of the extraordinary man who needs no help from others.

PART TWO
Chapter VI

Raskolnikov dresses and rushes out of his apartment, enjoying his new clothes and feeling a new "unshakeable resolution." He stops on the street and listens to a girl singing, then passes by a brothel where a young prostitute solicits him. He gives her some money but continues on his way. He feels like a "condemned man," which engenders in him a new lust for life.

Entering the Crystal Palace restaurant, he asks to read the last five days' newspapers. Zametov, the police clerk, coincidentally sits down next to him. Raskolnikov, suddenly delirious again, becomes irritable and mocks Zametov, who mentions that he thinks his police colleagues are on the wrong track with the murder. Raskolnikov insults the policemen with the moniker "cock-sparrow." Zametov thinks the murder was committed by an amateur. Filled with resentment toward Zametov's ideas, Raskolnikov passionately describes in detail how he would commit the murder. Zametov is astounded by Raskolnikov's ravings and writes them off to his delirious state.

Raskolnikov, still raving, leaves the restaurant. He runs into Razumikhin on the street and screams at him. Because Raskolnikov is ranting, Razumikhin assumes he is still delirious from his fever. Raskolnikov is so weak, he almost falls down on the street. He wanders off and witnesses a poor woman with a "yellow" face jump from a bridge in a suicide attempt. He looks down at the water and is repelled, and leaves the scene in "complete apathy." He stops and entertains the idea of suicide, then decides that suicide is a cowardly way out.

Raskolnikov makes a beeline for the apartment of Alena Ivanovna, where he finds two wallpaper hangers and tells them that a murder took place there recently. He asks them what happened to the blood on the floor. The wallpaper hangers are suspicious and warn that they will take him to the police. Raskolnikov dashes off and resolves to turn himself in to the police, but a commotion in the street distracts him.

UNDERSTANDING AND INTERPRETING
Part Two, Chapter VI

A Drastic Change in Mood: After his long illness, Raskolnikov feels a sudden lust for life. He enjoys the new clothes he recently hated, he feels resolute, and his conviction that he will soon be condemned gives him a new appreciation for life. "Only to live, to live! No matter how—only to live!" he tells himself. On reaching the restaurant, his pride fully intact, he takes the opportunity to flaunt his new-found energy. Zametov is a perfect target because he allows Raskolnikov to prove to himself that he is extraordinary. After all, any man who could taunt a policeman while talking about his own crime must be extraordinary. At the pinnacle of his strength and power, Raskolnikov comes close to an outright confession.

Another Plunge into Depression: Raskolnikov's tenure as "extraordinary man" is short-lived. He becomes hysterical and exhausted after talking to the policeman, and irritability sets in. Though he was able to return to rationality for a short time, he finds himself unable to keep up with his own machinations of reason. His humanity—his physicality, his health—creeps back.

Bumbling Zametov: Zametov, while practical, lacks imagination. He does not comprehend the significance of Raskolnikov's hysteria and intimate knowledge of the crime and fails to follow the leads that Raskolnikov dangles under his nose. Unlike his associate, Porfiry Petrovich, Zametov follows traditional methods of police work. Even when he infuriates Raskolnikov by describing the murderer as a bumbling thief who took the money and went "straight into the pub," Zametov suspects no connection between the crime and the man seated next to him.

The Dread Crystal Palace: The restaurant's name, "The Crystal Palace," affirms Raskolnikov's renewed ability to put aside his conscience and rely on rational theories. The Crystal Palace is an actual structure in England, and an important symbol in many of Dostoevsky's novels (see page 46). The Crystal Palace was the site of an international exposition that Dostoevsky attended during his travels before the publication of *Crime and Punishment*. For Dostoevsky, the Palace symbolizes the decadence of the West and of utopian Enlightenment thought. Chernyshevsky uses the Crystal Palace in his novel *What is to be Done?* to describe a utopian place where humanity lives in perfection as a result of universal rational behavior.

Searching for Redemption and Insanity: The wallpaper hangers are immediately suspicious of Raskolnikov. He accuses them of cleaning up the blood from the murder, but they know nothing of it. Raskolnikov returns to the scene of the crime in search of the painters, who symbolize redemption, and of the blood, which symbolizes his own deteriorating mind.

PART TWO
Chapter VII

Raskolnikov comes upon an accident involving a drunken man who has fallen under the wheels of a carriage. A crowd has gathered, but no one knows the injured man. Raskolnikov identifies him as Marmeladov and asks a policeman to help him take the injured man home in return for money. At the apartment, Katerina Ivanovna is beside herself with grief. She hysterically lashes out at everyone, saying her family is hungry and she has no money for a funeral. Raskolnikov tries to comfort her and offers to pay the expenses. He sends for a priest, and Katerina asks one of her children to fetch Sonya.

Their landlord, **Amalia Ivanovna Lippewechsel**, arrives and complains of the commotion in the house. Katerina insults her and defends the family, then breaks down in a fit of tubercular coughing. The doctor arrives and declares Marmeladov a hopeless case. Marmeladov, with his last breath, apologizes to Katerina and to Sonya, who has arrived in prostitute's clothing. It is the first time he has seen his daughter dressed as a prostitute, and he is deeply ashamed that he has forced her into this position.

Raskolnikov gives a wad of money to Katerina and leaves for his apartment. A policeman outside remarks that he is covered in Marmeladov's blood. Katerina sends one of her young daughters to discover Raskolnikov's identity since no one knew who he was. When the girl arrives at Raskolnikov's apartment, Raskolnikov is kind and asks her to pray for him. After she leaves, he is full of pride and self-confidence. He resolves to continue living his life and not to confess to the crime. He walks over to Razumikhin's party to apologize for being rude. Razumikhin decides to leave with Raskolnikov and accompany him back to his apartment. Razumikhin mentions that Zametov described Raskolnikov's delirious ravings at the restaurant earlier that day. Dr. Zosimov is worried that Raskolnikov is slightly mad. Back at Raskolnikov's apartment, they find Pulkheria and Dunya, Raskolnikov's mother and sister.

UNDERSTANDING AND INTERPRETING
Part Two, Chapter VII

A Kind Murderer: Raskolnikov showed compassion when he first met Marmeladov, and he is kind again when Marmeladov is injured. Raskolnikov's bouts of sympathetic behavior contrast sharply with his acts of homicide. Compassion again overtakes him when he sees Katerina, and later, her daughter. He doles out money and assurances, asks for prayers on his behalf, and generally behaves kindly. The conflicted Raskolnikov can rationalize the murder of an old woman, but cannot stand to watch people suffer.

Keeping Calm While Covered in Blood: Blood bothers Raskolnikov only when it indicates his guilt. After killing Elena, Raskolnikov is horrified by a small, blood-soaked sock. After helping to move Marmeladov's body Raskolnikov reacts calmly to the blood that soaks him. Even though policemen swarm around the scene of Marmeladov's accident, Raskolnikov keeps cool. When Raskolnikov is focused on helping other people, blood loses all of its symbolic potency.

Sharing the Suffering: Constant suffering characterizes the Marmeladov family. Semen Marmeladov is a hopeless drunk who steals from his family, Sonya is a prostitute, and Katerina approaches the brink of madness after losing her husband. By showing compassion for these sad people, Raskolnikov shares their suffering.

PART THREE
Chapter I

Dunya and Pulkheria are waiting for Raskolnikov in his apartment. He faints when he sees them. Razumikhin explains that Raskolnikov has been very ill. Soon, Raskolnikov regains consciousness and begins raving, reproaching his sister for agreeing to marry Luzhin. He demands that she break off the engagement. Pulkheria and Dunya are beside themselves, but Dunya forgives her brother and blames his behavior on his illness. Pulkheria cries, "Oh, this illness! Something terrible will come of it!"

Razumikhin escorts the two women back to their shabby hotel. He promises to go back and check on Raskolnikov and to get Dr. Zosimov to examine him again. Razumikhin says, "I like people to talk nonsense. It is man's unique privilege, among all other organisms." On the way to the hotel, Razumikhin reveals Zosimov's concern that Raskolnikov might be slightly mad. He also bluntly admits to his low opinion of Luzhin. Razumikhin seems infatuated with Dunya and at one point falls to his knees in awe of her "kindness, purity, reason and . . . perfection." Razumikhin's ramblings bother Pulkheria and Dunya. Razumikhin leaves them momentarily and returns with Zosimov, who tells the two women about his concern that Raskolnikov has "monomania." Later, Razumikhin tells Zosimov of his passion for Dunya.

UNDERSTANDING AND INTERPRETING
Part Three, Chapter I

The Temporary Star of the Show: The close third-person narration, which to this point has followed Raskolnikov, here shifts to follow Razumikhin, who plays the pivotal role of intermediary on his friend's behalf. He sets the secondary elements of the plot in motion, including Dunya's relation to Peter Luzhin and, later, the introduction of Raskolnikov to his nemesis.

Pulkheria's Pessimism: Motherly, worried, and not quite as intelligent as her children, Pulkheria has the most pessimistic outlook on her children's fates. She looks to others to solve her problems and is happy to find a sensible friend in Razumikhin. Pulkheria also has a remarkable sense of intuition. When she sees her son's confused mental state and physical exhaustion, she cries, "Oh, this illness! Something terrible will come of it!"

Fyodor Dostoevsky

Razumikhin's Good Nature: Razumikhin is a good friend and a decent person, if somewhat brash and loose-lipped. He quickly earns the respect of Pulkheria and Dunya, even after calling Luzhin a "scoundrel." His sudden passion for Dunya shows his impulsive nature, but it also seems to be a true, strong emotion. In Dunya, Razumikhin sees the strength of purpose and depth that he lacks. Razumikhin's flaw is his inclination to talk too much, as he does here, letting slip that the doctor fears for Raskolnikov's sanity. Razumikhin also likes to engage in intellectual discussions, even if he is just talking to himself or talking nonsense, as he does in this chapter.

The Limits of Theory: Dostoevsky attacks Enlightenment theories through the mouthpiece of Razumikhin, who says, "I like people to talk nonsense. It is man's unique privilege, among all other organisms." This sentiment attacks rational Enlightenment theories that human beings are unique among animals because of their innate reason. Dostoevsky suggests that, on the contrary, man is unique because he is *irrational*, not because he is rational. Dostoevsky also suggests that the foundations of rational inquiry are unoriginal and usually pointless. As Razumikhin says, "We are all, without exception, in the kindergarten with respect to science, progress, thought, invention, ideals, desires, liberalism . . . everything! We have been content to rub along on other people's ideas—we have rusted away!"

PART THREE
Chapter II

Razumikhin wakes up alone the next day and feels ashamed of his behavior the previous night. He resolves to set aside his cynicism and slovenly appearance, so he washes and dresses handsomely. He visits Dr. Zosimov and discusses Raskolnikov's condition with him. Zosimov worries aloud about Raskolnikov's apparent monomania. After his visit with the doctor, Razumikhin visits Pulkheria and Dunya at their hotel. Pulkheria says they are grateful for his assistance the night before. Razumikhin again assures them that Raskolnikov will be fine.

Razumikhin says he has known Raskolnikov for two years. During that time, he has noticed that Raskolnikov seems to have "two separate personalities": one morbidly depressed and taciturn, the other proud and haughty. Razumikhin describes his friend as kind and generous, if a little self-obsessed. He fears that Raskolnikov may not be capable of loving anyone. Raskolnikov was once engaged to the daughter of his unpleasant landlady. The girl was quiet, ugly, and strange, and she died before the marriage could take place.

Razumikhin again admits that he dislikes Peter Luzhin, Dunya's fiancé. Pulkheria produces a new letter from Luzhin in which he demands a meeting. Luzhin stipulates that Raskolnikov must not come. If he does, Luzhin will leave the city immediately and end the engagement. Luzhin says he witnessed Raskolnikov's actions at the Marmeladov household and describes Marmeladov as a known drunk and Sonya as a prostitute—an "ill-conducted female." Luzhin writes that he saw Raskolnikov give Sonya a large amount of money "on the pretext of funeral expenses," insinuating that Raskolnikov was paying Sonya for sexual favors.

After seeing the letter, Razumikhin suggests that Dunya should decide how to proceed with the engagement and brings both women to see Raskolnikov.

UNDERSTANDING AND INTERPRETING
Part Three, Chapter II

A Lowdown Suitor: Luzhin's letter reveals him to be a despicable man. He accuses Raskolnikov of paying for sex with Sonya when it was obvious to those observing the scene that Raskolnikov gave money to the Marmeladovs to ease their suffering. Luzhin also tries to create a rift between Dunya and Raskolnikov, demanding that Dunya choose between Luzhin and her own brother.

A Fondness for Suffering: Raskolnikov does not appear in this chapter, although we learn more about him from other characters. Razumikhin relates the details of Raskolnikov's engagement, a story that gives weight to the idea that suffering attracts Razumikhin's sympathy. Their suffering drew Raskolnikov to the Marmeladovs, and perhaps the suffering of the landlady's daughter is what attracted Raskolnikov to her. The daughter was poor, ugly, and sickly, the very qualities that appeal to Raskolnikov. As he says later, "she was always ailing; she liked to give to beggars . . . If she had been lame as well, or humpbacked, I might very likely have loved her even more." The pain of others provokes Raskolnikov's sympathy, but he also responds to it because he, himself a lonely misfit, identifies with the downtrodden.

A Pre-Freudian Split Personality: Razumikhin describes Raskolnikov as possessing "two separate personalities," one dark and depressed, the other proud and confident. Dostoevsky's use of the phrase "two separate personalities" is eerily ahead of his time. Austrian psychoanalyst Sigmund Freud theorized about split personalities at the turn of the century, and psychological illnesses known as multiple personality disorder and dissociative personality disorder became well-known in the latter half of the twentieth century. With his distinct personalities, Raskolnikov could be a case study in these sorts of disorders.

PART THREE
Chapter III

Razumikhin visits the doctor with Pulkheria and Dunya. Dr. Zosimov tells them that Raskolnikov's condition has improved and suggests that Raskolnikov remove himself from the "radical causes" that induced his illness, although he does not know what these causes might be. He speculates that Raskolnikov's departure from his university studies might have brought on the illness. Raskolnikov seems to agree, but he quietly mocks Zosimov.

Raskolnikov apologizes to his mother and sister for not meeting them at the train station, blaming his behavior on delirium. He admits it was "unforgivable" to give all his money to Katerina Ivanovna, since Pulkheria had borrowed the money for him. He suddenly gets up to leave, but they beg him to stay. Discussion turns to Dunya's engagement, and Raskolnikov again demands that Dunya break off her relationship with Luzhin. He sees the letter from Luzhin, and it surprises him. Raskolnikov then changes his tone and tells Dunya that she can marry whomever she pleases. He says that what Luzhin wrote about the Marmeladovs is pure slander against him and the Marmeladovs. Dunya decides that Raskolnikov should accompany them to the meeting that night with Luzhin.

UNDERSTANDING AND INTERPRETING
Part Three, Chapter III

Between Reason and Compassion: Raskolnikov drifts between compassion and reason, the two opposite impulses that are strongest within himself. Reason gains the upper hand, to Raskolnikov's detriment. He begins by criticizing Dunya's engagement out of compassion, but eventually he becomes coldly rational and sees sense in the marriage. Dr. Zosimov says Raskolnikov must remove the "radical causes" that led to his illness, unaware that these "radical causes" are ideas spawned by an extreme form of reason. Reason drove Raskolnikov to commit the crime in the first place, and reason now drives him to fits of self-righteousness, delusion, and alienation.

Struggling to be Extraordinary: Raskolnikov now thinks of himself as an extraordinary man who acts as pure reason dictates and does not let emotion interfere. It is because Raskolnikov thinks of himself as extraordinary that he reacts so harshly to his sister. Dunya rationalizes her marriage by saying, "If I destroy anybody it will be myself and nobody else," and instead of protesting at the idea of Dunya destroying herself, Raskolnikov only recognizes the sound reasoning of her arguments. Thinking of the same rationalization that urged him to commit the murder, he says, "You must marry whom you please!" Raskolnikov wants to operate like a rational machine, but his guilty conscience continues to haunt his ordinary, compassionate self. Acting solely according to reason does not come easily to him. He knows that an extraordinary man who committed a crime would have detached himself from his family and from everyone else. The prospect of this isolation makes him act insane.

PART THREE
Chapter IV

Before the group leaves for the meeting with Luzhin, Sonya comes to Raskolnikov's apartment. She enters the room meekly and invites Raskolnikov to her father's funeral. She is embarrassed to sit in the presence of Raskolnikov's mother and sister and is further embarrassed when she sees Raskolnikov's shoddy apartment and obvious poverty. Dunya fixes her gaze on the poor girl. She realizes that Raskolnikov has given all his money to this girl's family. Pulkheria and Dunya leave after bidding respectful goodbyes to Sonya. Outside, Pulkheria says that Raskolnikov and Sonya seem to have something "very important" between them.

Raskolnikov leaves the apartment with Sonya and Razumikhin. Raskolnikov asks if Razumikhin can arrange a meeting with Porfiry Petrovich, the magistrate. A mysterious, well-dressed man—whose name, we will later learn, is **Svidrigaylov**—follows the trio on the street, listening to their conversation. After Sonya leaves the group to go home, the mystery man follows her. He realizes that she lives in the same building as he does and greets her, although we do not yet learn his name.

On the way to meet Porfiry, Raskolnikov thinks to himself that he must put up his best front for Porfiry to prove to him that he could not possibly be the murderer. He decides to make the most of his delusional illness (Dostoevsky's original Russian uses the colloquial expression "I shall have to sing like Lazarus to him") to make it seem as though the illness is to blame for his ravings and strange behavior. Razumikhin describes Porfiry as "incredulous, skeptical, cynical," a man who confounds criminals. When they arrive at Porfiry's door, Raskolnikov teases Razumikhin about his obvious attraction to Dunya, and the two rib each other about romantic entanglements. They enter Porfiry's apartment laughing loudly together.

UNDERSTANDING AND INTERPRETING
Part III, Chapter 4

Comings and Goings: Abrupt arrivals and departures characterize this chapter, which advances several different parts of the plot: Sonya invites Raskolnikov to her father's funeral; Raskolnikov's attraction to Sonya begins to develop; Razumikhin introduces Raskolnikov to Porfiry Petrovich; and a mysterious figure makes an ominous first appearance.

Shy Sonya: Sonya makes her first significant appearance in this chapter. The narrator describes her as childlike, modest, and somewhat timid, defined by her innocence and shame. Sitting with Pulkheria and Dunya embarrasses her because, according to custom, a girl of Sonya's class would not sit in the presence of her social superiors. Dostoevsky establishes a connection between Sonya and Dunya, who fixes her gaze on the shy girl. Both women are self-sacrificing and endure pain gracefully.

A Cynical Magistrate: Razumikhin describes Porfiry as a hardened, cynical officer who has his own method of dealing with criminals. Razumikhin also tells Raskolnikov that Porfiry is eager to meet Raskolnikov, a menacing revelation in light of Raskolnikov's crimes.

Maneuvering Against the Tactician: Raskolnikov fires the first shot in his psychological battle against Porfiry by entering Porfiry's apartment in gales of laughter. He wants to seem confident and carefree to Porfiry and starts playing mind games with the man even before meeting him.

The First Mention of Lazarus: Raskolnikov's reference to Lazarus is used in an idiomatic Russian expression, but the biblical story of Lazarus will later become a central metaphor for redemption. Dostoevsky will suggest parallels between Jesus' resurrection of Lazarus and Raskolnikov's spiritual rebirth.

PART THREE
Chapter V

Raskolnikov is introduced to the police magistrate, Porfiry Petrovich. Making small talk, Raskolnikov mentions that he once sold a few items to Alena Ivanovna and wants to retrieve them now that she is dead. Porfiry, acting unconcerned, tells him that retrieving the items is a simple matter. Raskolnikov immediately becomes suspicious of Porfiry. He is sure that Porfiry winked at him. Raskolnikov grows more suspicious as Porfiry says he has actually been expecting Raskolnikov to drop by since everyone else who sold things to Alena already checked in to see if they could reclaim them. Porfiry says he heard that Raskolnikov raved to Zametov at the Crystal Palace restaurant and that he knows about Raskolnikov's illness. Because he is a police official, Porfiry has also heard about Raskolnikov's kindness to the Marmeladovs after the carriage accident.

> " It is worthwhile to remember that *Crime and Punishment* is not only a religious, metaphysical, psychological, sociopolitical, documentary, and Realist, but also a detective novel."
>
> **LAUREN G. LEIGHTON**

Raskolnikov thinks that Porfiry is baiting him and is gripped with the fear that Porfiry's "cat and mouse game" will prove his undoing. He again contemplates confessing and wonders if Porfiry can sense his terror. Porfiry reveals that he read an article that Raskolnikov recently published in a magazine. The article advanced an interesting theory on crime, and Porfiry asks Raskolnikov to elaborate on his ideas.

The article's main argument is that people are either ordinary men or extraordinary men. Ordinary men, Raskolnikov argues, live in submission to laws and have no right to break them. Extraordinary men, on the other hand, have the right to commit crimes because they aspire to great things. For extraordinary men, the right to commit crimes is not a legal one, but rather, an internal one, inherent in their nature. The extraordinary man, such as Napoleon, decides with his conscience whether to break a law in pursuit of noble ends. Some ordinary men mistakenly consider themselves progressives or "destroyers" who will bring about great change, but they "never go far."

Razumikhin points out that the truly original part of Raskolnikov's theory proposes that the extraordinary man not only commits murder, but he also "uphold[s] bloodshed *as a matter of conscience*." As Raskolnikov says, extraordinary men have the right to commit murder if the crime will benefit humanity. They are benefactors of humankind, even if they commit heinous crimes, because they bring something "new" to the world. But extraordinary men are rare, totaling only one in a million, and the great geniuses perhaps one in many billions.

Porfiry and Raskolnikov debate the theory. Porfiry wonders aloud if Raskolnikov thinks of himself as an extraordinary man, and Raskolnikov says he does not. At one point, Porfiry asks Raskolnikov about his religious beliefs, in particular whether he believes in God, the Apocalypse, and the raising of Lazarus by Jesus. Raskolnikov firmly replies that he believes in all three.

Raskolnikov starts to leave, but Porfiry detains him for another minute with a few questions about the pawnbroker. He asks Raskolnikov if he saw any painters on his last visit to the pawnbroker. Raskolnikov senses that he is being trapped and replies that he saw no painters. Razumikhin chides Porfiry, saying the painters were only there on the day of the crime.

UNDERSTANDING AND INTERPRETING
Part Three, Chapter V

A Battle of Wits: With subtlety and ingenuity, Porfiry presents himself as Raskolnikov's worthy intellectual opponent. Porfiry uses a relaxed, informal manner. He tries to trap his suspects with his sincerity and cordiality. While Porfiry may already suspect Raskolnikov of the crime, we are led to believe that sharpness and suspicion are also part of Porfiry's regular conversation. In contrast to Porfiry's self-command, Raskolnikov cannot act natural, as he had wanted to, because his conscience troubles him and Porfiry's tactics upset him. Porfiry speaks abstractly about the crime but drops small hints that he is speaking about Raskolnikov. He forces Raskolnikov to share his opinions on crime and extraordinary men, all the while insisting that he is simply discussing Raskolnikov's article. Raskolnikov accepts the challenge of battling wits with Porfiry, but in this initial encounter, Raskolnikov seems outmatched by Porfiry's breezy intellect.

An Explanation of a Ruthless Theory: When Raskolnikov discusses his article on the criminal mind, we finally hear a full explanation of his ideas about ordinary and extraordinary men. In his view, ordinary men live in submission and have no right to transgress the law. Some ordinary men wrongly consider themselves extraordinary, but such men do not accomplish much. For extraordinary men, "everything is permitted." If the extraordinary man wants to fulfill the promise of an idea and benefit humanity, he can transgress laws. This means, as Razumikhin points out, that if extraordinary men know that a murder would benefit humanity, they must kill to satisfy their consciences. Raskolnikov argues that truly great men still feel suffering and pain.

Illusions and Delusions: Raskolnikov denies that he is an extraordinary man, although he secretly believes himself to be one. In fact, he seems to fit into the category of the men he scorns: ordinary men with delusions of grandeur. Porfiry asks Raskolnikov about a theoretical case of a young man who believes himself to be extraordinary and devises a "long campaign" for which he needs money. Raskolnikov writes these people off as "stupid and conceited, especially the young." Ironically, nothing describes Raskolnikov better than his own words. His flawed murder of the pawnbroker —committed in the name of a greater good—was really nothing more than a simple crime. By testing Raskolnikov's reaction to the theoretical ordinary young man, Porfiry indicates that he is on to Raskolnikov.

Thoughts of Lazarus: Porfiry asks Raskolnikov whether he believes in the resurrection of Lazarus, and while Porfiry does not pry any deeper into the meaning of the story, his mention of it sparks a thought in Raskolnikov's mind. Later, Raskolnikov will look to the story of Lazarus as one that holds meaning for his own redemption and salvation.

> "Dostoevsky undermines our contemporary illusions not only by satirizing them mercilessly, but more simply by showing that many supposedly brilliant innovations of ours, stupendously original creations, are really just warmed over nineteenth-century ideas, just a little more shrill and imprudent with each passing decade."
>
> **RENÉ GIRARD**

PART THREE
Chapter VI

After meeting with Porfiry, Raskolnikov tells Razumikhin he is convinced that Porfiry suspects him of the murder. Razumikhin promises that he will meet with Porfiry to dissuade him of this notion. Raskolnikov goes home feeling more fearful than ever. When he arrives outside his apartment building, he notices the porter pointing him out to a small tradesman. The tradesman looks at Raskolnikov and then rushes off. Raskolnikov follows the man down the street to find out why he was looking for him. The tradesman suddenly cries out "Murderer!" and runs off.

Raskolnikov returns to his room, horrified. He ponders the murder and begins to feel weak. He realizes that his own situation pales in comparison to that of Napoleon, his model of an extraordinary man for whom "everything is permitted." He concludes that he did not kill a human being, but killed a

EMPEROR NAPOLEON, EXTRAORDINARY MAN

Napoleon Bonaparte (1769–1821), perhaps the greatest conqueror in European history, embodies Raskolnikov's idea of the "extraordinary man." Amid the instability and terror of the French Revolution's most radical phases at the end of the eighteenth century, Napoleon was a general in the French Revolutionary Wars, rising to fame with his victories against other European powers. He returned to France and assumed dictatorial control, stabilizing the country with the Napoleonic Code, a series of legal reforms. He crowned himself emperor in 1804, a seizure of power that caused coalitions of European nations to align against him. Napoleon crushed the armies of Austria and Russia during what became known as the Napoleonic Wars, and by 1807, the entire political map of Europe had changed in France's favor. The giant Holy Roman Empire—institutionalized nearly 900 years before Napoleon's reign—dissolved and was split into new kingdoms. Napoleon's brothers ascended the thrones of Spain, Holland, and Italy. Russia broke the new peace in 1812, and Napoleon launched an invasion that would lead to his exile and, ultimately, to his famous defeat at Waterloo in 1815. Napoleon died in exile on the isle of St. Helena in 1821, just months before Dostoevsky's birth in Russia.

"principle." He begins to think of himself as a "louse," more vile than the pawnbroker herself. He again contemplates making a confession to the police.

Raskolnikov falls asleep and dreams of murdering the pawnbroker. In the dream, Alena does not die as he strikes her with the axe, but laughs at him. He wakes in a cold sweat to find Svidrigaylov—his sister's former employer—in his doorway.

UNDERSTANDING AND INTERPRETING
Part Three, Chapter VI

Debunking the Theory: After his meeting with Porfiry, Raskolnikov's rational justification for the murder deteriorates rapidly as his conscience takes over. Raskolnikov is shaken by Porfiry's suspicions and his intellectual appraisal of the extraordinary-man theory. When the tradesman calls him a murderer, it rattles him further. He no longer sees himself as an extraordinary man and is ashamed to recall that he compared himself to Napoleon. Reexamining his motives for the crime, he concludes that the murder is just one effort of many he could have made to help his family. He realizes that he is not extraordinary enough to see the theory through to the end, and that he could not have benefited humanity with his one puny act. He refers to the ideal of the rational utopian worlds as the "common weal" and feels impatient that utopia has not arrived during his lifetime.

Dreaming of Impotence: Raskolnikov again dreams of murdering, but this time, his dream reflects his new embarrassment. He fails to kill the pawnbroker in his dream because in real life, he has begun to understand the folly of his theories. Raskolnikov is ashamed by his powerlessness and his failure to prove himself to be one of the extraordinary men of his theory. Everyone laughs at him, as the pawnbroker does in his dream. Raskolnikov's dreamed failure reinforces the fact that his crime has had no effect on the world at large; it has affected only him.

Shadowy Svidrigaylov: Again, the mysterious figure of Svidrigaylov appears in a sinister way. He seems to materialize out of Raskolnikov's dreams. As we will see in the second half of the novel, Svidrigaylov brings Raskolnikov a possible way to escape his punishment.

NIETZSCHE'S *ÜBERMENSCH*

Philosopher **Friedrich Nietzsche** (1844–1900) was inspired by Raskolnikov's theory of the extraordinary man. Through the use of a dialectic in which the dueling conceptions of master and slave moralities confront each other, Nietzsche argues that the ordinary man conforms to a slave morality, while the extraordinary man—the *Übermensch*, or superman—rejects the slave morality and replaces it with a heroic master morality. Raskolnikov's extraordinary man, for whom everything is permitted and who commits evil with a clear conscience if it leads to a greater good, is a clear precursor to the *Übermensch*. In fact, Nietzsche once wrote, "Dostoevsky [was] the only psychologist . . . from whom I had something to learn." Nietzsche vehemently disagreed with Dostoevsky, however, about the role of Christianity, which Nietzsche blamed for the subjugation of the individual and the cause of slave morality.

PART FOUR

Chapter I

As Raskolnikov gazes at Svidrigaylov, he thinks he is still dreaming. The unexpected visitor tells Raskolnikov that he always wanted to meet him and now he wants to enlist his help in arranging a meeting with Dunya, the object of his obsessive affection. Svidrigaylov describes himself as a "vulgarian and sensualist" and says that he and Raskolnikov have a lot in common. He recounts striking his wife, **Marfa**, with a riding whip and extrapolates from that experience to conclude that humankind loves to be affronted. More specifically, he says, "women are highly gratified at being outraged." Svidrigaylov's words disgust Raskolnikov, but he wants to hear more. He feels a strange, inexplicable affinity for Svidrigaylov.

Svidrigaylov wishes to offer Dunya 10,000 rubles to break off her engagement to Luzhin. He argues that she is prostituting herself to Luzhin, so she might as well take money from him. His offer, he insists, has no ulterior motive. He simply wants to "do something for her good." Svidrigaylov denounces the intellectual life of St. Petersburg's political clubs as full of "hair-splitting discussions." He wants to save Dunya from such a life.

On his way out, Svidrigaylov casually mentions that Dunya has inherited 3,000 rubles from Marfa as a result of her recent death, money she will get regardless of whether or not she takes the 10,000 from him.

UNDERSTANDING AND INTERPRETING

Part Four, Chapter I

Debauched Svidrigaylov: The emergence of Svidrigaylov adds new interest to the narrative. He is a man about whom we know little except for his reputation as a lecherous and possibly violent lothario. Instead of contradicting those rumors, Svidrigaylov adds more fuel to the fire and cheerfully admits to his "idle and depraved" nature. Despite his descriptions of his own lewd behavior, Svidrigaylov has a clear conscience. The reports that he whipped his wife are irrelevant or, perhaps, a point in his favor, because his wife enjoyed the whipping. Svidrigaylov explains that in his ethos, pleasure and pain mingle and reinforce each other. A loner, Svidrigaylov depends on no one, and he has apparently visited St. Petersburg solely to pursue his carnal desires.

Effortlessly Extraordinary: Some critics argue that Svidrigaylov is the archetypal extraordinary man. He answers to no one, cares little for what people think of him, and goes about his evil business with impunity. More important, he does all of this effortlessly. Svidrigaylov suspects that Raskolnikov shares

UTOPIA ON EARTH

French social philosopher **Charles Fourier** (1772–1837), a predominant thinker of his day, came up with his own notion of the ideal society, or utopia. He conceived of an economic system based around a "phalanx"—a type of commune—in which people share living space and divide work according to their needs and abilities. Fourier based his ideas on Sir Thomas More's *Utopia*, written three centuries before, as well as Plato's *Republic* and St. Augustine's *City of God*. A theory of utopian Socialism grew from Fourier's philosophies, and communities were actually built in France, the United States, and elsewhere in accordance with his theories during the latter part of the nineteenth century. The movement was short-lived due to the world wars of the twentieth century.

these instincts, and Raskolnikov feels an affinity for Svidrigaylov. Still, Raskolnikov is unlike Svidrigaylov in the frailty of his resolve and the inner turmoil that has prevented him from becoming an extraordinary man. In their discussion, Svidrigaylov subscribes to reason when he agrees with Raskolnikov about Dunya's marriage of convenience to Luzhin, yet he also derides St. Petersburg's intellectuals, characterizing them as being obsessed with unimportant details.

PART FOUR
Chapter II

Razumikhin and Raskolnikov make their way to the meeting with Luzhin, Dunya, and Pulkheria. Razumikhin says he met again with Porfiry and Zametov, but things went badly. He could not quite articulate what was objectionable about Porfiry's insinuations. In fact, he thinks he might have made the situation worse and stoked the police's suspicions. Raskolnikov thinks nothing of it, for he is busy thinking over his meeting with Svidrigaylov. He says to Razumikhin, "I am very afraid of that man [Svidrigaylov], I don't know why."

At the meeting, Luzhin tells the group more stories about Svidrigaylov. He says that Svidrigaylov molested a deaf fifteen-year-old girl who later hanged herself. Dunya retorts that those stories are just rumors. Luzhin is insulted that she is taking Svidrigaylov's side. He tries to belittle Dunya in front of her own family by insinuating that he has heard rumors of her impurity. Raskolnikov surprises everyone by revealing that he just met with Svidrigaylov. He tells them that Marfa Svidrigaylov willed 3,000 rubles to Dunya. Raskolnikov refuses to say any more about his conversation with Svidrigaylov, which offends Luzhin further. Raskolnikov scolds Luzhin for the letter he wrote insinuating that Sonya is a tramp and Marmeladov was a useless drunk. Luzhin has had enough. He lashes out at Raskolnikov and insults Dunya. Dunya and then the other Raskolnikovs ask him to leave, and he furiously obliges.

UNDERSTANDING AND INTERPRETING
Part Four, Chapter II

Loathsome Luzhin: Luzhin is selfish, vain, and entirely odious. He vilifies the people around him to make himself look better. He heaps scorn on Svidrigaylov, the only person who is arguably more loathsome than he is. Luzhin is already known to have spread rumors about Sonya and Marmeladov, so we cannot be sure that his stories of Svidrigaylov's depraved exploits are true. Finally, he tries to belittle Dunya in front of her own family by suggesting that she is sexually impure .

Fair-Minded Dunya: Dunya sits in judgment in this chapter, showing her forthrightness and intelligence. She listens to Luzhin's defense and decides he makes an unconvincing case even when he is badmouthing Svidrigaylov, a man she has more reason to detest than does Luzhin. Dunya stands as a symbol of justice and goodness.

Sadistic Svidrigaylov: We glean bits of information about characters offstage from the stories told by other characters. Luzhin's descriptions of Svidrigaylov's misdeeds and violence make Svidrigaylov sound like a man in the mold of the notorious Marquis de Sade, sexual sadist. This description might not be so far off base, considering what Svidrigaylov told Raskolnikov about his sexual adventures and predilection for whipping. Luzhin paints a portrait of Svidrigaylov as a depraved, criminal beast, although we cannot automatically trust Luzhin.

> "An artist can wander and still maintain essential form. Dostoevsky did it. he usually told 3 or 4 stories on the side while telling the one in the center (in his novels, that is)."

CHARLES BUKOWSKI, "CHRISTMAS POEM TO A MAN IN JAIL"

PART FOUR
Chapter III

A bitter Luzhin returns to his lodgings, plotting a way to bring Dunya back to him. He fears Svidrigaylov the most. Meanwhile, Raskolnikov tells his sister about Svidrigaylov's offer of 10,000 rubles if she breaks off her engagement to Luzhin. Dunya says that Svidrigaylov must have a "terrible purpose" in mind. Razumikhin vows to protect Dunya, and everyone decides to keep their distance from Svidrigaylov. Raskolnikov then tells his mother and sister that he is not well. He says that no matter what happens to him, he wants to be alone. Dunya, upset, calls her brother wicked and heartless. Razumikhin whispers to her that Raskolnikov is mad, not heartless.

Raskolnikov leaves, and Razumikhin follows. He senses that Raskolnikov is trying to get away for a reason and wants to talk with him before he leaves. Raskolnikov asks Razumikhin to watch over his mother and sister and never to leave them. Then, with a minute of silent staring, he conveys to Razumikhin that he is involved in something terrible and shocking. From that moment on, the narrator says, Razumikhin becomes "a son and a brother" to Pulkheria and Dunya.

UNDERSTANDING AND INTERPRETING
Part Four, Chapter III

Confessing to a Trusted Friend: This chapter reaffirms Razumikhin's role as trustworthy intermediary. Because Razumikhin agrees take over Raskolnikov's role and care for Pulkheria and Dunya, Raskolnikov is free to focus on coming to terms with the murder and his conscience. In one way, Razumikhin is the first person to whom Raskolnikov confesses. When the two men stare at one another in silence, the unspoken truth of Raskolnikov's trouble is conveyed. Because the friendship between Raskolnikov and Razumikhin is strong, they can understand each other without speaking.

Trapped by Theory: Raskolnikov gradually becomes a victim of his own theory of crime. He argued that crime isolates the criminal from society, and now he formally parts from his mother and sister. Svidrigaylov, like Raskolnikov, is isolated. Raskolnikov suspects that he can learn something from Svidrigaylov, but he has not yet noticed Svidrigaylov's isolation.

PART FOUR
Chapter IV

Raskolnikov goes straight to Sonya's house, where he questions her about her life and about Katerina Ivanovna. Sonya describes Katerina as a clever, passionate, generous woman, unhappy but eager to find justice in the world. Raskolnikov then assaults Sonya with grim images of her potential future, saying Katerina will die of tuberculosis, Sonya's stepsiblings will be forced to beg, and her younger stepsister will have to become a prostitute to support the children.

Distraught, Sonya responds, "God will not allow it!" and when Raskolnikov counters that God may not exist, she begins to sob. Suddenly, he bows down before her and kisses her feet, saying he kneels to prostrate himself "before all human suffering." He cannot reconcile her shame and baseness as a prostitute with her holiness. He asks her why she does not contemplate suicide, given the desperation in her life. Sonya responds that she has not committed suicide because the children must be supported. Raskolnikov gathers from her haunted expression that these questions have tormented Sonya for years.

THE STORY OF LAZARUS

The story of Lazarus is one of the episodes in the Bible most often cited for its depiction of salvation through Jesus Christ. The story appears in John 11:1–44. Lazarus, who died after an illness, was miraculously raised from the dead by Jesus. Jesus says, "This illness does not lead to death; rather it is for God's glory, so that the Son of God may be glorified through it." When he promises that Lazarus will rise from the dead, he says, "I am the resurrection and the life. Those who believe in me, even though they die, will live, and everyone who lives and believes in me will never die." Some Christians say that, with these words, Jesus offers people the opportunity to be reborn or "saved" from a life of sin. The Lazarus story is also well known for containing the shortest verse in the Bible: "Jesus wept." (11:35)

Raskolnikov discovers that Sonya and Lizaveta are devout "religious maniacs." He muses, "I shall become one myself here! It is catching!" He grabs a Bible and asks Sonya to read him the story of Lazarus. Sonya mentions that the Bible used to belong to Lizaveta Ivanovna (the murdered sister of the pawnbroker), who was a friend of hers. She says that Lizaveta was a good, God-fearing woman. Raskolnikov realizes that Sonya keeps her tormented feelings about suicide from her family and that reading the Bible helps alleviate her torment. As Sonya reads the story of Lazarus, Raskolnikov sees her strength return.

Raskolnikov tells Sonya she must join him, that they are similarly cursed and that their "paths lie together." He insists that she cannot continue her life of prostitution. They must "demolish what must be demolished, once and for all, that is all, and take the suffering on ourselves" in the name of power. Finally, Raskolnikov says that if he sees her the next day, he will tell her who killed Lizaveta. As the chapter ends, we discover that Svidrigaylov has been hiding behind the door in the next room. He has heard everything said between Sonya and Raskolnikov.

UNDERSTANDING AND INTERPRETING
Part Four, Chapter IV

Tormenting Sonya: Raskolnikov taunts Sonya to test her strength and see how much suffering she can endure. He paints a bleak but plausible picture of her future, finally suggesting that God may not exist. This last comment offends Sonya and causes her to bitterly resent Raskolnikov. Raskolnikov views Sonya's suffering as a badge of nobility and a sign of the unending goodness within her.

Using Sonya: When Raskolnikov learns that Sonya seeks out God in her times of need, he decides to become a "religious maniac," not because he seeks religious redemption for himself, but because he seeks salvation in Sonya. Sonya brings Raskolnikov strength just as the Bible brings Sonya strength. Sonya reads the Bible for redemption, and Raskolnikov goes to Sonya for redemption. As Sonya reads from the story of Lazarus, her strength floods back into her, and Raskolnikov is amazed at her passion. He feels reborn from her strength.

Commandeering Sonya: Raskolnikov's rebirth through Sonya leads him to believe that he and Sonya are on the "same path." In Sonya, he finds a kindred spirit who struggles to escape suffering. By linking himself to her, he puts aside his isolation.

Likening Sonya to Jesus: The story of Lazarus is identified as symbolic of rebirth and redemption. Just as Lazarus died and was entombed, Raskolnikov's crime isolated him from society. Lazarus was raised from his tomb by Jesus Christ, and Raskolnikov hopes to be restored to life again through Sonya. The story of Lazarus has appeared twice before this chapter, notably when Porfiry asked Raskolnikov if he believed in the literal meaning of the biblical story. Porfiry's use of the story indicates that he too could be a source of redemption for Raskolnikov.

Remembering Lizaveta: Until Sonya reveals that she was a friend of Lizaveta's, Raskolnikov does not give a thought to the innocent victim of his second murder. The Bible from which Sonya reads once belonged to Lizaveta, emphasizing the connection between the two women, both of whom are innocent sufferers.

PART FOUR
Chapter V

The day after meeting with Sonya, Raskolnikov goes to Porfiry's office to file a claim to retrieve the items he left with Alena. He is worried that Porfiry will try to trap him into confessing. Their meeting begins pleasantly, and Porfiry tries to keep matters social. Raskolnikov asks Porfiry if he still intends to cross-examine him about the murder. Porfiry dances around the subject of the investigation, but Raskolnikov threatens to leave unless it begins immediately.

To calm Raskolnikov, Porfiry begins to talk of the methods he uses in an investigation. He usually lets his suspect go free for a time but assumes that the suspect will come back like a "moth to a candle" to provide his own theory of the crime. Finally, the suspect will come closer and closer until he flies "straight into [Porfiry's] mouth." Porfiry then reveals that he knows about Raskolnikov's suspicious return to the scene of the crime. Again, he implies that he does not consider Raskolnikov a suspect. He says that he had hoped their meeting could be a friendly social call. Porfiry motions to the door behind him, where he has his apartment, and says he has a "surprise" for Raskolnikov. Before he has a chance to open the door, there is a commotion outside the office in the police station.

UNDERSTANDING AND INTERPRETING
Part Four, Chapter V

Cat and Mouse: Porfiry employs subtle tricks in an attempt to coax a confession from Raskolnikov. The key element of Porfiry's strategy is acting as if he is *not* in pursuit of Raskolnikov. As Porfiry says, the job of an examining magistrate is an art. Porfiry does not want to arrest Raskolnikov, perhaps because Raskolnikov will no longer feel the burden of his crime once in jail. Instead, Porfiry leaves Raskolnikov free so he can continue to contemplate his crime. He suspects that, eventually, Raskolnikov's conscience will get the better of him and he will confess.

Breaking Down the Criminal: Porfiry realizes that Raskolnikov's theory of crime will prevent him from confessing. Before Raskolnikov will admit to murder, Porfiry has to convince him that his theories about the extraordinary man are illogical. Thus, Porfiry appeals both to Raskolnikov's intellect and to his morality. Once Raskolnikov's intellectual rationalizations collapse, he will be forced to conclude that his crime was the act of an ordinary man. Then Raskolnikov's conscience, heavy with remorse and suffering, will take over, rendering his guilt unbearable.

Why Raskolnikov Suffers: Porfiry understands why Raskolnikov is suffering. He knows that Raskolnikov has begun to doubt his own theory of crime, and that Raskolnikov's rationalization for killing Alena no longer eases his conscience. Raskolnikov compassion causes him to suffer for the crime, and this suffering makes him realize that he is not an extraordinary man, because extraordinary men would not feel pain or remorse. This realization causes Raskolnikov to suffer more, filling him with self-loathing for being weak and ordinary.

PART FOUR
Chapter VI

Outside Porfiry's office, the police bring in one of the painters from the murder crime scene. This painter confesses to the murders, which confuses Porfiry completely. He does not believe the painter. He tells Raskolnikov to leave, saying that they will see each other again soon.

Raskolnikov considers himself out of danger for the time being. Still, he worries that Porfiry knows all his weaknesses. When Raskolnikov arrives at home, he is met by the tradesman who had screamed "Murderer!" The tradesman confesses that it was he who was hiding behind the door in Porfiry's office. The man now apologizes and says he was wrong about Raskolnikov's guilt. After the man leaves, Raskolnikov glides along with a renewed sense of power and resolve.

UNDERSTANDING AND INTERPRETING
Part Four, Chapter VI

Stealing the Sins of Others: The painter arrives in time to save Raskolnikov from being implicated by Porfiry. We find out later that the painter belongs to a religious sect that says suffering for the sins of others will win you salvation. The painter, in an attempt to save his own soul, grants Raskolnikov a reprieve.

Get-Out-of-Jail-Free Card: After the painter gives him a free pass, Raskolnikov is reenergized and says to himself, "Now we shall fight again." He is ashamed of his cowardice with Porfiry and resolves to put behind him what he now considers an insignificant and bungled crime. He wants a new chance to become an extraordinary man.

PART FIVE
Chapter I

Peter Luzhin, wounded from his broken engagement to Dunya, ponders the mistakes he made at their previous meeting. Meanwhile, his friend and roommate, Lebezyatnikov—an intellectual and committed Socialist—rambles about a variety of Socialist theories and ideas popular at the time.

The discussion turns to Sonya, who is across the hall from their apartment with Katerina Ivanovna, hosting the funeral dinner for Marmeladov. Luzhin says Raskolnikov told him that Lebezyatnikov was violent to Katerina and propositioned Sonya. Lebezyatnikov vehemently denies both rumors and says that the violent Katerina attacked him, and he was only trying to persuade Sonya to join a commune with him, not proposition her sexually. Lebezyatnikov says, "I only understand one word: *useful*!"

Luzhin counts large stacks of money he just received from cashing in some bonds. He decides he wants to meet Sonya and asks Lebezyatnikov to stay and conceal himself in the room while he talks to the girl. When Sonya arrives, she immediately notices the stacks of money on the table. Luzhin tells her he wants to start a fund for Katerina and the family. Before Sonya leaves, he gives her a ten-ruble bill to prove his good intentions.

UNDERSTANDING AND INTERPRETING
Part Five, Chapter I

A Touch of Comedy: The stories we have heard about Lebezyatnikov make him sound like a violent, creepy person, but in this chapter, we see that he is actually a simple, one-dimensional man. He denies the rumors about his past and offers plausible alternate explanations for his actions. From his rambling monologues about Socialism, we learn that he is a committed, if naïve, idealist and a lover of humanity. He bases his entire life on the Socialist theories he mentions in this chapter. He can sum up his beliefs and character in the exclamation, "I only understand one word: *useful!*" Lebezyatnikov's blind faith in theory provides comic relief in a work not famed for its humor.

Silly Pet Theories: Through Lebezyatnikov, Dostoevsky attacks the emptiness he sees in some of the theories of his day—ideas to which he subscribed before his experiences in Siberia. For Dostoevsky, these ideas are just the absurd machinations of naïve intellectuals like Lebezyatnikov. Raskolnikov is not so different from Lebezyatnikov. He too is a naïve intellectual with a pet theory of crime that he proves, by his own actions, to be flawed and absurd. Both men believe that the only good ideas are new ones, a belief Dostoevsky abhors. Dostoevsky thinks that radicalism is the most dangerous element in society, a theme he pursues in his novel *The Possessed*.

PART FIVE
Chapters II & III

At the funeral dinner, a number of guests walk around eating free food and gulping vodka. Katerina knows the party is beyond her means, but she invited everyone she knew, even Amalia Ivanovna, the landlady with whom she has had many disputes. Raskolnikov arrives late after having been detained at Porfiry's. Katerina talks with everyone but breaks down in fits of tubercular coughing, spitting blood into a handkerchief. She soon becomes irritable and begins blaming the landlady for her family's misfortunes. A ruckus breaks out as Luzhin enters the room.

Katerina implores Luzhin to take sides in her fight, but Luzhin pushes past her and says he needs to talk to Sonya. He announces that he is missing a 100-ruble note and that he suspects Sonya of stealing it from his table. Sonya denies it, but Katerina orders that Sonya be searched. The missing note falls out of one of Sonya's pockets. Lebezyatnikov says he witnessed Luzhin plant the money on Sonya in the other room, but Luzhin denies it. Lebezyatnikov cannot come up with a reason why Luzhin would do this, so he wonders if he is wrong.

Suddenly, Raskolnikov steps forward and offers a reason for Luzhin's actions: Luzhin wanted to make Sonya look bad so Raskolnikov would look bad. Luzhin hoped that this way, he could force Dunya to return to him. Exposed and defeated, Luzhin leaves. Sonya rushes off in despair, and Raskolnikov follows her. Someone throws a glass at him but hits Amalia Ivanovna by accident. The wounded landlady announces that she will evict Katerina Ivanovna.

Part Five, Chapters II & III

Pride Goes before a Fall: Katerina is a proud woman, as we have seen in past episodes, although her prideful boasts are usually about long-ago events and achievements. Her pride has led her to invite a huge crowd of people to the funeral so she can prove she is not poor. She even invited Lebezyatnikov from across the hall, the "scoundrel" with whom she once had a brawl. She also invites and then mocks her German landlady. This mockery, although exaggerated, is typical of the Slavophile attitude of the time, shared by Dostoevsky, that German immigration and influence were weakening Russia.

Mad on the Street: Katerina's eviction from the apartment—the only location where we have seen her throughout the novel—is a metaphor for her madness. As she leaves the building, she leaves her senses behind.

More of the Same: These chapters flesh out characters we already know well. Luzhin demonstrates, once again, that he is reprehensible. Sonya shows she can bear the worst circumstances and still remain honorable and graceful. Katerina becomes hysterical, and Raskolnikov flaunts his intellect and his theories.

PART FIVE
Chapter IV

As Raskolnikov arrives at Sonya's apartment, he decides he must tell her that he killed Lizaveta. When he arrives and mentions that Katerina is being evicted, Sonya gets up to go see Katerina. He persuades Sonya to stay and talk for a while. She begs Raskolnikov not to taunt her as he did the last time they met. Raskolnikov asks her a hypothetical question: who has more right to live, Luzhin or Katerina? Sonya answers that she cannot know what God intends. Raskolnikov hides his face in his hands, and Sonya sees that he is suffering.

He reminds her of his promise to tell her who killed Lizaveta. He asks her to guess, and gradually she realizes that he is the murderer. Raskolnikov notices that Sonya's helpless, frightened face upon hearing his confession is the same face he saw when he murdered Lizaveta. Sonya weeps and says, "There is no one, no one unhappier than you in the whole world!" Raskolnikov is amazed that she still clings to him after discovering that he is a murderer. He asks her not to forsake him, and she promises she will not. She says she will follow him to prison in Siberia.

At the mention of prison, Raskolnikov tenses up and pushes Sonya away. She asks him to explain why he killed Alena and Lizaveta. He offers a variety of reasons but then rejects them all and breaks down sobbing. He finally admits that his theory of the extraordinary man does not apply to himself and there was no reason for the murder. Raskolnikov says, "If I worried for so long about whether Napoleon would have done it or not, it must be because I felt clearly that I was not Napoleon . . . I longed to kill without casuistry, to kill for my own benefit and for that alone! . . . I did not commit the murder to help my mother—that's rubbish! I did not commit the murder in order to use the profit and power I gained to make myself a benefactor of humanity. Rubbish! I simply murdered; I murdered for myself, for myself alone." He begs Sonya to tell him what to do.

> "In *Crime and Punishment*, the reader, as well as Raskolnikov, must struggle to draw his own conclusions from a work which mirrors the refractory and contradictory materials of life itself, with their admixture of the absurd, repulsive, and grotesque."
>
> **GEORGE GIBIAN**

Sonya tells him to go immediately to the crossroads, kiss the ground, and confess his crime aloud. She tells him to accept suffering and achieve atonement through it. Raskolnikov asks if she will visit him in prison, and she says yes. Sonya offers him a cross that once belonged to Lizaveta. He declines and says he will retrieve the cross when he is ready. She agrees, saying that he should wear it when he has decided to suffer. Lebezyatnikov knocks on the door, surprising them .

UNDERSTANDING AND INTERPRETING
Part Five, Chapter IV

How Much Can Sonya Bear?: Sonya's capacity to bear suffering is at the center of this chapter. She asks Raskolnikov not to tease her as he did the last time they met, but he still pushes her to see how much she can take, shocking her with the news of the eviction and then plaguing her with difficult metaphysical questions. He puts an enormous burden on her shoulders by confessing to the murders and begging her to redeem him and stand by him.

The Bumpy Road to Confession: Raskolnikov's admission of guilt is not entirely smooth. When Sonya, who does not understand Raskolnikov's intellectualization of the crime, tells him to confess publicly and then go to prison,

Raskolnikov loses his courage. At the mention of prison, Raskolnikov reacts with fear, a demonstration of his reluctance to admit to others that he is an ordinary man. His intellectual redemption lapses, and he makes a last-ditch effort to convince himself, saying, "Perhaps I am *still* a man and not a louse . . . perhaps I can still put up a fight!" He tells Sonya that he can bear the torment, even for the rest of his life, and hopes he can escape Porfiry.

The Burden of Love: In the end, Raskolnikov glimpses the path to redemption that Sonya offers through her love. He realizes that she feels intense love for him, which makes him feel pained and burdened. He went to Sonya because he thought of her as his only hope. He wanted to lay his burden on her shoulders, thereby easing his own suffering. But Sonya's presence has the reverse effect: "when her whole heart turns toward him, he is suddenly conscious that his unhappiness is immeasurably greater than before." Sonya's love for him makes him realize the burdens of his conscience. The weight of this love only increases his suffering. But Sonya shows him how this suffering—this love—will lead to his redemption.

The Wounded Trinity: Lizaveta's wooden cross symbolizes the burden Raskolnikov must bear. This symbolism comes from the Bible, in which Christ bears a cross on his shoulders as a symbol of the world's suffering and his own. Raskolnikov cannot yet wear Lizaveta's cross, because he is not yet ready to suffer for the crime. When Sonya tells him they will bear the cross together, she takes part of Raskolnikov's burden onto herself. She also connects herself to Lizaveta, as does Raskolnikov when he realizes that Sonya's frightened face reminds him of Lizaveta's face.

PART FIVE
Chapter V

Lebezyatnikov informs Sonya and Raskolnikov that Katerina Ivanovna has gone mad. In her madness, he says, she has taken her children out of the house and taught them to sing on the street for spare change. Sonya rushes off to find her, and Raskolnikov suddenly loathes Sonya and wonders why he told her anything. Raskolnikov returns to his apartment, where he finds Dunya waiting to speak to him. She sympathizes with him, saying she has heard that the police are falsely accusing him of the murders. Tormented, Raskolnikov wants to tell her the truth about his crime.

Dunya rushes off, and Raskolnikov wanders the streets. He finds Katerina Ivanovna surrounded by a large crowd that is enjoying the spectacle of her madness. Katerina stumbles to the ground and injures herself. Blood pours from her mouth. Raskolnikov carries her to Sonya's apartment, where she lies dying. Svidrigaylov enters from his room across the hall and offers to pay for all the funeral arrangements. He tells Raskolnikov he will take all the money he had planned on giving to Dunya and instead give it to Sonya and to Katerina's children.

Svidrigaylov privately explains to Raskolnikov that he is doing this because he has no use for the money himself. He repeats words that Raskolnikov used in his confession to Sonya, and it becomes clear that Svidrigaylov overheard Raskolnikov's confession from a nearby room.

UNDERSTANDING AND INTERPRETING
Part Five, Chapter V

Considering Siberia: Raskolnikov is repulsed by Sonya, because she has asked him to choose prison and public shame. He is not ready to bear the cross of suffering with her, so he reverts to his usual state of isolation. He even wonders if it would be best to exile himself in Siberia, a place where he would feel completely alone.

The Menace of the Eavesdropper: Svidrigaylov inserts himself into Raskolnikov's business, showing a mysterious, foreboding interest in it. His knowledge of the murders puts him in a position of power over Raskolnikov. We do not know yet what Svidrigaylov has planned for Raskolnikov, but it seems possible that he either wants to enjoy tormenting him or plans to blackmail him.

PART SIX
Chapters I & II

Raskolnikov falls into deeper solitude, worried by Svidrigaylov's knowledge of the murder. He concludes that Svidrigaylov is a "riddle," but one who might provide an escape route. Meanwhile, Svidrigaylov makes good on his promise to pay for Katerina's funeral. He also finds institutions to accept the Marmeladov orphans. As Raskolnikov watches the funeral service, he realizes that Sonya has not dared to look at him for the past few days.

The next morning, Razumikhin arrives at Raskolnikov's apartment and reproaches him for abandoning his family. He informs Raskolnikov that his mother, Pulkheria, has fallen ill. Razumikhin tells him Dunya has received a disturbing letter and Porfiry still has the painter in custody for the murder of the pawnbroker. Raskolnikov again asks Razumikhin to take care of his mother and sister no matter what happens to him.

After Razumikhin leaves, Raskolnikov wonders if Porfiry will attempt to cross-examine him again about the murder, regardless of the painter's confession. As Raskolnikov prepares to leave to find Svidrigaylov, Porfiry appears at his door.

In his usual way, Porfiry acts as though his visit were a social one. He apologizes to Raskolnikov for the scene at his office and admits that he acted unfairly. He says he admires Raskolnikov and considers him "daring, proud, in earnest." Porfiry says he believed Raskolnikov was the murderer because Alena was holding one of Raskolnikov's pawned goods in her hand when she was found, the action fit with Raskolnikov's magazine article on the psychology of the criminal mind, and Raskolnikov returned to the scene of the crime.

Porfiry also mentions that the painter who confessed to the crime is a member of a religious order that prizes suffering, especially suffering for others' sins at the hands of the authorities. He concludes that the painter could not have been the murderer. Raskolnikov asks whom Porfiry suspects, and Porfiry says, "it was *you*, Rodion Romanovitch. You murdered them!" Raskolnikov vehemently denies the accusation.

Porfiry says he has a "scrap of proof," but will not arrest Raskolnikov for several days, hoping that Raskolnikov will eventually confess. He does not think that Raskolnikov will run away and says there might be a reduction in his sentence if he turns himself in. Porfiry advises Raskolnikov, "Find your faith, and you will live." He also tells him to suffer, because "suffering is a great thing." Porfiry notes that Raskolnikov is ashamed that his theory does not work in practice. He tells Raskolnikov to pursue justice, since only then will his pride return and his shame fall away. Porfiry leaves, and Raskolnikov rushes off to see Svidrigaylov.

UNDERSTANDING AND INTERPRETING
Part Six, Chapters I & II

Porfiry's Shocking Honesty: Porfiry's monologue shows the brilliance of his psychological methods. Porfiry has suspected Raskolnikov since Raskolnikov made his first ragged appearance at the police station. Porfiry uses what little circumstantial evidence he has—for instance, Raskolnikov's behavior when he returns to the crime scene —and unravels Raskolnikov's psychology, figuring out why he committed the murders and what happened afterward. Porfiry is amazingly honest with Raskolnikov, admitting that he admires him and calling him "daring, proud, in earnest." Porfiry also admits that he is mesmerized by Raskolnikov's "absurd and fantastic" article about crime. And he even admits to Raskolnikov that he has almost no concrete evidence. Porfiry's complete honesty with Raskolnikov is a sign of his supreme confidence.

> "No other narrative fiction drives itself onwards with the remorseless strength of *Crime and Punishment*, truly a shot out of hell and into hell again."
>
> **HAROLD BLOOM**

Porfiry Follows Sonya's Lead: Like Sonya, Porfiry tells Raskolnikov that he would do well to confess. He appeals to Raskolnikov's sense of reason, telling him it is to his advantage to confess because if he does, the courts will be more lenient with him. Porfiry sounds even more like Sonya when he reveals his own religious inclination, telling Raskolnikov, "Find your faith, and you will live." He tells Raskolnikov not to fear "the great fulfillment" that lies ahead, saying faith will bring justice and also restore his self-esteem, which he knows Raskolnikov now lacks. Confession takes courage, he says, but Raskolnikov will be able to endure the aftermath. He believes that Raskolnikov is an intelligent, good man with potential to be a productive citizen again. But without a confession, Porfiry will have to arrest him, and he suspects Raskolnikov will suffer a long life in prison without ever living up to his potential.

Svidrigaylov, Still Ominous: Svidrigaylov's appearances in the novel, until this point, have been shadowy. He has hardly appeared at all except as a sinister phantom of a character. He first appeared to Raskolnikov as half-dream, half-real man. After that, he made small appearances that hinted he might play a pivotal role. Now, we are sure that Svidrigaylov will become a central character in the novel.

PART SIX
Chapter III

After his long talk with Porfiry, Raskolnikov feels a "moral weariness." He does not look forward to figuring out the riddle of Svidrigaylov, but he does feel that Svidrigaylov has some kind of power over him. He thinks that Svidrigaylov probably has not talked to Porfiry and feels that for some reason Svidrigaylov would avoid going to Porfiry. Raskolnikov wonders whether Svidrigaylov still has designs on Dunya and fears that Svidrigaylov's knowledge of the murder may lead Raskolnikov to compromise his sister's safety. Raskolnikov decides he will kill Svidrigaylov before it comes to that point.

Raskolnikov finds Svidrigaylov in a restaurant, warns him to leave Dunya alone, and threatens to kill him. Svidrigaylov calmly tells Raskolnikov not to worry—he only wants to get to know him better. He finds Raskolnikov a "curious subject for observation" and muses that he may be able to learn something new from him. Svidrigaylov says he came directly to St. Petersburg after his wife's death so he could find women to satisfy his unrelenting desires. He says debauchery is one of his main pursuits, almost his job. Raskolnikov finds Svidrigaylov's talk disgusting and boastful and thinks Svidrigaylov the "most shallow and worthless scoundrel on the face of the earth." Raskolnikov makes a move to leave, but Svidrigaylov begs him to stay and hear why he is so infatuated with Dunya.

UNDERSTANDING AND INTERPRETING
Part Six, Chapter III

The Connection Between a Murderer and a Sensualist: Despite believing Svidrigaylov to be a "man of endless schemes and designs," Raskolnikov still feels a mysterious connection to him. In the restaurant, Raskolnikov asks him if the filth of his deeds has sapped his strength, which gives us the first hint of what this connection could be. Svidrigaylov lives a life of baseness without conscience—exactly what Raskolnikov hoped to achieve—but Svidrigaylov shows no signs of the moral weariness that now plagues Raskolnikov. After the initial euphoria he felt while committing the murders, Raskolnikov has found his life exhausting. Svidrigaylov has no such problem. Consequences are insignificant obstacles, and as long as he has his vices to enjoy, he is fulfilled. Svidrigaylov similarly recognizes the connection between himself and Raskolnikov and expresses great interest in observing Raskolnikov to better understand his position.

PART SIX

Chapter IV

Recounting his life to Raskolnikov, Svidrigaylov explains that he was in debtor's prison until his wife brought him out on condition that he confine his infidelities to the house servants and that he tell her about his affairs. She also asked him to tell her if he fell in love with someone. Dunya, the family governess, reproached Svidrigaylov for his exploits with various women. Because of her decency, Svidrigaylov immediately fell in love with her. Dunya felt sorry for him and wanted to save him from his life of debauchery. Her sympathy only made him love her more. Svidrigaylov then mentions to Raskolnikov that he has a new fiancée, a fifteen-year-old who lives in St. Petersburg.

Svidrigaylov's idle talk about his sister and women in general irritates Raskolnikov. He explodes and calls Svidrigaylov a "vile, disgusting, salacious creature." They leave the restaurant and walk down the street. Svidrigaylov tries to lose Raskolnikov, but Raskolnikov follows him. Svidrigaylov finally tells him, "Your way lies to the right and mine to the left, or perhaps the other way round."

UNDERSTANDING AND INTERPRETING

Part Six, Chapter IV

A Fastidious Murderer: Svidrigaylov seems to be testing Raskolnikov, trying to determine what effect his vile stories have on him. When Raskolnikov loses his temper, it shows that he is repulsed by Svidrigaylov's life, which is base and devoid of contemplation or intellect. In one way, it is strange that Raskolnikov, a murderer, feels morally superior to a man whose only crimes are carnal. In another way, though, Raskolnikov's response is understandable. The knowledge that his sister is the object of Svidrigaylov's desire torments him. Furthermore, his own vice involves violence, not sex, so sexual exploits repulse him slightly. That Svidrigaylov disgusts Raskolnikov shows that Raskolnikov is not, as Svidrigaylov is, an extraordinary man. Svidrigaylov stands alone and lives by his own conscience, not by the moral standards of the society around him. Raskolnikov cannot do this, and he cannot bear the thought of becoming a man like Svidrigaylov.

Death or Confession: Svidrigaylov's parting remarks at the end of this chapter acknowledge that he and Raskolnikov are different people and must choose different paths. Like Porfiry, Svidrigaylov sees potential in Raskolnikov, but unlike Porfiry, he sees potential for baseness. Svidrigaylov speaks of symbolic paths, one leading to redemption via death, another leading to redemption via confession.

Fyodor Dostoevsky

PART SIX
Chapter V

Raskolnikov follows Svidrigaylov because he still fears that Svidrigaylov will pursue Dunya. Raskolnikov berates Svidrigaylov for being the type of person who eavesdrops and hides behind doors, but Svidrigaylov counters that Raskolnikov is a fake idealist who murders old women. He challenges Raskolnikov to kill himself if the questions that torment him are too much to bear. Finally, he persuades Raskolnikov that he is not pursuing Dunya anymore. Raskolnikov wanders off, disgusted.

In a daze, Raskolnikov walks right past Dunya on the street. Dunya sees Svidrigaylov and catches up to him. The letter she received earlier was from him, and she has decided to face him in person. Svidrigaylov tricks her into coming up to his room and there reveals that Raskolnikov killed the pawnbroker, convincing Dunya that he is telling the truth by mentioning Raskolnikov's theory of the extraordinary man. Svidrigaylov then blackmails her, saying that only if she has sex with him will he help Raskolnikov flee the country.

Dunya pushes him away, but the door is locked. She pulls out a pistol and points it at him. Svidrigaylov is surprised, but he smiles and says, "You are making things very much easier for me." She shoots once and misses. She shoots again but only grazes his head. Svidrigaylov gives her one more chance to kill him, but the gun misfires. He then allows her to reload the pistol, and Dunya sees that he would rather die than let her go. She throws the gun down, unwilling to help him commit suicide. When she again refuses to submit to him, he produces the key to the door and lets her go, still smilingly despairingly. The revolver, still on the floor, has one shot left.

UNDERSTANDING AND INTERPRETING
Part Six, Chapter V

Desperate for Dunya: As Svidrigaylov told Raskolnikov, Dunya attracts him because she represents pure goodness and because she feels sympathy for him while most others felt repulsion. Svidrigaylov sees his salvation in Dunya, just as Raskolnikov sees his in Sonya. Dunya is not just an object of Svidrigaylov's sensual and vulgar desires. If this were the case, he would have attacked her in the locked room before she produced the pistol. It is her acceptance and love that he seeks.

Svidrigaylov's Death Wish: When Dunya rejects Svidrigaylov, he recognizes that his will has been broken in the face of overwhelming goodness. As a result, he yearns for punishment: death, the only thing he fears. Svidrigaylov lets Dunya fire at him repeatedly. When she takes out the gun, he admits that she is making things easier for him, by which he means she is helping him commit suicide. After Dunya leaves, Svidrigaylov is still smiling "the weak, pitiful, mournful smile of despair." The pistol left on the floor is his path and his way out.

PART SIX
Chapter VI

Svidrigaylov wanders the streets of St. Petersburg in search of carnal pleasures, but he ends his night without drinking or indulging in sex. He returns to his apartment and finds Sonya at home next door with Katerina's children. He gives her 3,000 rubles and tells her that arrangements have been made for the children. He wanders off to visit his new fiancée. He gives her family 15,000 rubles. Eventually, Svidrigaylov goes home and falls into a fitful sleep full of nightmares. He dreams first of a fourteen-year-old girl who took her own life because an "outrage" had overwhelmed her soul. Then he dreams of a five-year-old girl in the hallway outside his apartment. He brings her back to his bed and covers her in blankets. He notices that she is awake and looking at him longingly. Before his eyes, the girl's face turns into the face of a French prostitute. As she reaches for him lustily, he awakens with a start.

At dawn, Svidrigaylov wanders outside to a public park where he tells the sentry that he is going to America and then shoots himself in the head.

UNDERSTANDING AND INTERPRETING
Part Six, Chapter VI

He Does Have a Conscience: Svidrigaylov's dreams reveal that he does have a conscience, and he does feel vaguely guilty about his sexual sins. The fourteen-year-old he dreams of is one of his real-life conquests, and his dream of her shows his sadness at the knowledge that the girl died, in shame and horror, because of his actions. When he dreams that a little girl's face morphs into the face of a lusty prostitute, it shows his understanding that his vile thoughts and actions have the power to transform others into depraved souls. Dunya was the only possible means of redemption from his own vileness, and now that he has lost hope of being with her, vileness overtakes his soul.

Svidrigaylov's Suicide: Svidrigaylov's death feels inevitable. He has tried every-thing during his life and indulged all of his morally objectionable vices. He finds himself longing for redemption through Dunya. He loves her with a pure love, and when she rejects him, he is devastated. After Dunya fails to kill him, it is as if no force in the world can destroy Svidrigaylov but himself. His demise, like everything in his life, is left up to his own will. When he tells the sentry he is going to America—a country that was at that time still alien to Dostoevsky and to Russia—he is talking about achieving the final discovery of death and the afterlife.

The Failure to Commit Suicide: Raskolnikov contemplates the notion of suicide more than once. He thinks of it at the bridge in Part II and while walking through the streets in Part V. Raskolnikov always concludes that he does not have the will to go through with the deed. This failure of nerve is another reminder that Raskolnikov, unlike Svidrigaylov, who succeeds in killing himself, is not an extraordinary man. In earlier drafts of *Crime and Punishment*, Raskolnikov com-mited suicide. In the end, though, Dostoevsky decided that suicide is not in Raskolnikov's character. Raskolnikov's goal, in the wake of the murder, is to pur-sue life and to triumph over his own powerlessness.

PART SIX
Chapter VII

Raskolnikov visits his mother. She is alone and near madness. She says she has read his article about crime many times and finds it brilliant, which shames Raskolnikov. She bursts into tears, and Raskolnikov begs her to always love him as much as she does at this moment, no matter what people say about him. He tells her he loves her and says he is leaving. He asks her to pray for him. Raskolnikov feels his heart soften in his mother's presence.

He opens the door and finds Dunya standing there. Dunya has been with Sonya all day, waiting for him. They feared he would kill himself. Dunya tells him she knows about the murders, but she is glad he is going to confess. Winc-ing at the mention of the crime and confession, Raskolnikov says to her, "Crime? What crime? Killing a foul, noxious louse . . . no good to anybody . . . was that a crime?" He admits that he is a bad man and that he feels incompetent for having been caught. He says, "Oh, if only I were alone and nobody loved me, and if I had never loved anyone! *All this would never have happened!*" He says he is ready to face his suffering, even though he sees no point in it.

UNDERSTANDING AND INTERPRETING
Part Six, Chapter VII

A Half-Hearted Plan to Confess: Raskolnikov stops short of confessing to his mother, but he shows a love and affection for her that he never could have shown before. He asks her to pray for him as he looks to the suffering that lies ahead. When Raskolnikov meets Dunya, he relapses and attempts to rationalize his crime. Although he has decided to confess, he has made the decision because he thinks that confessing is his only way out. His confession will be based on his failure, not on his belief in his own wrongdoing and potential redemption.

A Diseased Understanding of Love: Raskolnikov whines, blaming love for his crime. He insists that if no one loved him and he loved no one, *"[a]ll this would never have happened!"* Raskolnikov does not understand love at this point. He is still thinking of his original theory. He thinks that because he is loved, he is unable to be an extraordinary man and is burdened with emotions and guilt. Earlier, he realized that Sonya loves him, and the realization scared him: "it seemed strangely painful and burdensome to be loved."

PART SIX
Chapter VIII

Raskolnikov arrives at Sonya's, and she is glad to see him. He tells her, "I have come for your crosses" and asks if she has changed her mind about his confession. She says no. He laughs and says he refuses to confess to Porfiry because he is sick of him, but he will confess to one of the police clerks instead. Sonya asks him to make the sign of the cross. She wants to accompany him to the police station, but he says he will go alone. She follows him anyway.

As Raskolnikov walks to the station, he decides to kneel down in the street and confess to the world, as Sonya suggested earlier. People laugh and mock him. He is humiliated and thinks about going home, but notices Sonya behind him on the street, watching him. He enters the police station and asks for Zametov, but Zametov is not there. In the background, he overhears someone say that Svidrigaylov has shot himself. He decides to turn around and go home, since Svidrigaylov is the only person who might report him to the police. When he gets outside, he again sees Sonya watching him, and he goes back inside. At last, he confesses to Porfiry. He says, in the chapter's final sentence, "It was I who killed the old woman and her sister, Lizaveta, with an axe, and robbed them."

Part Six, Chapter VIII

Crosses and Crossroads: When Raskolnikov tells Sonya he wants the crosses, he is approaching the crossroads of his redemption. Sonya gives him the two crosses, and he returns Lizaveta's cross to her, reemphasizing the connection between the two innocent sufferers. Raskolnikov also remembers the two crosses he took from Alena and thinks about how fitting they would be now. Raskolnikov's laughter at this thought can be interpreted as Dostoevsky's acknowledgment that crosses are obvious in their symbolism of suffering and redemption.

The Power of Love: Sonya will not let Raskolnikov go to the police station alone. Not only is Sonya a reminder of their suffering and Raskolnikov's redemption, she symbolizes how love prevents isolation. Sonya's love is so great that it inspires even a vacillating, rationalizing murderer to do the right thing.

A Small Beginning: The final chapter follows Raskolnikov as he wavers back and forth between confessing and shying away from confession. He attempts to bow down at a public crossroads and confess to the world, as Sonya suggested, but his shame is still too great. He almost leaves the police station, but Sonya's watchfulness stops him. Even when Raskolnikov finally confesses, he has only taken one step toward redemption. He still thinks he could have succeeded if he had not made mistakes and had not had the nuisance of loved ones in his life. He still clings to the last vestiges of his theory, and he does not understand the impact of his crime or the redemptive power of suffering.

EPILOGUE
Chapters I & II

Eighteen months have passed since the murder, and Raskolnikov has spent the last nine in a prison work camp in Siberia. He has been sentenced to eight years in prison. The trial went smoothly. Everyone who testified on Raskolnikov's behalf said he has been very ill, but Raskolnikov refused to defend himself. He blamed the murder on his poverty and called himself a coward. There was no evidence against Raskolnikov other than his confession. Porfiry testified that he never suspected Raskolnikov.

Pulkheria dies of a strange nervous illness that borders on madness. Dunya and Razumikhin, who are now married, never told her about Raskolnikov's confession and murder. Razumikhin and Sonya visit Raskolnikov in prison. Sonya takes the money from Svidrigaylov and moves to Siberia to be near Raskolnikov. She occasionally reports to the others that he is sullen and uncommunicative, even when informed of Pulkheria's death. He seems irritated by Sonya's visits and is even rude to her. Soon, he shuns everyone and the other convicts begin to dislike him.

Now in prison, Raskolnikov suffers not from privation but from the deep wounds to his pride. He hopes to feel remorse for his crime, but it does not come. For a while, he clings to the idea that his actions were the first moves of a great benefactor who serves humanity. But the failure of his first moves has revealed to him that he is not a great man. He now torments himself with thoughts of suicide but realizes he does not have the strength to overcome his will to live.

During Lent, Raskolnikov attends prison religious services with the other convicts. They loathe him for being an atheist and threaten to kill him. Sonya continues her visits. Everyone likes her, but no one can understand why she stands by Raskolnikov.

Ill, Raskolnikov enters the prison hospital. During his illness, he dreams of an unknown pestilence that kills most of Europe. This plague is made up of microscopic creatures endowed with intelligence and will. The people who have been stricken with the plague believe that all of "their judgments, their scientific deductions, or their moral convictions and creeds" are infallible. Convinced of their infallibility, they band together in armies and begin killing one another. The plague spreads and kills most of humanity. Raskolnikov is distressed that this nightmare repeatedly torments him.

Two weeks after Easter, Raskolnikov notices that Sonya has stopped visiting him, and he becomes concerned. He learns that she is bedridden with illness, but she writes and says she will be healthy soon. Raskolnikov is discharged from the hospital and goes back to work. Sonya suddenly appears on a riverbank and sits down beside him. She offers her hand and Raskolnikov holds onto it passionately for the first time. He weeps and realizes that he loves her and that his moment of ultimate redemption has begun.

Sonya and Raskolnikov will be separated for seven more years, but Raskolnikov feels "restored to life." His past and his crime seem distant to him. He reaches for the New Testament that Sonya has given him. He stored it under his pillow but never read it. Sonya is overjoyed. The couple reflect that they have only seven years to wait. It is the "dawn of their happiness."

"CROSSING THE IRTISH FERRY"

Like his fictional creation, Dostoevsky suffered through years in a Siberian camp, as did countless Russian prisoners and political dissidents who lived there in exile. Siberia is a vast region that makes up most of Russia's land area. While its borders are undefined, the region stretches across Asia from the Ural Mountains in the west, up through the Arctic, and east to the steppes of Mongolia, the Pacific, and the Bering Strait across from Alaska. Aside from the Trans-Siberian Railroad (completed in 1905), the primary means of transportation in Siberia are ferries that navigate the many rivers of the region. The Russian expression "to cross the Irtish ferry" refers to exile to Siberia and the end of a political career.

Epilogue, Chapters I & II

Tying Up the Loose Ends: The two chapters of the Epilogue answer questions in the way we expected they would be answered. Pulkheria dies, Razumikhin and Dunya marry, Sonya moves to Siberia thanks to the money she received from Svidrigaylov, and Raskolnikov finds true redemption.

The Last Dream: Most significantly in the Epilogue, Raskolnikov finally abandons the logic and reason of his theory. His dream of the plague shows him what would happen if everyone accepted the flawed theory of the extraordinary man. If people were incorrectly convinced of their own extraordinariness, violence and death would result. People would kill each other under the mistaken notion that they killed for the glory of a greater good. When people think they have the right to transcend moral law, nihilism is the outcome. Finally, Raskolnikov can see that his theory is wrong. Realizing this means his redemption can begin.

The Final Redemption: When life takes the place of logic in Raskolnikov, he begins the process of true suffering. He is finally able to recognize the evil of his crime and the strength of his yearning for love. He takes up the Bible and seeks his salvation just as Sonya does. He embraces his condition as an ordinary man who cannot be isolated from society, and he is "restored to life." The suffering expressed in Sonya's love makes him see the error of his ways and the beauty and goodness to be found in loving her and loving God. Dostoevsky suggests that love is the ultimate means of finding salvation.

Conclusions

Crime and Punishment is perhaps the greatest crime novel ever written, and it is the first to examine the psychology of the criminal mind in such detail. The novel is a cautionary tale about alienation and the destructive results of zealous theorizing. A story of profound moral and psychological depth, it reflects Dostoevsky's belief that suffering is the true path to human happiness, redemption, and salvation.

Raskolnikov is a conflicted man whose bouts of pride alternate with bouts of uncertainty and shame. The root of his name in Russian means "schism," and a schism exists within him. He possesses both intellect and compassion, and the two forces do battle for control of him. Raskolnikov is capable of murder but displays genuine compassion for the poor. He commits the murders as a result of his intellect but finds salvation when he understands that he cannot base his life on reason alone.

Raskolnikov separates himself from society and feels alienated from those around him. This isolation prompts him to conceive of the theoretical extraordinary man, which makes him believe that he is above society's law. Raskolnikov's crime isolates him even further. He suffers alone until he finds redemption in the love of Sonya, the innocent sufferer.

IV

THE
BROTHERS
KARAMAZOV

The Brothers Karamazov

An Overview

Key Facts

Genre: Tragedy; murder mystery

Date of first publication: 1879–80

Setting: 1860s. The town of Skotoprigonyevsk (translated as "pen of beasts" or "pigsty"), in the countryside outside Moscow, Russia; other scenes take place in the nearby villages of Mokroe and Tchermashnya.

Narrator: Omniscient, first-person, anonymous townsperson

Plot Overview: The depraved and negligent Fyodor Karamazov is murdered when his estranged sons are reunited.

Style, Technique, & Language

Style—Many Versions of Parricide: Dostoevsky uses parricide as a literal device and as an allegory, a symbolic story presented as an extended metaphor for something outside the text. On a literal level, the novel's parricide is the murder of Fyodor Karamazov and the complicity of his sons in the crime. On a political level, the parricide stands for the challenges to Tsarist authority that shook Russia in the 1860s and 1870s and culminated in the assassination of Tsar Alexander II (the symbolic father of Russia) in 1881, after the novel was published. On a religious level, the parricide is the rejection of God the father by people like Ivan, who disavow their faith.

Fyodor Dostoevsky

Technique—Many Novels in One: *The Brothers Karamazov* is part family drama, part exposition on faith, morality, and salvation, and part murder mystery. An omniscient (all-knowing) narrator assembles the plot and its grand themes. This narrator is familiar with all of the characters and can describe their inner thoughts and feelings as well as their actions.

> "There is probably more sheer substance in *The Brothers Karamazov*, as well as more spiritual and psychological insight than there is in any other novel, in any language."
>
> JOHN BAYLEY

The early books develop the conflict between two sets of beliefs: the Christian beliefs of Father Zossima, who preaches "active love" and "responsibility for all, by all," and the skepticism and intellectual rationalizations of Ivan, who preaches, "if there is no immortality, then all things are lawful." The three Karamazov brothers question their individual beliefs over the course of the novel. Alyosha questions his faith, Dmitri realizes the power of suffering and discovers his own compassion, and Ivan finds his intellectual skepticism challenged.

Along with the novel's philosophical explorations, Dostoevsky weaves a murder mystery. He also makes a mystery of Dmitri's inexplicable source of money, which adds tension and depth to the main plot.

Language—Dialogue Reveals Characters' Debauchery, Morality, and Intellect: Dostoevsky masterfully portrays a large cast of characters from all walks of Russian life. Dialogue, in part, is what makes the characters so convincing. Among the Karamazovs, differences in speech and manner reflect great differences in character. Fyodor is brutish and vulgar; his speech is peppered with risqué anecdotes and boastful crudities. Dmitri, the emotional son, fills his language with grand romantic pronouncements about beauty and lust for life. His language also reflects his struggle between debauchery and moral resolve. Ivan, the intellectual, speaks almost exclusively in logical, rational arguments. Alyosha, the spiritual brother, speaks in the quiet, didactic manner of a monk— a style he learned from Father Zossima. His non-judgmental and gentle demeanor draws everyone to him with a desire to confess and be decent. Smerdyakov, the illegitimate brother, affirms his illegitimacy and corruption with his duplicitous and inscrutable way of speaking.

Characters in *The Brothers Karamazov*

Fenya: The young servant to Grushenka. On the night of the murder, Fenya lies to Dmitri about Grushenka's whereabouts.

Father Ferapont: The ascetic monk who challenges Father Zossima's system of beliefs. He fears his fellow monks may be possessed by demons. After Zossima's death, he is asked to leave for stirring discord in the monastery.

Fetyukovitch: Dmitri's defense attorney. Fetyukovitch is famous throughout Russia for taking on notorious cases.

Gorstkin (alias Lyagavy): A merchant in the countryside town of Tchermash-nya, he wants to buy some parcels of Karamazov land. He chooses to go by the name of Gorstkin and ignores anyone who calls him Lyagavy.

Grand Inquisitor: The main character in Ivan's prose-poem about moral authority and the rejection of faith. In real life, the Grand Inquisitor was the leader of the Spanish Inquisition in the sixteenth century. In Ivan's poem, he threatens to execute Jesus Christ because Jesus' return to earth ruins the Church's authority over humanity.

Gregory: Fyodor Karamazov's head servant. He and his wife Marfa adopted and raised Smerdyakov. Gregory also raised Dmitri for about a year after Dmitri was abandoned by Fyodor.

Grushenka (Agrafena Svyetlov): Dmitri's lover, she is a flirtatious, duplicitous "enchantress." Wickedly smart and confident, she seduces Fyodor too and then plans to run off with an old lover, Mussyalovitch, leaving both Dmitri and Fyodor behind.

Madame Hohlakov: Lise's mother. Vain and prone to gossip, she makes an insincere confession to Father Zossima, only to be taught a lesson about self-deception.

Ilusha: The proud, fiercely independent son of Captain Snegiryov. About ten years old, he refuses to let his father take any charity from the Karamazovs.

Alyosha (Alexey) Karamazov: The youngest son of Fyodor, he is about twenty years old and is a gentle, thoughtful, handsome seminary student. At the suggestion of his mentor, Father Zossima, Alyosha leaves the monastery to help mediate his family's conflicts. He considers children the hope of the future and spends much of his time teaching them and learning from them.

Fyodor Dostoevsky

Dmitri Karamazov: The oldest son of Fyodor, he is hot-headed and impulsive. Dmitri is twenty-seven years old, and like his father, he is a sensualist who hosts wild, expensive orgies. He hates Fyodor because he believes he was cheated out of his inheritance. This hatred is compounded by his jealousy over Fyodor's advances toward Grushenka.

Fyodor Karamazov: A vain, brash, depraved sensualist and buffoon, he is father to the three brothers Karamazov. He is in his late fifties. He lusts for Grushenka and refuses to give Dmitri any more money. Fyodor dies at the hands of one of his sons.

Ivan Karamazov: The intellectual middle son of Fyodor, he lived and studied in Moscow. He is about twenty-four years old. He invents the Grand Inquisitor story and puts forth the idea that everything is permitted when we reject the existence of God and the idea of immortality.

Adelaide Ivanovna Karamazov: The rich and beautiful first wife of Fyodor and the mother of Dmitri, she is hot-tempered, bold, and strong-willed. Fyodor filched all her money and used it to build his own fortune. Their marriage quickly fell apart because of Fyodor's depravity, and she ran off with another man, dying shortly thereafter.

Sophia Ivanovna Karamazov: The meek, gentle second wife of Fyodor and the mother of Ivan and Alyosha. A penniless orphan, she was raised by a wealthy guardian who hated and mistrusted Fyodor. In the midst of Fyodor's endless philandering, she fell ill and died of a nervous disease. Alyosha first returns to his father's town to search for her grave.

Katerina: The strong-willed, prideful, self-deceiving fiancée of Dmitri. Katerina loyally clings to Dmitri, even when he resolves to run off with Grushenka. Katerina's testimony in court seals the guilty verdict against Dmitri. She is probably in love with Ivan too, but is too stubborn and proud to admit to it.

Ippolit Kirillovitch: The public prosecutor who argues for Dmitri's guilt.

Kolya Krassotkin: An intelligent young boy who earns Alyosha's respect. Kolya trains the dog Perezvon (Zhutchka) to surprise his friend, Ilusha.

Lizaveta (Smerdyastchaya): A mentally deficient village waif whose nickname means "smelly." Fyodor Karamazov molests her, and she later dies while giving birth to their son, Smerdyakov.

Lise: The crippled young daughter of Madame Hohlakov. She loves Alyosha and plans to marry him when she is older.

Lyagavy: See Gorstkin.

Michael Makarov: The police captain of Skotoprigonyevsk.

Maria Kondratyevna: A neighbor of the Karamazovs and the daughter of Dmitri's landlady. She falls in love with Smerdyakov, who at one point serenades her with a guitar.

Marfa: Gregory's wife and Fyodor Karamazov's servant. She reports Fyodor's murder to the police.

Maximov: A homeless old mooch and former landowner, he becomes dependent on Grushenka's good will. He attends Dmitri's last party in Mokroe.

> "**D**ostoevsky paints like Rembrandt, and his portraits are artistically so powerful and often so perfect that even if they lacked the depths of thought that lie behind them, and around them, I believe that Dostoevsky would still be the greatest of all novelists."
>
> **ANDRÉ GIDE**

Miusov: A cousin of Fyodor's first wife. Miusov helped raise Dmitri for many years and is present at the meeting in Father Zossima's cell, where he shows his deep loathing for Fyodor.

Mussyalovitch: A retired Polish military officer, he is the past love of Grushenka and returns after five years to reclaim her. He cheats at cards and proves himself a disreputable cadger. He testifies against Dmitri at the trial.

Peter Perhotin: A minor town official who holds the dueling pistols Dmitri pawned him. He lends Dmitri a small sum of money on the night of the murder. When he becomes suspicious of Dmitri's bloody hands and excited manner, he investigates to see if a crime has been committed.

Trifon Plastunov: The innkeeper in Mokroe who testifies that Dmitri spent 3,000 rubles during each of his wild parties there.

Rakitin: A young divinity student who seems to know all the gossip of the town. He is cynical and mocking and betrays Dmitri Karamazov at the trial. He is a cousin of Grushenka but tries to keep this fact a secret.

Samsonov: An old, wealthy landowner and a friend and protector of Grushenka. Dmitri tries to con Samsonov out of 3,000 rubles, but Samsonov outwits Dmitri and sends him on a wild goose chase to the merchant Lyagavy (Gorskin).

Smerdyakov (Pavel Fyodorovitch): The bastard son of Fyodor and Lizaveta. His name means "stinky." Smerdyakov is about twenty-five years old. Fyodor's servants Gregory and Marfa adopted Smerdyakov, and later he became the cook and valet in Fyodor's house. He takes Ivan's intellectual arguments to heart.

Smurov: A young boy about twelve years old. He accompanies his friend Kolya Krasskotin to visit their sick friend Ilusha.

Captain Snegiryov: Ilusha's father. Dmitri beat him up, but he refuses to take money from Alyosha out of respect for Ilusha.

Vrublevsky: The Polish associate of Mussyalovitch. He is an unlicensed dentist.

Father Zossima: The monastery elder and mentor to Alyosha. Many monks and townspeople believe that Zossima is a saint. When he dies, his corpse decomposes rapidly, leading to widespread confusion and disillusionment because a saint's corpse supposedly maintains its integrity long after death. Zossima's teachings of love and human engagement are central to the novel and provide Alyosha with his belief system.

Reading *The Brothers Karamazov*

PART ONE, BOOK I
The History of a Family

The narrator tells us that the name Karamazov is well known throughout Russia because of the gloomy death of **Fyodor Karamazov** thirteen years earlier. Fyodor is an "ill-natured buffoon," a vicious, despicable man with a characteristic "Slavic senselessness." He dedicates his youth to hard drinking and carnal extravagance and begins his adult life with no riches of his own. He marries well and continues his excesses.

Fyodor's first wife, **Adelaide**, endures his depravity for a time, clinging to the belief that his passion is romantic and that he is "one of the bold and ironical spirits of that progressive age." But she leaves him after bearing him one son, **Dmitri**. Fyodor is crushed by her departure. Publicly, he plays the part of the injured, tragic husband, but privately, he hosts drunken orgies in his house and ignores his son Dmitri. Eventually, Fyodor's servant, **Gregory**, takes Dmitri into custody. Later, Adelaide's cousin, **Peter Miusov**, takes on Dmitri, and after that Dmitri passes through the custody of a series of relatives.

> "After *King Lear*, [*The Brothers Karamazov* is] the greatest work ever written to illustrate the moral horrors that ensue when family bonds disintegrate."
>
> **JOSEPH FRANK**

Dmitri eventually learns of his father's riches and excesses but does not meet with him until years later. As a young man, Dmitri receives small payments from his father's estate, repeatedly returning to claim more of his inheritance. His requests for more money fall on deaf ears, and Fyodor evades him. Dmitri is impulsive and emotional. He partakes freely in drinking and debauchery. After dropping out of school, he enters the military and has an inconsistently successful career. His life is wild, and he spends money wastefully.

Fyodor, meanwhile, invests his money well and becomes rich. He returns to the town and opens a string of taverns. He feasts on the poverty of the towns-people by lending them money. Fyodor soon marries again, taking as his bride a woman named **Sophia**, an orphan with no money of her own who was raised by a wealthy guardian. Fyodor marries Sophia for her beauty and meekness. The new couple have two sons, **Ivan** and **Alexey** (nicknamed **Alyosha**), and Fyodor continues his life of extravagant orgies in their house.

Sophia's nerves cannot bear the insult of Fyodor's behavior, and she soon falls into a delusional state. She dies when Alyosha is four. Since Fyodor has made it clear that he has no interest in raising children, the two boys are handed over to the servant, Gregory, and his wife, **Marfa**. Sophia's wealthy former guardian becomes the boys' benefactor and sets aside a sum of money for their education.

Ivan goes on to become a celebrated intellectual, publishing widely and joining the literary scene in Moscow. One of his articles on the role of Russia's eccle-siastical courts is read widely throughout the country, and Ivan becomes a minor celebrity in his hometown. After saving some of his own money, he has sufficient funds to travel outside Russia for two years. Meanwhile, Alyosha becomes devoutly religious as he grows into a young man. He becomes a monk at a local monastery and is well loved by the townspeople for his gentle, thoughtful nature. Neither Ivan nor Alyosha attempt to claim any inheritance from their father.

As the novel begins, the family is reuniting for the first time. At the request of Dmitri, Ivan returns to town, where Fyodor welcomes him. Dmitri wants Ivan to help mediate the financial conflict between himself and Fyodor. Alyosha has been back in town for a year already, studying at the monastery under the elder **Father Zossima**, who is revered as a saint by many of the monks and laypeople.

Alyosha and Dmitri, meeting for the first time, quickly become good friends. Alyosha also gets along with his father. He never judges Fyodor's decadent way of life. But Alyosha cannot seem to connect with Ivan, who has a subdued, intellectual nature. Alyosha is apprehensive about the unresolved dispute between Dmitri and Fyodor, and tensions between his father and brother rise. Fyodor has requested that Alyosha set up a meeting with Father Zossima so that he and Dmitri can settle their differences. Alyosha fears this meeting will be a disaster.

UNDERSTANDING AND INTERPRETING
Part One, Book I

An Inside Look at the Tragedy: The narrator, a resident of the town who speaks for his fellow townspeople, weaves together the many stories that make up *The Brothers Karamazov*. In Book I, the narrator uses a series of flashbacks to outline the background of each member of the Karamazov family. Because the narrator lives in the town, he has firsthand knowledge of the events that have transpired in the Karamazov family. The novel immediately has a tragic tone, because we find out right away that we are reading the story of the "gloomy and tragic death of Fyodor Karamazov."

Pen of Beasts: A wide variety of people populate the countryside town where the Karamazov family reunites. The town is meant to represent a typical Russian provincial village. By setting the story in this locale, Dostoevsky brings together a diverse cast of characters from all classes and walks of life. The name of the town, Skotoprigonyevsk, is not mentioned until later in the novel. Skotoprigonyevsk translates literally as "stockyard" or, perhaps more appropriately, "pen of beasts" or "pigsty." The name of the town reflects the grotesque and beastly behavior of the Karamazov family.

Orgies, Money, and Neglected Sons: Fyodor Karamazov is charming and savvy, but also depraved and corrupt. He is self-centered, cynical, and immoral. He pursues every action with personal interest in mind. He marries his first wife to advance his position in life and his second wife for her beauty and meekness. His greatest strength is his financial sense, and he keeps up his property so that he can retain his wealth. Owning taverns provides him with a bountiful source of income. Fyodor is not only financially savvy; he is greedy. We suspect he cheated Dmitri out of his rightful inheritance, for example. An admitted sensualist, Fyodor makes his home not with his family, but at drunken orgies he organizes. He hosts these orgies in the presence of his wife and children, flaunting his disrespect for family and propriety. He does not hate his children or physically abuse them, but he thoroughly neglects them. Fyodor discards three sons one after the other as if they are mere obstacles to his pursuit of pleasure.

The Role of Children: One of the novel's major themes is the role of children in society. The children of Fyodor Karamazov are case studies in the dangers of neglect, and other children in the novel demonstrate various aspects of childhood: sensitivity, vulnerability, impressionability, and, above all, hope for the future.

Volatile Dmitri: Fyodor's sons are quite different from one another. Dmitri, the eldest and the only son of Adelaide, resembles his father in many ways. He is impulsive and emotional, and, like Dmitri, he becomes a sensualist who drinks and sleeps around. Dmitri obsesses over money, and he is the only Karamazov brother who believes he has earned an inheritance from his father. Whatever Dmitri gains, he squanders frivolously. As a result, he always needs money, which is his primary reason for returning to see his father. Perhaps because Dmitri resembles Fyodor so closely, his defining characteristics of carnality and money lust put him in direct conflict with his father.

Intellectual Ivan: In contrast to the extroverted Dmitri, Ivan is an intellectual guided solely by his own thoughts and ideas. Unlike Dmitri, Ivan has largely paid his own way, earning money by teaching and writing articles for newspapers and magazines, and eventually emerging as a brilliant and well-known critic. Ivan takes pride in his financial independence. He gets along well with Fyodor when he returns home because he asks nothing of Fyodor. Ivan is quiet, educated, reflective, and proud.

Loving, Accepting Alyosha: Alyosha is unlike either of his brothers. Where Dmitri is volatile, Alyosha is placid and good-natured. Where Ivan is prideful, Alyosha is modest and self-sacrificing. People love Alyosha because of his supportive, caring manner. He was not brought up in a religious tradition but discovered faith as a young man. God interests him because he is "struggling from the darkness of worldly wickedness." Compassionate and nonjudgmental, Alyosha has a humanist, realist approach to life. Alyosha's quiet wisdom allows him to examine the relationships in his family, and his family trusts him to be objective. His father welcomes Alyosha into the house because Alyosha does not moralize or judge him. Alyosha, who originally came home to find his mother's grave, craves family connection and unity, things he did not have when he was growing up.

The Monk and the Atheist: Ivan and Alyosha, who share the same biological mother, have opposite views on faith—but both men arrive at their views through reason. Alyosha is the faithful servant of God, but he is also a realist. He approaches his faith not with fanaticism or mysticism, but with reason. He believes because he accepts the existence of God and of immortality. Ivan does not believe in God or immortality, but like Alyosha, he comes to his beliefs after rigorous contemplation. Alyosha perceives that Ivan is an atheist and that he is "absorbed in something—something inward and important." Ivan's inward struggle will come to define his character.

"The whole idea of the work is to affirm the notion of universal disorder, to show that this disorder is all over the place, in society, in its affairs, in its governing principles . . . and in the decay of the idea of family. If passionate convictions still exist, then they are destructive ones (socialism). Moral ideas no longer exist, suddenly not a single one remains."

FYODOR DOSTOEVSKY, EARLY NOTES ON *THE BROTHERS KARAMAZOV*

Zossima and Fyodor, Opposite Men: Fyodor Karamazov is the portrait of dissipation and negligence, and Zossima is his counterpart, a portrait of goodness and the activity of Christian love. Fyodor is no father at all to Alyosha, but Zossima is an ideal spiritual father to Alyosha. The narrator says, "An elder was one who took your soul, your will, into his soul and his will," and the sentiment applies to both Fyodor and Zossima, though in different ways. Fyodor ravages the soul and will of people, and Zossima has a "peculiar quality of soul" that comforts those who love him. So wonderful is Zossima that many of the monks and laypeople consider him a saint. And unlike Fyodor, Zossima does not judge people. He loves sinners more than the chaste. In the same way, Alyosha seems to get along best with the most sinful men in his family, Fyodor and Dmitri. Zossima stands for all that is good.

THE BROTHERS DOSTOEVSKY

Dostoevsky's older brother, Mikhail, was also one of his greatest friends and colleagues. The two were sent off to school together as youths and afterward they were lifelong correspondents. Mikhail supported Fyodor financially during many periods of Fyodor's life, and in 1858, when Fyodor was released from his prison sentence and subsequent military service, he lived with Mikhail for a time. The brothers launched two magazines —*Vremya* (*Time*) in 1861 and *Epokha* (*Epoch*) in 1864—that provided a forum for Dostoevsky's early post-Siberian work, including *House of the Dead* and *Notes from Underground*, along with other literary and political works of the 1860s. Both journals eventually went bankrupt. Mikhail died in 1864, just weeks after Fyodor's first wife passed away.

PART ONE, BOOK II
An Unfortunate Gathering

On the day of the meeting at the monastery, Fyodor and Ivan arrive first with a few others, including **Peter Miusov**, the relative who helped raise Dmitri. Dmitri is late, and everyone wonders if he will show up. While walking to Zossima's cell, Fyodor talks mockingly and crudely about monks, telling risqué stories. Miusov condemns the vulgarity of his words. The group enters Zossima's cell just as Father Zossima enters from another room with Alyosha. Two other monks are already present in the cell, along with **Rakitin**, a young divinity student. The monks kneel and kiss Zossima's hand to receive his blessing, but the Karamazovs just bow to him awkwardly. Alyosha is mortified that the meeting has gotten off to such a bad start.

Fyodor apologizes for Dmitri's absence and then continues talking loudly before anyone else has a chance to speak. He introduces himself as a "buffoon" and regales the room with crude, irreverent anecdotes. Zossima silently gazes at the group. Suddenly, Fyodor falls to his knees and asks Zossima to tell him the way to eternal life. Zossima quietly tells him to give up excessive drinking and, above all, to be honest with himself. Without truth, Zossima says, a man falls prey to vice and vindictiveness. He begs Fyodor to get up from his knees because he knows Fyodor is engaging in "deceitful posturing." Fyodor acts as if he has taken all Zossima's words to heart and then kisses the monk's hand. He returns to his loud buffoonery. After a few more minutes, Zossima excuses himself and goes outside with Alyosha to meet some people who have come to seek his blessing.

Zossima first greets some peasant women in the group and offers lamentations for their illnesses and sorrows. He tells them, "All things are saved by love." He meets a wealthy widow, **Madame Hohlakov**, and her young crippled daughter, **Lise**. Lise giggles in the presence of Alyosha and gives him a written note from someone named **Katerina**, who asks that Alyosha come to see her. Madame Hohlakov confesses to Zossima that she has lost her faith in the afterlife, but Zossima detects a hint of insincerity in her confession. He tells her to be wary of falsehood and to regain her faith through active love. Zossima promises that he will send Alyosha to visit them soon. They return to Zossima's cell to find the group engaged in an intellectual discussion.

Ivan discusses his article on the ecclesiastical courts with the monks. He argues that the separation of church and state is wrong and the state should not be allowed to mete out punishments when the church already has the power to punish and excommunicate a criminal. Zossima says that neither church nor state can punish a criminal and only guilt deters and punishes crime. The debate continues, and Alyosha is elated that his family is finally making a good impression.

Suddenly, Dmitri bursts into the room and apologizes for his tardiness. He kneels and receives Zossima's blessing, then sits and listens to the debate. Miusov says that Ivan's current arguments contradict a past discussion in which Ivan argued against faith in God, even saying that if people did not believe in God or immortality, then "everything would be lawful."

Zossima sees an insincerity in Ivan and asks if Ivan is unhappy because what he argues conflicts with what he truly believes. Zossima asks Ivan if he truly believes what he has said about immortality. Ivan says he does and continues to argue that believing in the idea of virtue is illogical without believing in immortality. If people did not believe in immortality, he says, they would commit crimes without fear of eternal punishment. Zossima pauses the conversation and raises his hand. Ivan kneels before him to receive his blessing.

After this pause, Fyodor begins to rant and rave again, and then he insults Dmitri. Fyodor accuses Dmitri of carrying on affairs with two women: one honorable woman, Katerina, and one "enchantress," **Grushenka**. Dmitri defends Katerina's honor and then accuses Fyodor of being jealous and infatuated with Grushenka. When the yelling builds to a roar, Zossima rises from his chair, silently kneels before Dmitri's feet, and then leaves without saying a word. Everyone ponders the meaning of Zossima's gesture.

The group breaks for lunch, and Fyodor says he wants to go home. Alyosha catches up with Father Zossima outside, and Zossima suggests that Alyosha leave the monastery and serve as his family's mediator. This advice upsets Alyosha, who wants to stay, especially because Zossima is very ill. The two men part. Alyosha runs into Rakitin, the divinity student, and the two walk to lunch. Rakitin says there will be a crime in the Karamazov family as a result of the rift between Dmitri and Fyodor. He thinks that Zossima's bow to Dmitri is nothing but "holy nonsense," but that it is also a prophesy that Dmitri will spill blood. Rakitin tells Alyosha all the sordid gossip of the Karamazov family: Dmitri is in love with Grushenka and wants to leave his fiancée, Katerina; Ivan wants to claim Katerina as his own bride; and Grushenka is toying with Fyodor, trying to get him to marry her so that she can get her hands on his money. Rakitin teases Alyosha, saying that the libidinous Grushenka wants to seduce him too.

Alyosha and Rakitin arrive at the luncheon and find a commotion. Fyodor is making a ruckus, yelling insults and accusing the monks of being falsely virtuous. As Ivan drags him from the room into their carriage outside, Fyodor screams at Alyosha to quit the monastery.

UNDERSTANDING AND INTERPRETING
Part One, Book II

Be Honest and Love: Father Zossima is quiet, but his presence dominates this chapter. He looks for love in people and does not judge them. Even the discord in the Karamazov family does not faze Zossima. He watches them and listens to their arguments without saying more than a few words. Fyodor's loud, brash buffoonery brings only quiet admonishments from Zossima. The elder monk can see the true nature of people, and he warns against dishonesty. Zossima uses strong words when giving advice to Fyodor: "Above all, don't lie to yourself." When a person deceives himself with a false front, he argues, the person "loses respect for himself and for others," "ceases to love," and without love, becomes no better than an animal. Zossima may seem passive, but he has great insight into human psychology. Knowing Fyodor for only a few minutes, Zossima sums up Fyodor's character flaws in a few simple words. He also spots Madame Hohlakov's dishonesty right away. He senses that she just wants his approval, and he gives her the same advice he gives Fyodor: avoid falsehood and take the difficult road of active love. Zossima's advice is simple, if challenging: be honest and love. Only a true belief in love—an active love of "labor and fortitude"—is the right path.

Alyosha's Call to the Outside: Alyosha watches and listens carefully to everything Zossima teaches him. As Zossima's protégé, Alyosha tries to live by the precepts of love and honesty. After the Karamazov family comes to the monastery in an attempt to settle its disputes, Zossima senses that the situation should be different: the family should stay at home, and Alyosha should be with them as a mediator. Zossima knows that Alyosha can go out into the world and live by example, to take the teachings of love outside the monastery and put them into practice. Zossima also knows that Katerina wants Alyosha's help. Zossima has faith that Alyosha can bring the power and order of love to the chaos of his family.

Arguing What You Do Not Believe: Ivan's discussion of the ecclesiastical courts reveals the contradictions within him. Ivan is an atheist, but he believes that only the church can be a practical force for reducing crime, for only the church can terrify potential criminals with its threat of excommunication and exclusion from heaven. In turn, Ivan believes, only if people believe in immortality will they be threatened by the idea that they could be barred from heaven, so the belief in immortality is essential for virtue in society. Despite these sound arguments, Zossima notices Ivan's strange insincerity and asks if he is unhappy because of the conflict between what he argues and what he truly believes.

Flustered, Ivan responds, "Perhaps you are right! . . . But I wasn't altogether joking." Zossima worries that Ivan has a "heart capable of such suffering; of thinking and seeking higher things." The conflict remains unresolved when Ivan kneels and accepts Zossima's blessing. Ivan is decent and intelligent, but troubled.

Good Underneath It All: Zossima sees a good but troubled soul in Dmitri, the only visitor to bow and accept a blessing immediately after arriving. In Dmitri, Zossima sees honor, but also a surging passion that leads him astray. At least Dmitri, unlike Fyodor, seems aware of his own self-deception and sins. Whereas Fyodor is self-absorbed, Dmitri shows decency toward others, as when he defends Katerina. He lets Fyodor lure him into a shouting match, but soon he musters enough control to just sit and stare. Zossima's bow to Dmitri symbolizes, in part, Zossima's faith in Dmitri's potential redemption. Dmitri may be misguided by his vices and vindictiveness, as he is in his indiscretions with Grushenka and his vengeful attitude toward Fyodor, but he is honest about himself and his faults. He may be a sensualist like his father, but he has good intentions.

Gossipy Rakitin: Rakitin purveys a mixture of ill-intentioned slander and gossip. A divinity student, he calls Zossima's bow to Dmitri "holy nonsense" and openly mocks Alyosha's dearly held idea of Zossima as a wise and respected elder. He considers Fyodor a "just man" and first plants the idea in Alyosha's head that Dmitri will harm Fyodor. Rakitin is a gossip who looks for the worst in all people, even Alyosha. Alyosha, by contrast, is ignorant of the sordid happenings in his family and looks only for the goodness in his brothers and father, attributing their faults to inner conflicts. Alyosha is perhaps too trusting and is certainly naïve. Both Rakitin and Alyosha are intermediaries, men involved in other people's affairs. The difference between them is that Rakitin intervenes to cause anxiety and spread rumors, while Alyosha intervenes to mediate and make peace.

Lusty Grushenka: Grushenka seems to be a calculating, lustful opportunist. She has reportedly even said of Alyosha, "I'll pull off his cassock," a remark that shows how shamelessly she wants to sully Alyosha's chasteness. Everything we learn about Grushenka we learn from Rakitin or, to a lesser extent, from Fyodor and Dmitri. Dostoevsky has a tendency to plant images of a character in his readers' minds, only to later reveal that character's hidden depths. Grushenka will be revealed as a complex personality. Her role is more dynamic than the initial descriptions of her lead us to believe.

PART ONE, BOOK III
The Sensualists

CHAPTERS 1–5

The narrator now tells us about **Smerdyakov**, the illegitimate son of Fyodor. After Dmitri was born and Fyodor's first wife had left him, Fyodor's servants, Gregory and Marfa, gave birth to a deformed child who died two weeks later. On the night of his baby's death, Gregory awoke to the sound of crying outside. He went to investigate and discovered a newborn child with his dying mother, **Lizaveta**, a mentally retarded girl commonly known in the town as Lizaveta Smerdyastchaya ("Stinking Lizaveta").

The townsfolk pitied Lizaveta, and many tried to help her. Still, she was usually found wandering around town and sleeping on the church porch. The town was outraged to hear that someone had impregnated her, because it meant someone must have raped her. Even if Lizaveta had lived past the birth of the child, she would not have been able to identify her assailant. Rumors implicated Fyodor Karamazov as the father of Lizaveta's child. He had been heard boasting that he would sleep with Lizaveta in order to prove that no woman was too unpleasant for sex. Gregory defended Fyodor, and the accusations eventually faded away. Gregory and Marfa decided to take in Lizaveta's baby and raise him as their own. Fyodor named the child Smerdyakov ("the Stinker") after his mother.

The narrative returns to the present. It is summer. Alyosha is upset at the prospect of leaving monastic life forever. He also worries about an upcoming meeting with Katerina, Dmitri's fiancée, who asked him to come see her. Although he vaguely fears Katerina, he thinks Dmitri is making a big mistake in abandoning her for Grushenka. On his way to meet Katerina, Alyosha runs into Dmitri, who bares his soul, telling Alyosha that he loves life and the earth. Dmitri describes the conflict he feels between his impulses toward good and evil. As a Karamazov, he feels he should be a sensualist and "leap into the pit" of degradation, yet even in his worst moments, he sings a hymn of praise: "Let me be accursed. Let me be vile and base, only let me kiss the hem of the veil in which my God is shrouded."

Dmitri talks of the contradictions between the ideals of Madonna (virtue) and Sodom (vice) and how people can embrace both of them simultaneously. He recites poems that show his lust for life and beauty, including a Schiller ode to Ceres, but he finds only a "riddle" in the beauty of the world.

SCHILLER AND THE ODE TO JOY

The idealism and tragedy in the work of
Friedrich Schiller (1759–1805) strongly
influenced Dostoevsky. Schiller is probably
best known as the author of the "Hymn to Joy"
(or "Ode to Joy") that comprises the choral
sections of Beethoven's Ninth Symphony.
Dmitri Karamazov sings parts of the Ode
to Joy, which demonstrates his decency,
hopefulness, and lust for life. Elsewhere in
Dostoevsky's work, when characters display
idealism or high-mindedness, other characters sometimes refer to them as "Schiller."
For example, in *Crime and Punishment*,
Svidrigaylov calls Raskolnikov "a Schiller, a
Russian Schiller, an absolute Schiller!" In
The Brothers Karamazov, Dostoevsky borrows
heavily from Schiller's play *The Robbers*, a
story of a parricide, fraternal rivalry, and the
disintegration of a family. Throughout *The
Brothers Karamazov*, Dostoevsky also references Schiller's *Moraltheorie*, a study of
ethics that argues for a meeting between
morals and aesthetics in humans, especially
in Dmitri's discovery of the riddle of beauty.

Dmitri tells Alyosha that when he was young, he lived a life of debauchery, loving vice and cruelty. He was an army officer and Katerina was the daughter of his commanding officer. At first, Dmitri kept his distance from Katerina, even though he found her beautiful. He soon discovered that her father was accused of embezzling 4,500 rubles from the army. He had lent the money to a friend who never paid him back. Dmitri told Katerina he would pay back the money if she would visit him in his room, implying that he would help her father in return for sex. When Katerina arrived, Dmitri had a change of heart and gave her the money without requiring anything in return. After Katerina's father died, she inherited money from another relative and paid back the 4,500 rubles to Dmitri. She offered to marry him, and Dmitri accepted.

After the engagement, Dmitri returned to the town where he had met Grushenka and become infatuated with her. He took Grushenka to an inn where he spent 3,000 rubles on a three-day binge, using money Katerina had given him to deliver to her sister. Now, Dmitri says, he must free himself of Katerina so that he can marry Grushenka. He feels a terrible self-hatred about the 3,000 rubles that he owes Katerina.

Dmitri asks Alyosha to tell Katerina the marriage is off. He also asks one more favor of Alyosha. He knows that Fyodor's infatuation with Grushenka is as deep as his own, and he has heard that Fyodor promised Grushenka 3,000 rubles if she would sleep with him. Dmitri says that if Grushenka ever visits Fyodor, Dmitri will be forced to kill him for defiling her. Fyodor allegedly keeps the money to pay Grushenka in an envelope in his bedroom. Dmitri asks Alyosha to get this money from his father so he can pay Katerina back and be free to go off with Grushenka once and for all. He also feels that Fyodor owes him more money from the family estate, since Fyodor made a fortune with Dmitri's mother's money. Dmitri admits to hating Fyodor so intensely that he is physically repulsed by him. Alyosha notices Dmitri's frenzied face and wonders if his brother is mad and harbors murderous impulses.

UNDERSTANDING AND INTERPRETING
Part One, Book III, Chapters 1–5

Madonna and Sodom: Dmitri pours out his internal suffering in a long confession to Alyosha. He is torn between his impulse toward degradation and his impulse toward virtue. He describes this internal battle as the dueling ideals of Madonna and Sodom, virtue and vice. Neither side prevails; if one side triumphed, Dmitri would feel better. It is their simultaneous existence that distresses him. He says, "What's . . . awful is that a man with the ideal of Sodom in his soul does not renounce the ideal of Madonna." Lust, the apparent mark of the Karamazovs, is Dmitri's strongest temptation. It drags him down into the pagan debauchery of Sodom. Even in the depths of his depravity, though, Dmitri feels an impulse to sing religious hymns like Schiller's "Hymn to Joy."

The Riddle of Beauty: Dmitri says his vile impulses are provoked by the beauty of the world—beauty that is "mysterious as well as terrible." Beautiful women especially trouble him, because they provoke both his lust and his moral appreciation for beauty. Dmitri finds that the joys of life—his sensual pleasures—often lead him into debauchery, and soon he feels he is drowning in the "cup of life." When swamped by "riddles" and disorder, Dmitri craves harmony and unity. He longs for a fusion of his morality and his aesthetic sense of beauty.

A Garden of Earthly Delights: Dmitri's confession takes place outside in a lush garden during the summer, a location that emphasizes Dmitri's love for sensual pleasures and his appreciation for earthly beauty. Dmitri's name reflects his personality. "Dmitri" comes from "Demeter," the Greek goddess of the earth, agriculture, and the harvest. Dostoevsky emphasizes the connection between Dmitri and Demeter when Dmitri recites not just "Hymn to Joy," which celebrates nature, man, and unity, but Schiller's ode to Ceres, the Roman equivalent of Demeter. Dmitri's character is strongly associated with the pagan and earthly —and with an appetite for the bountiful fruits of nature.

Beginning with Prostitution, Ending with Honor: Dmitri's relationship with Katerina is a microcosm of Dmitri's conflicted dual nature. When Dmitri first meets Katerina, his vile impulses make him encourage Katerina to prostitute herself for her father's sake. But when the moment arrives to have sex with Katerina, Dmitri retreats from the prospect of sin. His appreciation for good things pulls him back and allows him to perceive her beauty and generosity. He understands the self-sacrifice Katerina is willing to make for her father. For the moment ruled by his virtuous impulses, Dmitri gives Katerina the money without demanding anything in return. Katerina behaves honorably in turn by paying back the money when she has the means to do so. Dmitri's relationship with Katerina is based on honor, so he feels strongly that he should pay Katerina 3,000 rubles before parting ways with her. As Dmitri tells Alyosha, "Though I'm full of baseness, and love what's low, I'm not dishonorable."

Motive for Murder: In his confession, Dmitri admits to everything Fyodor has said about him and shows that he has more than one motive for wanting to kill his father. First, he is motivated by possessive jealousy. Dmitri is angry that Fyodor is his apparent rival for Grushenka's affections. He says that if Grushenka ever sleeps with Fyodor, Dmitri will be forced to kill Fyodor for defiling her. He is also motivated by money. He owes Katerina 3,000 rubles, and Fyodor apparently has the same amount of money ready to offer Grushenka. He is further motivated by wounded feelings, because he thinks his father should give him more money from the family estate. Finally, Dmitri is motivated by simple disgust. He admits to feeling physically repulsed by his father.

Alyosha as Confessor: Alyosha acts as listener and confessor to Dmitri. Alyosha, thought not truly a confessor, dresses in a priest's cassock. This priestly garb enhances his naturally kind manner and makes him an appealing confessor. When Dmitri explains himself, Alyosha begins to understand the complexity in Dmitri that Zossima already noticed. Alyosha has learned his philosophy of life from Zossima and has absorbed his capacity to learn about people by listening to them. Alyosha has not yet left the monastery for good, but he has already begun to practice Zossima's mandate to go out into the world and help his family.

PART ONE, BOOK III
CHAPTERS 6–9

After talking with Dmitri, Alyosha puts off visiting Katerina and instead goes to his father's house. There, Ivan and Fyodor sit drinking in the dining room while Gregory and Smerdyakov argue in the background. We learn that Smerdyakov, now a servant and a cook for his own father, suffers from epilepsy. He carries himself with a morose and irritable air. Gregory taught him to read and write, but he also belittled Smerdyakov, saying things like, "You're not a human being! You grew from the mildew in the bathhouse." As a child, Smerdyakov rejected the Bible and did not like books. He used to hang cats for pleasure. He despises everyone and is known for being exceedingly honest. Once, he found a small sum of Fyodor's cash on the ground and returned it to him instead of taking it for himself. Fyodor sent him to Moscow to learn to be a cook. Smerdyakov resents serving the man who is allegedly his own father.

Smerdyakov and Gregory argue about whether a man should publicly renounce his faith to save his life if he can later repent for his sin of renunciation. Smerdyakov says that one can successfully atone for the sin of renunciation. He holds his own in the argument, and Fyodor notices that Smerdyakov is interested in Ivan's intellectual ideas. Ivan mutters that Smerdyakov is a "lackey and a low person. Raw material for revolution when the time comes."

After the servants leave, the conversation turns back to religion. This time, Alyosha and Ivan argue. Ivan claims that neither God, immortality, nor the devil exist. Alyosha contends the opposite. Fyodor predictably turns the conversation to women. He talks of Adelaide and her insanity. Alyosha weeps to hear stories of his mother. Ivan reminds Fyodor that Adelaide was also Ivan's mother. Since the two brothers are so different, Fyodor has completely forgotten that Adelaide was mother to both.

Suddenly, Dmitri bursts into the room, chased by Gregory and Smerdyakov. Dmitri cries out that he believes Grushenka is in the house somewhere. He insinuates that his father is up to no good. Dmitri searches the house and finds nothing, then returns to the dining room and picks a fight with Fyodor. Fyodor accuses Dmitri of stealing money from him. Dmitri, enraged, flings his father to the floor and kicks him. Ivan and Alyosha stop his attack. Before Dmitri storms out, he again asks Alyosha to visit Katerina and tell her that their engagement is off. He threatens to return and vows to kill Fyodor. After the ruckus, Alyosha tends to his father for an hour.

As Alyosha leaves, he asks Ivan if he thinks the conflict will end in murder. Ivan says that all men have the capacity for murder and Dmitri is as capable as anyone else of shedding blood. He says to Alyosha, "One reptile will devour the other. And it will serve them both right, too." Then he takes it back and says he would never allow Fyodor to be killed. The two brothers shake hands for the first time and plan to meet the next day. Alyosha wonders if Ivan has an ulterior motive for their new friendship.

UNDERSTANDING AND INTERPRETING
Part One, Book III, Chapters 6–9

Smerdyakov's Alienation: In this chapter, we learn about Smerdyakov for the first time. His parentage does not bode well for his future. His mother was the village idiot, and his father is the vile Fyodor Karamazov. He seems an enigma at first. He has little affection either for Gregory, his foster father, or Fyodor, his natural father. Smerdyakov's attitude is unsurprising, for Gregory belittles him, and Fyodor sends him off to Moscow to learn to cook and then employs him as a servant. Naturally enough, Smerdyakov resents being a servant in his father's house. Fyodor also reveals that Smerdyakov has no fondness for either Alyosha or Ivan. Smerdyakov is a portrait of alienation. Isolated from everyone around him, he lashes out with contempt.

Smerdyakov's Problems: Smerdyakov can be read as a weaker, less intelligent version of Ivan. Like Ivan, he loves a good intellectual discussion, but Smerdyakov's intellectual arguments are almost silly: "God created light on the first day, and the sun, moon, and stars on the fourth day. Where did the light come from on the first day?" He tries to show off and impress Ivan, but Ivan dismisses him as a "lackey." As a shadow of his legitimate brothers, Smerdyakov is wickedly jealous of them. He relishes any opportunity to demonstrate his superiority over them, trying to impress even when his inferiority is apparent. Smerdyakov is hard to like for these and other reasons. He has a history of cruelty, as we learn from the fact that as a child he enjoyed killing cats. He denounces religion, a position that puts him in conflict with Alyosha. Smerdyakov's epilepsy stands for his psychological sickness. Even his nickname, "Stinker," points not just to the familial scorn that has so warped Smerdyakov, but also to the tinge of filth that marks him.

Alyosha's Active Love: Alyosha continues to act on Zossima's mandate of love. Just as Zossima did during the family meeting, Alyosha tries to practice only love in the face of Fyodor's buffoonery. When Fyodor mocks faith in God and sides with Ivan in the debate about religion, Alyosha replies, "I am not angry. I know your thoughts. Your heart is better than your head." When Fyodor pesters and insults Ivan, Alyosha begs him to stop. Only when Fyodor speaks sardonically of Alyosha's mother does Alyosha finally break down, but he does not strike back at his father or rebuke him. Alyosha reserves judgment. He tries to love his father despite all his faults and to show him the error of his ways. When the clash between Fyodor and Dmitri results in physical violence for the first time, Alyosha plays the role of peacemaker.

Ivan's Calm Amorality: Ivan is a puzzle. He has no love for Fyodor or Dmitri, and his feelings for Alyosha are ambiguous at best. Ivan helps stop Dmitri from hurting Fyodor, but when Dmitri threatens to return and finish the job, Ivan cares little about the prospect of the murder. Again, we cannot tell if Ivan really believes what he is saying. As casually as he writes off faith, he writes off the threat of his brother murdering his father. He claims, enigmatically and somewhat suspiciously, that the decision to murder is "decided in men's hearts." When he shakes Alyosha's hand for the first time, even the trusting Alyosha wonders about Ivan's motives. Ivan himself seems unsure where he stands on these questions. He is very intelligent and enjoys debate, but is not guided by any moral principles.

Dmitri's Impulsiveness: Dmitri threatens to murder Fyodor, and his rage and jealousy make the threat seem credible. Ivan claims that every man can commit murder, but Alyosha holds out. He believes in Dmitri's goodness. Dmitri's earlier confession about the dualities of his nature gives Alyosha hope that the good in Dmitri can save him.

PART ONE, BOOK III
CHAPTERS 10–11

Alyosha goes straight to Madame Hohlakov's house, where Katerina is boarding. Katerina believes that Dmitri is not completely lost and that his infatuation with Grushenka is merely a passing fancy. Alyosha tells her how seriously Dmitri takes his 3,000-ruble debt to her. Katerina says she hoped Dmitri would come to her to confess rather than feel shame. She says she is Dmitri's "truest friend." Her resolve to hold on to Dmitri is unwavering, but she speaks kindly of Grushenka, puzzling Alyosha.

Suddenly, Grushenka appears from behind a curtain—she was in the room before Alyosha even arrived. She and Katerina appear to have become allies in some way. Katerina says that Grushenka will soon be leaving town to reunite with a past lover. When Grushenka leaves, she says, Dmitri will have no choice but to return to Katerina, his rightful fiancée. When Katerina asks Grushenka to confirm the story, though, Grushenka betrays her and says she might change her mind and stay with Dmitri. Grushenka also mentions that Dmitri told her how Katerina had been agreeable to the prospect of selling her body for money. Katerina screams insults at her, but Grushenka just laughs and walks out. As Alyosha exits a few minutes later, Madame Hohlakov's maid hands him a letter.

Alyosha makes his way back to the monastery and bumps into Dmitri again. Alyosha tells him what happened between Katerina and Grushenka, and the story delights Dmitri. The mere mention of Grushenka's behavior lights up his face. He thinks of Grushenka as a magnificent "she-devil." But Dmitri suddenly feels ashamed of himself and predicts he will be disgraced. He pounds a spot on his chest "as though his dishonor lay precisely on his chest . . . or hanging round his neck."

Alyosha, feeling unsettled, returns to the monastery. He becomes further upset upon learning that Father Zossima's health has taken a turn for the worse. Alyosha decides he must stay at the monastery until Zossima dies, no matter what anyone tells him. Before going to bed, Alyosha opens the letter given to him at Madame Hohlakov's. It is written by Lise, who says she wants to marry him when she is old enough. She requests that he visit her soon.

UNDERSTANDING AND INTERPRETING
Part One, Book III, Chapters 10–11

Pride, Hysteria, and Resolve: A portrait of resolve, Katerina shows her self-assuredness and pride. She is sure that Dmitri will return to her despite his errant ways, and she even allows Grushenka to befriend her to prove the point.

Katerina's resolve is built on arrogance. She sees Dmitri's passion for Grushenka as nothing but the sensual lust of a Karamazov, failing to consider the possibility that Dmitri feels more for Grushenka than lust. When Grushenka turns on her, Katerina's pride collapses into hysteria, and she feels ashamed and pathetic. Her dedication to Dmitri throughout the novel is tenacious—perhaps even obsessive—and she puts herself through these ordeals just to prove that she can take anything for him.

The Two-faced She-devil: Grushenka is two-faced and whimsical. She pursues her own desires at the expense of others. Dmitri describes her as a "tigress" and a "she-devil." She has no reason to insult Katerina except for her own amusement, and her insolence is a reflection of her own fickleness. She and Dmitri make an dangerous pair.

PART TWO, BOOK IV
Lacerations

Father Zossima wakes the next day worried that he may not live through the day. He gathers together his fellow monks and offers a final prayer for them: "Love one another, Fathers. Love God's people. Because we have come here and shut ourselves within these walls, we are no holier than those that are outside." He tells them that every human being shares the responsibility for all human sins. Only with that knowledge, he says, can the monks fill their hearts with "universal, infinite, inexhaustible" love.

Many in the monastery anticipate that a miracle will accompany Zossima's death because of Zossima's saintliness. There are also factions within the monastery that are hostile toward Zossima. One monk, **Father Ferapont**, a reclusive ascetic, is especially antagonistic to Zossima and does not believe in his doctrine of love. Ferapont believes that fear of Satan is the key to living, and he has visions of devils lurking in the shadows.

Zossima again appeals to Alyosha to take care of his troubled family. Alyosha reluctantly agrees and goes home to find his father alone. Fyodor tells Alyosha that he intends to live a long life and will need all his money to pay for his endless debauchery. Fyodor adds that he thinks Ivan is a materialistic scoundrel and wonders if Ivan has a plan to kill him. Fyodor thinks that Ivan intends to marry

Katerina for her money. Alyosha dismisses all of his father's theories. Fyodor asks him if Dmitri would go away forever if he were given more money, and Alyosha timidly hints that 3,000 rubles might be enough. Fyodor laughs off this suggestion and says he will never give Dmitri any more money. Alyosha leaves and walks over to Madame Hohlakov's.

On his way there, Alyosha comes upon a group of schoolboys throwing rocks at another solitary boy. The abused boy looks tiny and weak, but Alyosha notices that he displays a fierce resolve. The boys tell Alyosha they are throwing rocks because the boy stabbed one of them with a penknife. After Alyosha himself is hit with a rock, the other boys blame it on the fact that he is a Karamazov. Alyosha follows the small boy when he runs off, but the boy will not talk to him. Instead, he yells "Monk in silk pants!" He bites Alyosha's hand and runs off. Alyosha resolves to track him down and find out if he can help. Alyosha cannot understand why the boy is so angry with him.

At Madame Hohlakov's, Lise tells Alyosha that the letter is really just a bad joke. Alyosha politely refuses to give it back to her, because he has no reason not to believe what it said. Alyosha finds out that Ivan is upstairs talking with Katerina. Madame Hohlakov says she thinks Ivan and Katerina are in love but too hardheaded to do anything about it. Alyosha agrees. He thinks of Katerina's loyalty to Dmitri as masochistic.

Alyosha goes upstairs and Katerina tells him and Ivan that she will never abandon Dmitri, even if he marries Grushenka. Alyosha says she is making a mistake with her loyalty and torturing Ivan in the process. Ivan denies that he and Katerina feel anything for each other, but he agrees that Katerina is hurting herself by remaining loyal to Dmitri. Ivan tells Katerina, "you need him so as to contemplate continually your heroic fidelity and reproach him for infidelity. And it all comes from your pride." Ivan announces that he is leaving for Moscow the next day, and Katerina acts pleased about his departure.

After Ivan leaves, Katerina tells Alyosha about a poor man, **Captain Snegiryov**, whom Dmitri senselessly beat right in front of the man's son. She is haunted by the memory of this violence and wants to give 200 rubles to the captain as recompense. Alyosha says he will deliver the money as a favor. He goes to the bleak Snegiryov house, which looks like it might collapse. The captain's wife is deranged, and one of his two daughters is a hunchback. Captain Snegiryov's son **Ilusha** is the boy who bit Alyosha's finger. When Alyosha sees Ilusha, he understands that the boy hates him because Alyosha is the brother of the man who beat Ilusha's father. Alyosha offers the 200 rubles to Snegiryov, and at first the captain takes the money. Then, however, the captain throws the money on the ground and stomps on it, saying that his son will never respect him if he accepts the money.

UNDERSTANDING AND INTERPRETING
Part Two, Book IV

You are Responsible for the Sins of Others: With his words of wisdom,
Zossima makes the same appeal to all the monks that he has made to Alyosha,
saying that they should not live alone in the monastery, isolated from the people
they are supposed to help. They are responsible, as all people are, for the sins of
all humanity. He does not go so far as to tell them all to leave the monastery, but
he does ask them to stay vigilant about their own weaknesses and sins, because
they have the same faults as common people. These words strengthen Alyosha's
mission. He spends the entirety of Book IV going from person to person, helping
with problems and trying to understand character flaws through the lens of his
own shortcomings. Zossima's idea that we share responsibility for the sins of
others resonates throughout the rest of the novel.

Quiet and Active Love: In accordance with Zossima's teaching, Alyosha practices both quiet and active love. As usual, he quietly expresses his love for Fyodor with patient listening and by withholding judgment on him and his
loathsome ways. When Alyosha visits his father, Fyodor tells his usual brash
stories of wild women and sordid ways, but Alyosha simply smiles and tells
him, "You are not ill-natured, but distorted." He holds out hope that his father
has just strayed from the path of good. Alyosha kisses Fyodor goodbye even
after listening to his angry rambles about Dmitri. Meanwhile, Alyosha practices
a more active love when he tries to help people. When he comes upon the boys
throwing rocks, he tries to intervene on behalf of the boy he perceives to be the
underdog. Even when the boy he helps bites him and runs away, Alyosha
resolves to find out what is bothering him and to help if he can. The episode
with Katerina and Ivan perplexes Alyosha. He wants to mediate the new conflict
he discovers between Dmitri and Ivan but knows that passive love will not do
the trick. He also knows that his active love will have to be used carefully. He is
uncertain about how to proceed.

Katerina's Pride and Martyrdom: Alyosha cannot comprehend Katerina's irrational impulse for "self-laceration." Her loyalty to Dmitri takes the form of pure
suffering and humiliation, and here she says she will stay loyal to him even if he
marries Grushenka. She wants to be a martyr for an impossible cause, not only
to enjoy her own pain, but also to enjoy feeling morally superior to Dmitri. Ivan
summarizes her psychology this way: "The more he insults you, the more you
love him—that's your 'laceration' . . . You love him for insulting you. If he
reformed, you'd give him up at once." Because of Katerina's pride, she can never

admit to her feelings for Ivan. Father Zossima would probably accuse her of the worst self-deception—the kind that prohibits people from loving one another. When Ivan leaves, Katerina feigns indifference, even though his departure probably pains her. Alyosha says nothing and feels powerless. His love is useless to a person like Katerina, who cannot accept love of any kind. All he can do for her is act as peacemaker to Captain Snegiryov. But as with the little boy who bites his hand, he hopes to resolve the situation with Katerina another time.

The Newness of Children: Alyosha learns a great deal from children like Ilusha, and often forms stronger connections with children than he does with adults. When Alyosha fails in his errand to Snegiryov, he perceives Ilusha's deep self-respect and realizes that he approached Snegiryov in the wrong way, because the son must have learned his self-respect from his father. Alyosha has a rapport with Lise because he understands the girl better than her mother does, and Lise trusts him more than she trusts anyone else. Their plans for marriage, whether real or not, are a sign that Alyosha instills a hopeful sense of the future in Lise. Alyosha sees the great potential for the future in Lise and Ilusha since their values are still malleable. Both children suffer in their own ways—Lise as an invalid, and Ilusha as the son of a destitute family—and Alyosha understands their suffering as a valuable influence on their emotional development. Because they suffer, they contemplate, and will probably attain a sophisticated understanding of life. The adults that Alyosha encounters have all constructed high walls around themselves and have left no room for introspection. The difference between children and adults is emphasized in Book IV, which sets the arguments of Katerina and Ivan in between stories of Ilusha and Lise. The self-deception of Katerina and Ivan does not exist in children, and Alyosha's examples of love and honesty have a more profound and lasting effect on younger souls.

PART TWO, BOOK V
Pro and Contra

CHAPTERS 1–4

Alyosha returns to Madame Hohlakov's to tell Katerina what happened with Captain Snegiryov, but he finds that Katerina has fallen ill with a high fever. He sits down with Lise, who is more than happy to see him again. He discusses the episode at Snegiryov's, and she asks questions and contributes to his analysis of his own failings. Afterward, both admit to a mutual admiration and love for each other. Lise also confesses that she really does want to marry him. The two decide to get married when she is old enough. Before he leaves, Alyosha worries aloud that the problems in his family are testing his will.

Alyosha decides not to return to the monastery that evening but instead to find Dmitri. He walks to the family's summer house, where he and Dmitri met the night before, but he finds no one there. He overhears Smerdyakov nearby singing a "lackey's song" and playing guitar for a neighbor's daughter, **Maria**. His song is a simple, popular ditty and Maria compliments his singing, but Smerdyakov replies, "poetry is rubbish!" Smerdyakov also says he hates Russia and wishes Napoleon had conquered the nation once and for all.

Alyosha interrupts their conversation and asks if they have seen Dmitri. Smerdyakov says Ivan is supposed to meet Dmitri for dinner at a restaurant in town. He tells Alyosha not to reveal who told him of Dmitri's whereabouts. Alyosha hurries to the restaurant Smerdyakov named, where he finds Ivan alone. Ivan invites Alyosha to join him, saying he wants to get to know him better. Alyosha tells Ivan that he has trouble understanding him, even though he sees him as "fresh and nice, green in fact!" Ivan agrees with Alyosha and tells him that he prizes his youth. Ivan loves life but worries that as he gets older he will begin to lose faith in the order of the world and see things as a "disorderly, damnable, and perhaps devil-ridden chaos." He worries that after he turns thirty, he will become disillusioned.

Alyosha enthusiastically listens to Ivan and agrees that "everyone should love life above everything in the world. . . . Love it, regardless of logic. " He then tells Ivan that he is half way to being saved, although Ivan protests that he does not need saving. Alyosha says he worries that Dmitri may attack Fyodor again after Ivan leaves for Moscow. Ivan becomes upset and says he cannot stay in town "to be their keeper." He has put these episodes behind him, even his love for Katerina, and is ready to return to Moscow.

Ivan revisits the debate about God and immortality. He believes that if there were no God, then humans would invent one to believe in. He can accept the idea of God, but he cannot accept that God would create the world they live in. If God does exist and did create the world, humans should be able to understand the purpose of creation. But since we cannot understand creation, we must reject the world God created. Alyosha asks him to clarify what he means, and Ivan smiles and says, "It's not a secret. That's what I've been leading to. Perhaps I even want to be healed by you."

Ivan does not think we should love our neighbors as ourselves. He can love people at a distance, he says, but loving his neighbor is almost impossible. The chaos, brutality, and suffering of the world make it impossible for him to accept that the world is a creation of God. The pain leads him to question God's existence. When the world is so indifferent to children's suffering, for example, how can God exist? He concludes that "there is suffering and that there are none guilty." What he desires above all is justice on earth, not in some unknowable afterlife. He says that if the suffering of children is the price of knowing the meaning of God's universe, "I most respectfully return Him my ticket."

Alyosha is distressed to hear Ivan's theories, calling them rebellious. Ivan proposes one final question for Alyosha: if he could torture to death one tiny creature to make the world a perfect place, would he do it? Alyosha says he would not, nor can he admit that any human would. He reminds Ivan that only Jesus Christ could sacrifice himself in such a way. Ivan decides to respond with a prose-poem he has created about Jesus called "The Grand Inquisitor."

UNDERSTANDING AND INTERPRETING
Part Two, Book V, Chapters 1–4

Alyosha and Lise: Alyosha's relationship with the young Lise might seem odd to the modern reader, but it is meant to be innocent. Alyosha feels instantly comfortable in Lise's presence. Following Zossima's example, he gently explains to her the wisdom he gained from his failed meeting with Captain Snegiryov. Alyosha's intuition seems to be developing well. He dissects Snegiryov's psychology and carefully examines the mistakes he made in talking to the poor man. Lise chimes in from time to time, at one point calling the conversation "our analysis." Together, Alyosha and Lise form a harmonious whole, which will be solidified by their plans for marriage. In Lise, Alyosha sees first a child, but beyond that, a moral potential for the future. He tells Lise at one point, "You laugh like a little child, but you think like a martyr." This indicates Alyosha's belief that Lise has the worldly, moral wisdom of an adult.

The Karamazov Curse: Alyosha worries that he too has Karamazov blood in his veins, and that he is not an entirely saintly figure. His doubts about himself and his family lead him to question his own moral sense. He says to Lise, "My brothers are destroying themselves. My father, too. It's the 'primitive force of the Karamazovs'. . . . A crude, unbridled force. Does the spirit of God move about that force? Even that I do not know. I only know that I, too, am a Karamazov. . . . Me a monk, a monk! Am I a monk, Lise?" Alyosha worries that not only is he cursed with the Karamazov blood, but that perhaps it is God's will that instills crudity in the Karamazovs.

Pale, Shadowy Smerdyakov: Smerdyakov sings to Maria in the same garden where Dmitri talked to Alyosha the day before. Smerdyakov's guitar playing and singing are a stark contrast to Dmitri's poetic exaltation. Smerdyakov sings, in a "sugary falsetto," a simple popular tune. His mindless artistry has nothing in common with Dmitri's passionate recitation of the grand themes of Schiller's poetry. Smerdyakov even shows his disdain for poetry by calling it "rubbish." His remarks about his hatred for Russia—the earth, the motherland—are the opposite of Dmitri's glorious love of life. Smerdyakov is like a pale shadow of Dmitri. His biological illegitimacy makes him a pale version of a brother, too. He is not a "real" brother, but a shadowy man of mockery, deceit, and duplicity. When he reveals the information about Dmitri's somewhat secret whereabouts, he asks Alyosha not to betray him. The notion of betrayal is central to Smerdyakov's character and foreshadows further developments in the family crisis.

God Does Not Exist: Ivan is deeply conflicted. He loves life, but he cannot bear the idea of the suffering of the world. He cannot believe in a God that would allow such disorder and suffering, especially the suffering of children. Ivan is rational and intelligent, and he cannot find a rational, intelligent explanation for God's actions. He cannot transcend his own reasoning in order to find meaning in God's brutal world. He reasons that if God wanted humans to understand this world, then God should have given humans a way of understanding it. God allows suffering to take place, but God does not give humans a way of understanding why he made creation the way he did, so Ivan concludes that God does not exist.

A Dilemma of Faith: Ivan quotes the philosophical idea that "If God did not exist, he would have to be invented." These words were written by French Enlightenment scholar Voltaire in the eighteenth century, and Ivan's familiarity with them reflects his education. Ivan is surprised that humans, who are brutal animals, could have needed to invent such a benevolent deity as God. He does not reject God categorically, but he rejects a God who created a world of such unacceptable disorder. Ivan is an idealist and a humanist at heart, and he loves humankind and his own free will. Free will and freedom of thought have given him the chance to reject the divine order and authority of the universe. But the implications of this rejection trouble him.

PART TWO, BOOK V
CHAPTER 5 ("THE GRAND INQUISITOR")

The **Grand Inquisitor** prose-poem, which Ivan wrote, is set in sixteenth-century Spain at a brutal moment of the Spanish Inquisition "when fires were lighted every day to the glory of God." One day, Jesus Christ appears on the streets of Seville, and people surround him. Jesus performs miracles for the crowd and virtue radiates from his mere presence. The Grand Inquisitor, an old cardinal of about ninety, comes upon the scene and orders Jesus arrested.

"**D**ostoevsky had virtually to create God—and what a Herculean task that was! Dostoevsky rose from the depths and, reaching the summit, retained something of the depths about him still."

HENRY MILLER

That night, the Inquisitor comes to visit Jesus in his cell and rebukes Jesus for returning to earth and hindering the work of the Inquisition. The Inquisitor explains that Jesus does not have the right to add anything to what he said or did in his first life. "All has been given by Thee to the Pope," the Inquisitor says, "Thou must not meddle for the time, at least." The Inquisitor says that humankind has paid a steep price for the freedom of faith, and the Church is completing Jesus' work by vanquishing freedom to make men happy.

The Inquisitor explains that the source of this quandary of freedom is rooted in Christ's rejection of the temptations long ago offered to him by the devil during his forty days in the wilderness. The three temptations were the security of bread, power, and authority over all the kingdoms of the world, and the prospect of performing a miracle by surviving a fall from the highest pinnacle in Jerusalem. If Jesus accepted any of the three temptations, then humankind would follow him.

But Jesus rejected them, and when he did, he rejected them for all humankind. His decision gave humans the freedom to choose, even the freedom to choose or reject faith if they so desired. If Christ had accepted the bread, he would have given humankind security instead of freedom. And if he had let himself be cast down from the pinnacle of Jerusalem, he would have let humans worship him only because of his power to perform miracles, not because they freely chose to have faith in him.

But this freedom, the Inquisitor says, is incomprehensible and frightening to humans. The Inquisitor insists that human beings are "weaker and baser" than Christ expected. Christ asked too much of them by expecting them to choose good and virtue. Freedom often leads to suffering, and suffering often leads to the denial of God, because people cannot reconcile the existence of God with great suffering.

The Church, the Inquisitor argues, has corrected Christ's work, changing the basis of faith from freedom to "miracle, mystery and authority." Humans are happy again, because the "terrible gift of freedom" is lifted from their hearts. He argues that if Christ had accepted the last offer of the devil, authority, he could have accomplished all that humankind seeks on earth. That is, Jesus would be someone to worship and to unite humankind in a "universal state" of peace.

Because Jesus did not accept the last offer, the Church has started to do so. With the Inquisition, it has taken up the "sword of Caesar" in the name of this universal state. Thus, it has rejected Christ and followed the temptations of the devil. Humans willingly submit to the authority of the Church in exchange for the happiness and security that the Church provides. Under the Church's system, everyone benefits and lives in happiness, whereas under Jesus' teachings, only the strong survive, and the weak suffer and die. Christ's return to earth can only destroy this new equilibrium, so the Inquisitor asks that Jesus leave or be put to death again.

Christ has not said a word during the Inquisitor's long explanation. Finally, he rises without a word, kisses the Inquisitor on the forehead, and departs. The Inquisitor, perplexed by the silence, tells Jesus never to come again.

When Ivan is finished telling the story, Alyosha worries that if Ivan truly believes it, Ivan will go mad or commit suicide. Ivan assures him that he can endure anything because of the notorious Karamazov blood that he inherited from Fyodor. The Karamazov way is to follow the creed "Everything is lawful." With that, Ivan thinks he can survive. Ivan asks if Alyosha will renounce him for his beliefs. Alyosha says nothing and kisses Ivan on the forehead. Alyosha leaves knowing that Ivan's conflict with faith will later erupt. The two part on friendly terms and walk in separate directions. Ivan hobbles as if his body has been contorted into a crooked misalignment.

UNDERSTANDING AND INTERPRETING
Part Two, Book V, Chapter 5

The Grand Inquisitor's Argument: The Grand Inquisitor chapter is one of the most famous passages in all of Dostoevsky's works. It highlights Ivan's intense inner conflict and stirs up a powerful intellectual and theological debate. Ivan asks one of the most difficult, reasonable questions about faith: how can we believe in God when there is such suffering in the world? In his epic prose-

THE SPANISH INQUISITION

Inquisitions were used throughout Europe in the Middle Ages to root out nonbelievers or to find traitors. The Spanish Inquisition is remembered as the most brutal and the bloodiest of all inquisitions. After the Holy Crusades of the fourteenth and fifteenth centuries, Spain remained a divided nation of Catholic, Protestant, Jewish, and Muslim populations. In 1478, King Ferdinand and Queen Isabella—the monarchs who sent Columbus to America—resolved to unite the nation under Catholicism. In 1483, Tomás de Torquemada became inquisitor-general of the new Inquisition. Torquemada's tenure was notorious for its ruthlessness. He brutally tortured Spanish citizens in the name of *sangre limpia* (pure blood). Citizens with a drop of Jewish, Muslim, or Protestant blood were brought before tribunals and forced not only to recant their faith, but also to name other so-called heretics. If they refused, they were imprisoned or burned at the stake. The Inquisition became a tool to suppress the political power of Jews and to drive the Muslim Moors from the south. Within their first fifteen years, Torquemada's rampages killed nearly 2,000 Spaniards. The Spanish Inquisition continued in various forms for nearly 350 years, and was formally abolished only in 1834.

poem, Ivan reduces this question to one of human freedom and conscience. The Grand Inquisitor argues that Jesus Christ threw away the security and perpetual happiness of humankind by rejecting the last temptation of the devil (the biblical story is chronicled in Luke 4:1–13). Humans are simple beings who crave comfort and security, and freedom of choice and of conscience is far too difficult for them. By giving humans freedom, Jesus condemned them to an existence of suffering in which they must have faith in him, but without having a concrete, tangible reason for their faith. Jesus believed—wrongly, according to the Grand Inquisitor—that faith cannot be forced from people but must be freely chosen by them. Under the Inquisition, the Church makes humankind secure by accepting the third temptation of the devil and taking authority over the kingdom of earth. By gaining absolute authority, says the Grand Inquisitor, the Church abolishes freedom but creates happiness for all people.

Security versus Freedom: The Inquisitor's grand plan brings harmony and unity to humankind and forever abolishes suffering, but the price is freedom of choice. Ivan points out that freedom has a great price too: when people have the freedom to choose, incomprehensible suffering is the result. This is the price that makes him want to "return his ticket" to God. This is the crux of the issue for Ivan and the other characters in the novel: is it better to be free and suffer, or to be enslaved and feel safe? For Ivan, the issue remains unresolved. He does not side with the Inquisitor of his creation, but he cannot believe that God would create a world so full of suffering. Ivan says he relies on the Karamazov will, which is based on the credo "everything is lawful," to survive.

Parricide—Literal, Spiritual, Political: This novel of parricide—the murder of a father—is also a novel of spiritual parricide. In Ivan's story, the Grand Inquisitor effectively kills God, and in Ivan's theories, Ivan himself kills God by refusing to believe in him. Parricide also relates to the political situation at the time when *The Brothers Karamazov* was published. The main events of the novel take place in the 1860s, at a time when radical Socialists in Russia incited violence against the government of the Tsar, the national father of Russia. By the 1870s, when this violence culminated in numerous assassination attempts on Tsar Alexander II (the final, successful attempt occurred in 1881, just months after Dostoevsky died), Dostoevsky believed that there were "no moral ideas left" in Russia and that the radicals were "liars who do not admit that their ideal is . . . the coercion of the human conscience and the reduction of mankind to the level of cattle." Dostoevsky believed that the radicals rejected moral and religious beliefs in order to control people. *The Brothers Karamazov* is read by some critics as a defense of religion and of Dostoevsky's belief in the Russian system of government.

PART TWO, BOOK V
CHAPTERS 6 – 7

Ivan feels depressed as he leaves Alyosha. He has settled business at home, and now he will return to isolation, unsure of the future. Ivan arrives at Fyodor's house and realizes that he loathes the place. When he sees Smerdyakov, he realizes that Smerdyakov is actually the source of his loathing, even though Ivan originally liked Smerdyakov for his intellectual spark.

Smerdyakov tells Ivan that he is worried about the situation with Dmitri and Fyodor. He worries that the tension and stress around the house might cause him to have an epileptic seizure. He predicts he will have a fit and fall down the basement stairs. Fyodor has shut himself in his room and will only answer the door for Gregory. But Gregory is sick, and Fyodor has ordered Smerdyakov to stay out of the house at night. Meanwhile, Fyodor has developed a series of secret signals that Grushenka will use if she comes to see him. Smerdyakov says he told Dmitri about the signals because Dmitri threatened to kill him otherwise.

Smerdyakov says he fears that as soon as Ivan leaves for Moscow, Dmitri will have a chance to sneak into the house to kill Fyodor. He also mentions that Dmitri may steal the envelope containing the 3,000 rubles meant for Grushenka. Ivan dismisses the notion that Dmitri would steal the money. Smerdyakov pleads with him not to go to Moscow but to withdraw instead to a nearby town, Tchermashnya. Nevertheless, Ivan resolves to go to Moscow.

The next morning, Fyodor also asks Ivan to go to Tchermashnya to conduct some business for the family with a man named **Gorskin**. Ivan reluctantly agrees to go. On his way out, Ivan tells Smerdyakov he has changed his mind, and Smerdyakov replies, "It's always worth while speaking to a clever man." Ivan does not quite understand what he means. Later, when Ivan reaches the train station, he decides to forgo the trip to Tchermashnya and wait for the train to Moscow. As his train speeds toward Moscow, he whispers to himself, "I am base."

That night, as predicted, Smerdyakov has an epileptic fit, falls down the basement stairs, and is rendered unconscious. Gregory is incapacitated with back pain. Fyodor, meanwhile, sits and eagerly awaits the secret knocks that will signal Grushenka's arrival.

UNDERSTANDING AND INTERPRETING
Part Two, Book V, Chapter 6–7

Dropping Hints: Smerdyakov drops many hints to Ivan, testing him to see whether he would object to the murder of Fyodor. Ivan is oblivious to these suggestions. Smerdyakov reveals all the pieces of the murder plot: the secret signals that could be used by Dmitri to gain entrance, the envelope, and his own alibi of an epileptic fit. Smerdyakov's mysterious comment—"It's always worthwhile speaking to a clever man"—is his way of signaling to Ivan that he knows the murder will be committed that night in Ivan's absence. Because Ivan does not balk at any of these clues, Smerdyakov concludes that Ivan does not object to the murder.

A Dangerous Listener: Many of the ideas we hear Smerdyakov muttering to others in previous chapters are rehashed from conversations he probably had with Ivan. In Smerdyakov, Ivan found an active listener. Smerdyakov was far more receptive than Fyodor, Alyosha, whom Ivan perceives as too saintly, or Dmitri, with whom he has nothing in common. Although Smerdyakov may be a good audience, he is also a simpleton. He butchers philosophical ideas, and his pronouncements on aesthetics are almost comical. Ivan is happy to find a willing listener in Smerdyakov, but he still thinks of him as a "lackey" and a "low person" not fit to discuss the intellectual concepts that Ivan has mastered.

Justifying Murder: Ivan argues that immortality does not exist, a position that frees men from the fear of hell. If we do not have to fear hell, we can act as if "everything is lawful." Conscience does not play a role. The murder of Fyodor is rationalized according to this negative idea. While he is not the actual murderer, Ivan is complicit in the murder because his ideas justify murder.

PART TWO, BOOK VI
The Russian Monk

Father Zossima is ailing, and he surrounds himself with friends and fellow monks. He asks Alyosha if he has seen Dmitri and says he bowed in front of Dmitri at their meeting because he foresees great suffering for him. He sees a different future for Alyosha and again advises him to leave the monastery and pursue good works for the benefit of his family and the rest of the world. He knows that Alyosha has a gift that will help people learn to love one another. Zossima tells all those assembled that he especially loves Alyosha because he resembles Zossima's older brother, who long ago inspired him to join the monastery.

The narrator recounts Zossima's life story, which he bases on Alyosha's written account of Zossima's last conversations. This account is called "Notes of the Life of the Deceased Priest and Monk, the Elder Zossima, Taken from His Own Words." Zossima is born to a modestly wealthy noble family. He is two when

A QUIET TOWN
FOR A CRUEL RETIREE

Ivan is supposed to conduct business in
Tchermashnya, a town whose name closely
resembles the name of a village that was
part of the Dostoevsky family estate.
Dostoevsky's father retired to this village
and descended into a life of debauchery
and cruelty during his final years. It was
rumored that serfs murdered Dostoevsky's
father on his estate, but this theory was
later called into question on the basis of
scientific evidence.

his father dies, and he is reared by his mother and his beloved older brother. The brother is a freethinker in his youth and ridicules his mother's devout religious beliefs. The brother suddenly contracts tuberculosis at seventeen and dies a few months later. Before his death, he has a spiritual transformation and often speaks to the young Zossima of the power of God's love, exhorting him to love all of God's creatures.

Zossima's other major influence is the Bible itself, which he reads eagerly as a child and in which he still finds wonder even in his old age. He says, "What a book the Bible is, what a miracle, what strength is given with it to man! . . . Everything is there, and a law for everything for all the ages." He especially loves the story of Job with its parable of suffering and faith. The story reveals to him the extent of God's glory, a mystery to humankind. Only with this mystery can the majesty of God be celebrated. Zossima asks, "What is the use of Christ's words, unless we set an example?" When he is young, Zossima makes a trip around Russia to raise money for the monastery. On his journey, he learns about God's love and the beauty of God's work in "every insect, ant, and golden bee," and especially in the animals that serve humans, like the horse and the ox.

Zossima's life is not always devoted to God. He spends eight years in the Cadet Corps in St. Petersburg and then lives a corrupt existence as a young military officer. At one time, he courts a beautiful woman, but the woman decides to marry another man. Zossima challenges the man to a duel. On the morning of the duel, he remembers his brother's words about loving all God's creatures, and he devises a plan for the duel. He lets the other man take the first shot, and then he drops his gun and begs for forgiveness. He immediately resigns from the military and joins the monastery.

One night, a mysterious stranger visits Zossima. The man confesses that he killed a woman many years ago. Someone else was suspected of the crime, and when the suspect died, the case was dropped. This man has become a respected part of the community and a great philanthropist. Still, he has never been happy and has always needed to confess. The man falls ill a short time later but thanks Zossima before he dies, saying, "The Lord vanquished the devil in my heart."

Zossima then describes his views on what it means to be a Russian monk. Monks, he says, are closest to the Russian peasant, and monks should "go on educating him quietly." By living an ascetic life of obedience, fasting, and prayer, a monk achieves a "freedom of spirit" that is rich soil for important ideas. The salvation of the nation will be brought about by the peasants because the peasants always remain faithful in their beliefs. Zossima talks about the notion of equality. He thinks it is impossible that there will be no servants in the world, but he urges people to act so that their servants feel "freer in spirit."

He concludes with an exhortation to love all creatures, both human and animal: "Love a man even in his sin, for that is the semblance of Divine Love and is the highest love on earth." He tells the monks never to judge their fellow humans and to pray for all of those outside the church. There is no physical hell, he thinks, but there is a spiritual hell that is voluntary and self-consuming for those who live without God's love. After offering these words of wisdom, Father Zossima lives on for another few hours and then dies "quietly and joyfully," surrendering his soul to God.

UNDERSTANDING AND INTERPRETING

Part Two, Book VI

A Prose-Poem and a Handbook: The previous book focused on Ivan's logical arguments against faith and immortality, and this book celebrates the deep faith and Christian beliefs of Father Zossima, providing an almost direct rebuttal to Ivan's theories. Unlike Ivan's highly conceptual Grand Inquisitor tale, the collection of Zossima's beliefs is written in the "Notes of the Life of the Deceased Priest and Monk"—a formal, edifying format designed almost as a handbook for monks. The difference between the two texts reflects the nature of each character. Ivan's prose-poem is full of his intellect and the unresolved arguments that lead Ivan to reject faith. His prose-poem is an abstract narrative in which rejection and cruelty feature prominently. The Grand Inquisitor tale ends with the contradictory kiss of Jesus. Zossima's handbook, on the other hand, is a peaceful work. It relates a calming story and has a positive, accepting, and fulfilling outlook. Zossima's belief system is grounded in both earthly experience and abstract faith.

The Value of Worldly Experiences and Suffering: Zossima was not always such a saint. His worldly experiences are not a mark against him but, to the contrary, an essential part of the faith he gains as an adult. His beliefs could not exist without the death of his brother, his duel, and his interaction with the guilty stranger. Zossima is both a man and a monk—that is, both an earthly creature and a heavenly one. His religious dedication comes later in life after he has learned certain truths during his secular life. His beliefs are formed not by blind faith, but in part by reason, knowledge, and experience. In Alyosha, Zossima sees a man and a monk, but he knows that Alyosha must leave the monastery to learn about the world. Alyosha has already begun to understand the importance of suffering. He sees suffering in his brothers, especially, who are tormented by internal conflicts. The value Zossima places on suffering is at the heart of many of his beliefs, and it is the ultimate refutation of Ivan's atheistic ideas.

The Mysterious Suffering of Job: Dostoevsky's interest in Job spans his novels. The case of Job provides a reasonable answer to Ivan's questions. The suffering of Job seems unnecessary, and that is precisely the point. Zossima argues that the story of Job explains that meaningless suffering is part of God's plan for humankind and that we can never hope to understand it. Job can only be happy once he stops trying to understand why God does what he does and accepts the fact that he can never fathom God's plan. Ivan bases his rejection of God on the presence of irrational suffering. He cannot conceive of a logical reason why suffering should exist, or why a just God would allow suffering, and so he believes that God must not exist. Zossima would argue that we must accept mystery and realize that God is too great to be comprehended by humans and their logic.

> "*The Brothers Karamazov*'s genre might best be called Scripture rather than novel or tragedy, saga or chronicle. Dostoevsky's scope is from Genesis to Revelation, with the Book of Job and the Gospel of John as the centers."
>
> **HAROLD BLOOM**

The Importance of Freedom: Zossima also addresses Ivan's idea that freedom makes humans unhappy. Zossima says that freedom of spirit leads to great ideas. The Russian monk gains freedom of spirit by pursuing an ascetic life of obedience, fasting, and prayer. Through isolation and simplicity, a monk discerns that the true meaning of life is the great love of God. Only when we have freedom, Zossima says, can we come to understand the towering importance of love. This love, as Zossima continually reemphasizes, is the basis of all human interactions.

Punishing Criminals: Zossima believes that no one can judge a criminal. Criminals will see the error of their ways as a result of their own consciences, not because the Church or society punishes them. During the debate in Zossima's cell, Ivan initially held that the Church, not society, should deal with criminals by excommunicating them and isolating them from society, thereby causing them to see that they were wrong. But Zossima considers it useless for the Church to condemn the sinner to hell, because hell is not a real place. Hell is a state of the soul. It is the spiritual punishment for the unrepentant. Only a criminal's recognition of his sin can lead to true redemption and salvation. And only love for a criminal can help him recognize his wrong.

THE BOOK OF JOB

The Book of Job is one of the most literary and mystifying stories of the Old Testament. Included among the books of wisdom (Job, Proverbs, and Ecclesiastes), it is also grouped with the books of poetry (Psalms, Song of Solomon, Lamentations). The story of an ordinary man, it addresses the problem of evil and suffering in the world and insists on the supremacy of God. Job is a "blameless and upright" man who becomes a pawn in a wager between Satan and God. God points to Job as a good man, and Satan argues that Job is good because he is lucky and prosperous. In response, God takes away all of Job's property, kills his family, and afflicts him with illness and boils. The book then turns to a dialogue between Job and his friends, who wonder if it is proper to blame God for Job's suffering. Job inveighs against a God who "destroys both the blameless and the wicked. When disaster brings sudden death, He mocks the calamity of the innocent. The earth is given into the hand of the wicked; He covers the face of its judges." Yet, in the end, Job recovers his faith in an all-powerful, if mysterious, God. God has demonstrated his authority over the universe, and when Job is humbled, God restores Job's fortunes and grants him a new family.

PART THREE, BOOK VII
Aloysha

After Father Zossima dies, his body is prepared for burial, and the monks and townspeople gather and await a miracle. No miracle occurs, and the body begins to decompose rapidly. The stench drives away many of the mourners. They take it as a sign that Zossima was not good, but evil. The monks who were ideological enemies of Zossima seize the moment and announce that the odor is proof that Zossima was no saint and that all his credos about God's love are false. The laypersons of the town are mystified by the experience. Even Alyosha is afraid and wonders how God could have allowed this to happen. Father Ferapont, Zossima's monastic adversary, rushes around the monastery trying to exorcise demons. Ferapont is ordered to leave. Finally, a disillusioned Alyosha makes his final departure from the monastery.

Alyosha questions the justice of Zossima's rapid decay. He is distraught that Zossima has been disgraced by the odor of decomposition. He knows he cannot question God's will, but he wonders how God could have allowed this to happen. That evening, Rakitin, the divinity student, finds Alyosha lying face down, asleep under a tree. Alyosha tells him about his disillusionment and echoes Ivan's words: "I am not rebelling against my God. I simply 'don't accept his world.'" Rakitin tempts Alyosha with vodka and sausage, both of which are prohibited to monks, and Alyosha accepts them freely. Rakitin suggests they pay a visit to Grushenka.

When they arrive, Grushenka says she is waiting for a message from her old lover, a soldier who is rumored to be coming back to reclaim her after five years. Grushenka notices Alyosha's low spirits and tries to cheer him up by sitting on his knee. Alyosha's sorrow is so great that "his heart swallowed up every sensation that might have been aroused." Grushenka is devastated to hear about Father Zossima's death and offers her sympathy to Alyosha.

Alyosha speaks kindly to Grushenka, saying, "I came here to find a wicked soul—I felt drawn to evil because I was base and evil myself, and I've found a true sister, I have found a treasure, a loving heart . . . You've raised my soul

THE RUSSIAN ORTHODOX CHURCH

The Russian Orthodox Church is one of the strongest branches of the Eastern Orthodox Church, which split from Roman Catholicism in the fifth century. The schism between the Eastern and Roman Churches was formalized in 1054 when Pope Leo IX condemned and excommunicated the Eastern patriarch who resided in Constantinople (Istanbul in present-day Turkey). Constantinople was the capital of the massive Byzantine Empire. Since 1859, the Russian Church has had its own patriarch in Moscow. Russian Orthodox masses are sung (not spoken) in a dead language, Old Church Slavonic. With the forced secularism of the Russian Revolution, the Church's foundation was weakened, but after the collapse of the Soviet Union in the early 1990s, it regained members in Russia and throughout Eastern Europe.

from the depths." Grushenka, touched, bares her soul to Alyosha. She talks of the burdens on her conscience, calling herself a "wicked woman." She confesses that she paid Rakitin to bring Alyosha to her.

Then, the letter from Grushenka's old lover arrives. She prepares to meet him in the nearby town of Mokroe. She asks Alyosha to say goodbye to Dmitri and tell him that she loved him, but only for "one short hour." After Grushenka leaves, Rakitin mocks Alyosha, saying, "Well, so you've saved a sinner? Have you turned the Magdalene into the true path?" Alyosha dismisses this comment and says he holds no grudge against Rakitin for luring him to Grushenka's.

That night, Alyosha returns to the monastery and visits Zossima's cell. He kneels and prays, but his thoughts still trouble him. He hears one of the other monks reading the Bible story of the wedding in Cana of Galilee. Alyosha falls into a deep sleep and dreams that he is in Cana, watching Jesus and the wedding from a distance. Zossima is there too, and he tells Alyosha to join the celebration, reminding him to love life. Zossima says that Grushenka will find her salvation because of Alyosha's kindness to her. Alyosha wakes with "tears of rapture" in his eyes. He goes outside and kneels on the ground, kissing the earth and feeling a new energy. He now understands the joy and meaning of his life.

UNDERSTANDING AND INTERPRETING
Part Three, Book VII

Alyosha in the Desert: With Father Zossima's death and unexpected decay, Alyosha must confront his doubts and the darker side of his nature. Like Jesus in the wilderness, Alyosha faces temptations. The rapid decomposition of the saintly Zossima baffles him, as does the lack of miracles accompanying the monk's death. Alyosha is tempted to question his faith. Rakitin offers him sausage and vodka, and he is willing to succumb to earthly pleasures. Grushenka offers him a frisson of sex, and he is tempted to enjoy carnal pleasures. In the end, these temptations only strengthen Alyosha's faith. During his meeting with Grushenka, he sees that his redemption comes from serving and listening to others. By saving Grushenka, it seems, Alyosha redeems himself. Grushenka's compassion for him stirs his own tenderness ("a feeling of intensest, purest interest without a trace of fear"). The doubts that plague Alyosha, once quieted, actually reaffirm his faith. Like Jesus, he is able to reject temptation.

Grushenka's Confessions: In this book, we see another side of Grushenka. At first, she is fearful of Alyosha since his purity and decency contrast with her scheming and licentious life. Alyosha is afraid too, because Grushenka is an alluring temptation of the flesh. She offers an element that Alyosha has been missing in his ascetic life, and she is a typical object of the Karamazov men's lust. But both Alyosha and Grushenka transcend their expected roles. Alyosha does not indulge himself in Karamazov lust, and Grushenka is not distant or seductive. Instead, Alyosha and Grushenka fashion a priest-confessor relationship. Grushenka sees Alyosha as someone she can talk to, someone to whom she can pour out her tale of sin. She asks, "Do you see now, Alyosha, what a violent, vindictive creature I am? I have shown you the whole truth!"

Turning Water into Wine: Dreams of joy and love assuage Alyosha's suffering soul. In the Bible, at the wedding in Cana of Galilee, Jesus turns water into wine. Such a miracle adds abundance and generosity to the marriage itself, which symbolizes unity and love. As the water cisterns are filled with wine, Alyosha is filled with faith and love and joy. When he dreams that Zossima is there with him, it lessens the pain of Zossima's death. When Alyosha wakes, he runs outside and kisses the earth, just as Zossima instructed. Alyosha is again ready to confront the world outside the monastery.

PART THREE, BOOK VIII
Dmitri

Dmitri knows nothing of Grushenka's imminent departure for Mokroe. He tries to figure out a way to pay back his 3,000-ruble debt to Katerina, which would allow him to run off with Grushenka. His first scheme is to get money from **Samsonov**, an old merchant and landowner in town who is a friend and protector of Grushenka. Dmitri tries to sell Samsonov the timber rights to some of the Karamazov family land, saying that the land will soon be part of his inheritance. Samsonov secretly thinks of Dmitri as a "beggar," and plays a trick on him. He tells Dmitri that a merchant in the countryside named **Lyagavy** might be interested in making a deal.

Dmitri immediately rushes off to find Lyagavy. Strapped for cash, he sells his pocket watch to pay for a carriage to take him out to the countryside. When he finds Lyagavy, the man is obviously drunk and cannot do business. Dmitri notices that a peasant calls the merchant by the name **Gorskin** instead of Lyagavy. The peasant tells Dmitri that the merchant never does business with anyone who calls him Lyagavy. Dmitri waits in the countryside overnight for Lyagavy to come to his senses. The next day, Lyagavy/Gorskin is still drunk, and Dmitri leaves frustrated.

Back in town, Dmitri seeks out Grushenka. She lies and says she cannot see him, telling him she is awaiting the letter from her former lover. Dmitri leaves annoyed, but happy that she is not with Fyodor. Dmitri then realizes he needs more pocket money since he used all the proceeds from the sale of his watch to meet Lyagavy. He decides to pawn his prized possessions, a pair of dueling pistols, to a local official named **Peter Perhotin**.

Next, Dmitri seeks out Madame Hohlakov, from whom he hopes to borrow the 3,000 rubles. Madame Hohlakov will have nothing to do with him. She has no love for Dmitri since she sympathizes with Katerina, her boarder. She mockingly tells Dmitri that he should go off to the gold mines and seek a fortune there. Once again, Dmitri tries to find Grushenka, but she has left for Mokroe. Her servant, **Fenya**, pleads ignorance of Grushenka's whereabouts. Dmitri becomes enraged and suspicious that Grushenka has gone to see Fyodor after all. He grabs a brass pestle from a table and runs to his father's house.

At Fyodor's, he sneaks over a wall to the garden window, where Grushenka had been told to tap the secret signals. He peers in the window and sees only Fyodor pacing back and forth. Dmitri taps the signal on the window, and Fyodor rushes over to see if Grushenka has come. When Dmitri sees that Fyodor is still waiting for Grushenka, he is relieved.

Dmitri thinks of the great loathing he has for his father, and he pulls the brass pestle from his pocket. The narrator says that later Dmitri would think about this moment, "God was watching over me then." As Dmitri scales the wall, the servant Gregory, who has come outside for some air, notices him and cries out, "Parricide!" Dmitri jumps down from the wall in a panic and hits Gregory with the brass pestle. Gregory falls down unconscious, and his head bleeds all over the ground. Dmitri heads back up the wall but then he returns to Gregory's body to see if he is dead. He says to Gregory, "You've come to grief, old man."

Unsure if Gregory is dead, Dmitri leaves in panic and returns to Grushenka's. There the servant Fenya finally confesses that Grushenka has left for Mokroe to be with her lover, a Polish military officer. Fenya notices the blood on Dmitri's hands and is frightened. Dmitri realizes he forgot all about Grushenka's past lover. He decides he must step aside and let Grushenka marry her long-lost love. He resolves to see her one last time and then shoot himself at dawn. Dmitri retrieves the pistols from Perhotin, who notices the blood on him and also sees that Dmitri is now carrying a new wad of cash.

With Perhotin in tow, Dmitri goes to a store in town and uses his cash to buy a carriage filled with food and wine. Ignoring Perhotin's protests that he is wasting all his money, Dmitri only says, "My whole life has been disorder, and one must set it in order." Dmitri makes arrangements to have everything sent to Mokroe. After Dmitri leaves in another carriage, Perhotin launches into an investigation of the clues he had seen. Dmitri is at his wit's end during the ride to Mokroe, facing the prospect of his own death and asking his carriage driver to absolve him of his sins. He ruminates over his suicide plans and deliriously calls out to God for forgiveness.

In Mokroe, Dmitri finds Grushenka in a tavern with a group of people, including her lover, **Mussyalovitch**, and another Pole, **Vrublevsky**. Grushenka is shocked to see Dmitri, but soon the group begins to enjoy the food and wine he has had delivered. As the group plays cards, the two Poles are caught cheating and insult the rest of the group. The party falls into disarray. Dmitri finds the two Poles and pulls out his wad of cash. He offers them 3,000 rubles if they will go away and leave Grushenka alone.

Later that night, Dmitri finds Grushenka hiding behind a curtain, distressed. She admits that she cannot marry her Polish lover after all. Grushenka decides she loves Dmitri. She begs his forgiveness and says she will be devoted only to him: "I'll be your slave now, your slave for the rest of your life." She says it was spite that made her torment him. As Dmitri and Grushenka embrace, the police arrive. The police captain, **Michael Makarov**, arrests Dmitri. Dmitri thinks they have arrested him for murdering Gregory, but they tell him he is being charged with the murder of Fyodor Karamazov.

UNDERSTANDING AND INTERPRETING
Part Three, Book VIII

Two Mysteries and a Frenzied Pace: In Book VIII, the novel's pace picks up, and the primary story line moves toward its climax—the murder of Fyodor. The murder itself is not described here, and confusion surrounds the identity of the murderer. Although Dmitri's earlier comment that God was watching over him makes it sound as though he did not kill Fyodor, his emotional frenzy makes him suspect. His ravings around town increase people's suspicions. Dostoevsky emphasizes Dmitri's hysterical state of mind by structuring this book to parallel his frenzy. The action quickly moves from scene to scene, leading to the arrest at the end of the book, an arrest that feels inevitable. In addition to the mystery of who murdered Fyodor, there is the mystery of how Dmitri got the large wad of cash he uses to buy guns and food and drink for the party. The source of this money will later be of crucial importance.

Craving Order: Dmitri acts frantically and illogically. He rushes from one conversation to another, always demonstrating a lack of common sense and intuition. He misjudges Samsonov, a friend of Grushenka who would naturally try to do whatever is in Grushenka's best interest, and lets himself be sent on a wild goose chase. He approaches the business transaction with Lyagavy/Gorstkin without any forethought, and as a result the merchant mocks and ignores him. Dmitri also misjudges Madame Hohlakov, an ally of Katerina, and she sends him away in disgust. When all else fails, Dmitri rushes to his father's house and assaults Gregory for no good reason. He then rushes back into town covered with blood, so frenzied that he does not consider what others will think of him. His common sense fails him even in the matter of Grushenka, the woman who obsesses him. Her defection takes him by surprise, because he has completely forgotten about the possibility of Grushenka's past lover returning for her. Finally, Dmitri resolves to commit suicide, the ultimate irrational act. Disorder defines Dmitri, but what he craves is order, whether he finds order by running off with Grushenka or by putting an end to his disordered misery.

A Shot at Salvation: Despite Dmitri's resolve to kill himself, a mortal sin in the eyes of the Church, it seems that redemption is not impossible for him. He begs forgiveness from God and reveals the suffering of his soul. On the carriage ride to Mokroe, Dmitri faces the prospect of his own death with a hymn-like intonation: "Lord, receive me, with all my lawlessness. . . . Do not condemn me, for I love Thee O Lord." Dmitri is sinful and debauched, but he clings to his love for an all-powerful God. Father Zossima envisioned this kind of love as the salvation of humanity. When Dmitri asks his carriage driver to absolve him of his sins, as if the peasant could do a priest's work, he acts in accordance with Zossima's belief that all humans are responsible for one another under God's love. Dmitri leans on the carriage driver as if the carriage driver were as responsible as a priest for hearing his sins.

A Wicked Beast Who Wants to Pray: Like Dmitri, Grushenka feels the need to suffer for her own redemption. Just as Dmitri asks the carriage driver to forgive him, Grushenka looks to Dmitri to redeem her. When she renounces her Polish lover, she comes to grips with the suffering she has inflicted on Dmitri. She asks him, "You will forgive me for having tormented you? It was through spite that I torment you all. . . . Beat me, ill-treat me, do what you will with me. . . . I deserve to suffer." She even jokes that she will enter a nunnery, and begs God to forgive her, calling herself a wicked beast and saying she wants to pray.

Fyodor Dostoevsky

PART THREE, BOOK IX
The Preliminary Investigation

The narrator explains the events leading up to Dmitri's arrest, which took place while the narrative followed Dmitri into the countryside. While Dmitri is in Mokroe, Peter Perhotin decides to do some investigating. He is curious about Dmitri's frantic behavior, mysterious wad of cash, and bloodied hands. Perhotin visits Fenya, who tells him how Dmitri grabbed the brass pestle from Grushenka's house and returned later with blood on his hands. Perhotin next visits Madame Hohlakov, who says she did not give Dmitri the cash and speculates that Dmitri must have killed Fyodor and stolen the money. She writes a note for Perhotin attesting that she did not give Dmitri any money.

Perhotin decides he must go to the police with the information. When he arrives at the police station, he finds that the murder has already been reported by Marfa, Gregory's wife. She woke and found Gregory outside moaning in pain. She also found Fyodor Karamazov in his bedroom with his head bashed in, probably by the same brass pestle with which Gregory was assaulted. An envelope printed with the words "For my little chicken" is found in Fyodor's room, empty.

Dmitri said he would shoot himself before dawn. Perhotin informs the police of Dmitri's intentions, and they rush to Mokroe to stop him. They find him alive at the inn with Grushenka and arrest him for the murder of his father. This brings us back to the end of Part VIII.

Dmitri admits that he assaulted Gregory. Eventually they tell Dmitri that Gregory survived, which is a relief to Dmitri. He vehemently asserts his innocence, but no one believes he could have assaulted Gregory yet not murdered Fyodor. Even Grushenka believes Dmitri is guilty. She takes responsibility and cries out that she drove Dmitri to murder. She says that despite the murder, she will love Dmitri forever.

Under cross-examination, Dmitri speaks truthfully. He reveals information that might implicate him in the murder and leaves out facts that might exonerate him. He admits to hitting Gregory but does not mention that he went back and checked on the old man. He admits that he hated Fyodor, attacked him, and threatened to kill him. He mentions that he knew about the 3,000 rubles in the envelope that was found empty. He reveals that he was at the house that night, in the garden, with the brass pestle. Most damningly, Dmitri says he believes the money is his rightful inheritance and admits that he was desperate for that exact amount of cash to pay back his debt to Katerina.

The only information Dmitri will not reveal is the source of the large wad of cash he had in his possession on the night of the murder. The police assume it is the stolen 3,000 rubles. Another important piece of evidence is lodged against him. Dmitri testifies that when he left his father's house, the door from Fyodor's room to the garden was closed. But Gregory has already testified that the door was open, implying that Dmitri had access to the house and could have murdered Fyodor. Dmitri protests and insists that Smerdyakov must be the murderer. He says Smerdyakov was the only other person who knew the secret tapping signals that would rouse Fyodor.

After the police press Dmitri further and strip-search him, Dmitri realizes that he is their prime suspect. He tells the police about his vile behavior in the past—his debauchery, his treatment of Katerina, his general baseness. He feels shame for his past sins, for his hatred of Fyodor, and for his mistreatment of Katerina. He finally tells the police where the money came from. The wad of cash was 1,500 rubles, not 3,000. It was part of the original 3,000 that he had obtained from Katerina. He says he had not spent the whole 3,000 on his first party in Mokroe. Instead, he kept the leftover 1,500 in a cloth pouch hung around his neck. He says he was unable to spend it because he felt so guilty for having spent the first half.

When Dmitri found out that Grushenka was leaving him for good, he decided that he would kill himself. He saw no reason not to spend the money, as he would be unable to use it himself, so he spent most of the remaining 1,500 on the party in Mokroe on the night of the murder. However, many others testify that Dmitri claimed to have spent 3,000 on the first party and said he needed the full 3,000 to pay back Katerina. The innkeeper in Mokroe, **Plastunov**, claims that Dmitri spent at least 3,000 at the first party in Mokroe and another 3,000 on the night of the murder. The two Poles testify that Dmitri tried to buy them off with 3,000 rubles. Even Grushenka testifies that Dmitri claimed he spent 3,000 on the first party.

Dmitri pleads his innocence to Grushenka. She crosses herself and says she believes him. After the police interviews, Dmitri falls into a deep sleep and

> "It can scarcely be owing to chance that three of the masterpieces of the literature of all time—the *Oedipus Rex* of Sophocles, Shakespeare's *Hamlet* and Dostoevsky's *The Brothers Karamazov*—should all deal with the same subject: parricide."
>
> **SIGMUND FREUD**

OEDIPUS

Sigmund Freud includes *The Brothers Karamazov* in his list of the three great masterpieces of literature, with Shakespeare's *Hamlet* and the Greek tragedy *Oedipus Rex* by Sophocles—all three of which share the theme of parricide. In Greek mythology, Oedipus was the son of King Laius and Queen Jocasta of Thebes. His parents were warned by an oracle that Oedipus would rise up to kill his father and marry his mother, so they abandoned the infant boy on a mountainside. He was adopted and later heard about the prophecy, so he fled his adoptive parents and went to Thebes. Along the way, he came upon Laius and killed him, then arrived in Thebes where he married Jocasta. When they learned the truth, he blinded himself, and Jocasta committed suicide.

dreams he is a soldier again, years ago, in the barren steppes of the Caucasus Mountains. A peasant drives him in a carriage through a burned-out village. Rows of peasant women line the road. One woman holds a crying infant. Dmitri asks his driver why these people suffer so much. He feels pity for them and wishes that their suffering could be alleviated. He wakes feeling contrite, with tears in his eyes.

The police decide to pursue the case against Dmitri. He signs a written record of his own testimony and delivers a final speech to the police, proclaiming his innocence but accepting his imminent punishment and suffering, saying it will purify him. Dmitri and Grushenka ask forgiveness of each other and part tearfully. Then Dmitri is hauled off to prison to await trial.

UNDERSTANDING AND INTERPRETING
Part Three, Book IX

Grushenka Brings Suffering upon Herself: Grushenka feels guilty and wants to suffer. Before, she asked Dmitri to make her suffer. Now, she tries to bring suffering on herself by telling the police that her corrupt nature makes her equally guilty of the murder. Grushenka's self-accusations are a sign that she wants to continue down the road to her own redemption.

Dmitri Brings Suffering Upon Himself: When first interviewed by the police, Dmitri shows his usual lack of common sense. He does not defend himself and does everything he can to cast suspicion on his actions. He shows the police his brazen manner, his irresponsibility with money, and his desperate emotional condition. Most damaging to himself, he confirms his motive for killing Fyodor. Dmitri also downplays his own compassion, withholding the reason he went back to check on Gregory after striking him with the pestle. When asked why he returned to Gregory, he says, "I don't know why," instead of telling the police truthfully that he returned because he felt remorseful and worried. Dmitri refuses to grasp the gravity of his arrest. Since he knows he is innocent, he thinks he is safe.

Honor Breeds Trouble: Dmitri's deep-seated honor delays him in telling the police about the source of the money until it is almost too late. The tardy admission makes Dmitri sounds like a liar. Understandably, Dmitri puts off telling the police about his misuse of Katerina's money and confesses only when he feels he must. The fact that he withheld the information for so long renders his story, when he finally tells it, unconvincing.

A Spiritual Stripping: After declaring his innocence time and again, and while the evidence mounts against him, Dmitri finally realizes the seriousness of his plight. He will not plead guilty to a murder he did not commit, but he begins to examine himself and feel guilty about his sins. The police physically strip him, removing his clothing, and Dmitri spiritually strips himself, peering into his soul and making a "full confession." He admits the sordid truth about misusing Katerina's 3,000 rubles, saying, "I'm a beast, and an untrustworthy scoundrel." He admits to all his other faults too: his debauchery, his carelessness with money, and his lies. He confesses that he has a savage pride and a brazen personality. Too proud to let others judge him, Dmitri judges himself guilty of possessing a vile Karamazov nature.

A Dream and a Step toward Redemption: In Book VII, Alyosha's dream of the wedding in Cana of Galilee solidified his faith. Now, Dmitri's dream confirms his own transformation and redemption. In his dream, Dmitri identifies with the poor sufferers, especially the infant. His compassion is overwhelming. When he wakes with tears in his eyes, he feels an exalted love for his fellow humans. In his words to the police, Dmitri declares, "By suffering I shall by purified." Dmitri takes the final steps toward redemption, looking ahead with calm to his trial and trusting that from the ordeal he will emerge a more humble man.

PART FOUR, BOOK X
The Boys

It is now November, three months after the crime and a day before the trial. The action shifts to Alyosha's interactions with the children of the town, particularly **Kolya Krassotkin**, the intelligent thirteen-year-old boy whom Ilusha stabbed with the penknife. Ilusha and Kolya are still friends. Ilusha is now ill and bedridden, and Alyosha has been arranging for all the schoolboys to visit him. Kolya meets up with another friend, **Smurov**, to visit Ilusha. On the way there, Smurov mourns the loss of Ilusha's dog, Zhutchka. He thinks the return of Zhutchka would bolster Ilusha's spirits. Kolya brings along another dog, Perezvon, hoping the new dog might cheer Ilusha up.

Kolya stays outside Ilusha's and asks Smurov to fetch Alyosha from inside. He wants his entrance with Perezvon to be a surprise. Kolya has heard about Alyosha's respect for youth and wants to talk with Alyosha so he can show him that they are equals. When Alyosha comes outside to meet Kolya, Kolya tells him that Ilusha drove away the dog Zhutchka by feeding him a hunk of bread with a sharp pin lodged inside it (the joke was Smerdyakov's idea). Kolya was angry with Ilusha for doing this to the poor animal, and Ilusha stabbed him with the penknife.

Alyosha brings Kolya inside. Ilusha is happy to see his friend for the first time in weeks. Kolya starts teasing Ilusha about feeding Zhutchka the pin, and the others wonder why Kolya would want to upset Ilusha. Kolya calls for Perezvon, and Ilusha rejoices and pronounces that the dog is indeed Zhutchka. Kolya's surprise has been a success.

Everyone leaves the room when a doctor arrives to examine Ilusha. As they wait outside, Kolya regales Alyosha with his knowledge of literature and philosophical ideas. Alyosha realizes the boy is trying hard to earn his respect, and he carefully analyzes and corrects Kolya's arguments. He tells Kolya that he likes him because he has the rare quality of admitting to his own faults. The doctor leaves, and everyone is sad to hear that Ilusha will probably not live much longer. Ilusha knows he is dying and tries to comfort his father, Captain Snegiryov, as the rest of the family weeps. Kolya says goodbye to Ilusha and then bursts into tears outside. He vows to visit Ilusha often, and Alyosha does too.

UNDERSTANDING AND INTERPRETING
Part Four, Book X

A Break in the Action: Book X takes an abrupt detour from the main action, veering away from the murder investigation and the start of Dmitri's trial. The sentimental stories of Kolya and Ilusha do not directly affect Dmitri's trial. Instead, they bring focus to one of the novel's peripheral themes: the role of children in society. Alyosha is pivotal in this section since his ministry serves children. He practices Father Zossima's philosophy of love and responsibility, passing the monk's message on to a new generation.

Rare Familial Happiness: The intimate, affectionate relationship of Captain Snegiryov and Ilusha contrasts sharply with the relationship between Fyodor Karamazov and his sons. The Karamazov family suffers from rivalry, bitterness, and excess, and the Snegiryovs live a life of dignity, deprivation, and love. Their great love for each other heightens the pain caused them by Ilusha's illness. The final embrace among Ilusha, Snegiryov, and Kolya exemplifies the unity and harmony of the love Zossima preached. At the end of Book X, Ilusha weeps with his father and mother, a gesture demonstrating that even in the midst of grief, families can be harmonious. This is the first instance of family harmony in the novel.

A Loving Teacher: The intellectual discussions between Kolya and Alyosha show how Alyosha imparts his knowledge and wisdom to a new generation. In an echo of Zossima's method of teaching, Alyosha quietly and carefully corrects the faults in Kolya's logic and literary analysis while conveying a sense of equality and respect between them. In this way, Kolya learns to respect, listen to, and love Alyosha. At the end of their conversation, Kolya remarks, "Do you know, Karamazov, our talk has been like a declaration of love." The love between them would make Zossima proud.

PART FOUR, BOOK XI
Ivan

Ivan visits Smerdyakov in the hospital for the first time. Smerdyakov is recovering from his epileptic seizure. He swears to Ivan that his seizure on the night of the murder was real. Smerdyakov says he suspected Ivan knew the murder was going to take place. He thought Ivan went to Moscow to get as far from the murder scene as possible. Ivan counters that he is sure Smerdyakov faked the seizure. Ivan promises not to tell anyone about the fakery, and Smerdyakov promises not to tell anyone about their conversation immediately before Ivan left for Moscow. Ivan leaves believing that Dmitri was guilty of the murder.

On their second meeting, Ivan demands to know what Smerdyakov meant when he said, "It's always worth while . . ." Smerdyakov says he thought Ivan would leave town, tacitly allowing Dmitri to commit the murder. He assumes Ivan wanted the murder to happen so Dmitri would be locked up, leaving a larger inheritance for Ivan. Ivan angrily says he will turn Smerdyakov in, but Smerdyakov says he will implicate Ivan as an equal partner in the conspiracy to kill Fyodor. As Ivan leaves, he begins to feel guilty about the murder. He goes to Katerina for comfort, and she soothes him by showing him a letter Dmitri wrote, saying that he would kill Fyodor to repay Katerina's money. The letter temporarily convinces Ivan that Dmitri is guilty.

On the third visit, the night before the trial begins, Smerdyakov finally admits that he killed Fyodor. He says that he committed the crime only as an "instrument" of Ivan's desires. Smerdyakov cries, "*You* murdered him! You are the murderer! I was only your instrument, your faithful servant." He shows Ivan the missing 3,000 rubles stolen from Fyodor's room. Smerdyakov concludes that Ivan gave him the moral justification for the murder and then left town to let the actual crime play out.

Ivan returns to his apartment in disbelief, feeling terribly guilty. A haggard, shabby apparition appears across the room. It is the Devil, the monster Ivan mentioned to Alyosha. The Devil debates with Ivan about the nature of God, death, and the afterlife. Ivan says, "You are an incarnation of myself, but only of one side of me . . . of my thoughts and feelings, but only the worst and most stupid of them." The Devil says that "[h]esitation, suspense, conflict between belief and disbelief" are such torture to a man like Ivan that he should kill himself. He says, surprisingly, that his goal is Ivan's salvation. If Ivan refuses to believe in the Devil's existence, then the Devil's goal will be met. He will have planted in Ivan a speck of faith that will grow into a profound faith. Ivan finally throws a glass at the Devil, and the apparition disappears. At the same moment, Alyosha shows up at the door.

As Alyosha knocks, the Devil returns and mocks Ivan's Grand Inquisitor story. He laughs at the grand vision of the Devil Ivan created in the story and says that Ivan is angry because the Devil is showing himself not dramatically, but in a humble shape. The Devil speaks ironically to Ivan, mocking his theory that "all things are lawful." Ivan grows increasingly frustrated and angry.

At last Ivan feels himself released and moves to the door. Alyosha brings news that Smerdyakov has hanged himself. Ivan tells Alyosha that he already knows and confesses that he, too, is guilty of the murder because he provoked Smerdyakov. Ivan seems tormented and anxious, as if on the verge of madness. Alyosha tries to comfort Ivan, but he worries that Ivan has lost his mind. He tries to persuade Ivan that he is not to blame for the murder. Ivan eventually falls unconscious, mumbling incoherently in his sleep. Alyosha spends the night at Ivan's house, praying for him and thinking to himself, "Ivan will either rise up in the light of truth, or . . . he'll perish in hate."

UNDERSTANDING AND INTERPRETING
Part Four, Book XI

Smerdyakov the Murderer: Smerdyakov's confession to Ivan is genuine. He murdered Fyodor Karamazov and successfully shifted suspicion to Dmitri. The police have been almost convinced of Dmitri's guilt, which shows that Smerdyakov's devious scheme to frame Dmitri has worked perfectly. Even when he confesses to the murder, Smerdyakov is unwilling to shoulder responsibility for what he did. He spreads the blame around, laying it mostly on Ivan.

DOSTOEVSKY'S EPILEPSY

Dostoevsky was an epileptic and suffered severe attacks while imprisoned in Siberia. Epilepsy, once known as "falling sickness," is a disorder that involves rapid, unregulated brain activity, sometimes causing violent seizures. Brought on by haphazard electrical impulses in different parts of the brain, the seizures can incapacitate the sufferer to varying degrees, from simple loss of perception (such as a kind of daydreaming state known as "petit mal" seizures), to more dangerous convulsions that lead to unconsciousness ("grand-mal" seizures). No single factor has been isolated to explain why people suffer from epilepsy, but fever, alcohol withdrawal, head injuries, and prenatal injuries are thought to account for many chronic cases. Dostoevsky's fictional creation Smerdyakov occasionally suffers, as his creator did, from grand-mal seizures.

Shared Responsibility for the Murder: Ivan has already realized that he shares blame for the murder. On some level, he knew when he left for Moscow that Fyodor would be killed. He assumed that Dmitri would be the murderer, not Smerdyakov. Ivan breaks down upon learning that Smerdyakov is the killer, because it means he must shoulder a large part of the responsibility. Dmitri is an intelligent man who can make decisions for himself, but Smerdyakov is not. Ivan gave Smerdyakov a sound ideological basis to justify the murder, and then he left town. Smerdyakov, in every way the shadow of his brothers, has now acted on Ivan's and Dmitri's dark desires to see their father dead. Ivan already felt guilty because he wanted to see Fyodor dead, but after his last meeting with Smerdyakov, he feels responsible for the murder. His guilt confirmed, he falls into a deep illness that first manifests itself in his delusional nightmare of the Devil.

Ivan's Devilish Conscience: Ivan is the last of the Karamazov brothers to have a significant dream. Like Alyosha's and Dmitri's dreams, Ivan's dream forces Ivan to confront his deepest self-doubts. The Devil who visits Ivan is a manifestation of his own conscience. As Ivan says, the Devil is perhaps the evil, terrifying part of Ivan's being. The Devil torments Ivan with questions and confronts Ivan with his own intellectual arguments. The Devil lays bare the poverty of Ivan's logical reasoning, showing how logic withers in comparison to the strength of Ivan's overwhelming guilt about the murder.

The Devil as Foil to the Grand Inquisitor: The apparition that appears to Ivan is a shabby creature, which could implicate Ivan, the atheist intellectual, as a paltry beast himself. Dostoevsky might also mean that the devil does his evil not by being grand, but by being inconsequential. The Devil, as he appears to Ivan, wears a dirty jacket and has bad manners. Ivan tells him he is a "paltry, trivial devil." In the Grand Inquisitor tale, Ivan created an unseen Devil full of grandeur and terror, from whom the Inquisitor accepts the temptation of world authority. The Devil of Ivan's dream resembles a "lackey," which is what Ivan called Smerdyakov. Perhaps, Dostoevsky suggests, great evil comes not from great, intelligent, dangerous people, but from stupid, cowering, easily influenced people. The Devil cannot bring justice to the world, as Ivan hoped, because he is no more than a measly, impotent slug. He asks Ivan not to expect much of him, proof that he is not capable of the power Ivan imputed to him in his intellectual arguments. Like Smerdyakov, the Devil is a product of Ivan's intellectual powers. In the final paragraphs of Book XI, the narrator says, "God, in whom Ivan disbelieved, and His truth were gaining mastery over his heart, which still refused to submit." Ivan's redemption will occur only if he can trade his intellectual faith for faith in God.

Fyodor Dostoevsky

PART FOUR, BOOK XII
A Judicial Error

Dmitri's trial begins in front of a packed courtroom. The case has aroused interest all over Russia because of the nature of the crime and because of the fame of Dmitri's lawyer, **Fetyukovitch**. The jury consists mostly of peasants. The courtroom crowd believes that the case against Dmitri is strong. When the judge reads the indictment, Dmitri pleads not guilty but says, "I plead guilty to drunkenness and dissipation, to idleness and debauchery . . . but I am not guilty of the death of that old man, my enemy and my father."

A series of witnesses—Gregory, Rakitin, Captain Snegiryov, Plastunov, and various guests at Dmitri's last party—testify against him. Fetyukovitch manages to discredit each of them in turn. Medical experts are called, but their contradictory testimonies cancel each other out. The doctor of the village makes an impact with his testimony. He talks about Dmitri's sad and fragmented childhood and arouses sympathy for Dmitri. Alyosha testifies and speaks of talking to Dmitri one night. Dmitri kept striking himself on the upper chest and talking about the cause of his dishonor. Alyosha assumes Dmitri was indicating the pouch with the 1,500 rubles. Katerina recounts Dmitri's generosity to her father long ago. Fetyukovitch uses Katerina's story to argue that Dmitri's past generosity is incompatible with an impulse to kill and steal.

Ivan's illness makes his testimony barely coherent. He asks to leave, but as he does, he pulls out the 3,000 rubles that Smerdyakov gave him and shows the wad of cash to the courtroom. He testifies that Smerdyakov is the murderer and that he is also to blame for letting Smerdyakov commit the crime. He cries out that the Devil visits him at night and can corroborate what he is saying. Still raving, Ivan is dragged from the courtroom and his testimony is dismissed as the gibberish of a madman. Before the hubbub settles, Katerina offers to testify again. This time, she produces the letter that Dmitri wrote to her stating that he would kill his father if he could not get his inheritance money. She testifies that he needed the money to repay her and to finance his new life with Grushenka. She says that Dmitri murdered and robbed his father and then ran off to Mokroe to spend the money on Grushenka.

Dmitri protests loudly, saying that he wrote the letter when he was drunk, but Katerina stands by her new testimony. Suddenly, Grushenka rushes to the front of the room and tells Dmitri, "Your serpent has destroyed you!" She is subdued by court officials and removed from the room, but the courtroom is now in a frenzy. When order is restored, Fetyukovitch and the prosecutor, **Ippolit Kirillovitch**, give their closing arguments.

Kirillovitch sums up the evidence against Dmitri, emphasizing his debts and violent temper. He argues that Smerdyakov could not have been be the killer because he was motiveless and incapacitated by epilepsy on the night of the murder. Dmitri's motive is the only one that explains the crime. Kirillovitch points to Dmitri's letter to Katerina as proof. He ends with a stirring appeal to the jury's moral and nationalist sensibilities, calling parricide the worst of all crimes because it is a crime against enlightened Russian civilization.

Fetyukovitch begins his closing argument by saying that all the evidence against Dmitri is circumstantial. There is no positive proof that Dmitri committed the murder or robbery. He argues that a robbery may not have even occurred. Fyodor's envelope with the 3,000 rubles was just a rumor, and Dmitri's explanation of his money's origin is logical. In his most significant argument, Fetyukovitch maintains that Fyodor's murder was not, in fact, a parricide. Fyodor was never really a father to Dmitri, he says, because Fyodor did nothing to raise Dmitri. Fetyukovitch says that Dmitri was about to embark on a new, decent life with Grushenka and should be set free and redeemed. The purpose of justice, he says, is not punishment, but salvation. By freeing Dmitri, the jury will give him the chance to redeem himself and start his life anew. The courtroom audience applauds and cheers, now fully sympathetic to Dmitri.

Yet, when the jury returns an hour later, it finds Dmitri guilty on all counts. Dmitri delivers a final speech declaring his innocence, forgiving Katerina for her damning testimony, and asking pity for Grushenka. As Dmitri breaks into sobs, Grushenka shrieks, and he is taken into custody again. The courtroom audience ponders Dmitri's sentence and concludes that he will get at least twenty years in Siberia.

UNDERSTANDING AND INTERPRETING
Part Four, Book XII

The Danger of Parricide: The prosecutor, a representative of state and moral authority, appeals to the moral and patriotic sentiments of the jury and the courtroom audience. He raises the idea, shared by Dostoevsky, that parricide destroys the harmonious moral order of the universe. Parricide is a disaster whether it is committed against an individual's father, against the tsar (the national father), or against God (the spiritual father). The prosecutor makes the connections among these three clear by referring to the recent spate of revolutions in Western Europe, arguing, "We have already heard voices of alarm from Europe; they already begin to sound. Do not tempt them! Do not heap up their growing hatred by a sentence justifying the murder of a father by his son!" These words are cautionary. They sum up one of the main ideas of the novel, the notion that when moral authority disappears, disorder takes over and the family dissolves. Dostoevsky's novel refers not just to the fate of one man, but to the fate of nations and religions. When the moral authority of Russia or of God is called into question or destroyed, moral chaos is the result, and the social fabric of a nation or the family of man dissolves.

The Slippery Definition of Parricide: Fetyukovitch presents a convincing argument that the murder of Fyodor cannot be considered a parricide. Because Fyodor abandoned his children, he destroyed the moral order of the family and abdicated his position as father. Fyodor's irresponsibility creates the original disorder that leads to his murder. We hear a second position on parricide, equally important as the first, the claim that when the father (literal, national, or religious) abdicates responsibility, the children will rise up against him and cannot be blamed for doing so. Wrong as most parricides may be, when the father refuses responsibility, parricide is the natural result. The solution is for the father to create a peaceful and harmonious family that does not have cause to question his authority.

Dmitri is Guilty: Dmitri is wrongly convicted of murder, but he does share some responsibility for the death of Fyodor, as do all the brothers. He fostered an atmosphere of violence in the house, attacking and threatening to kill Fyodor. Dmitri's wild actions affected the impressionable Smerdyakov and encouraged him to commit murder.

Ivan is Guilty: Dostoevsky suggests that the blame for some murders must be shared by many people, not just by the official murderer. Although Ivan was far from the crime scene, his logic that "everything is lawful" was the primary rationalization for the murder. He left town after ignoring a number of hints that the murder was about to take place, he did not act on his suspicions about Smerdyakov's enigmatic comments, and he treated Smerdyakov like an impotent, stupid audience, filling his head with dangerous ideas. As a result, Ivan feels responsible for the death of Fyodor even though he had nothing to do with actually committing the murder.

Alyosha is Guilty: Aside from his temporary failure of faith, Alyosha neglected to stay away from the monastery to take care of the crisis of his family, as Zossima suggested. Alyosha was away when Fyodor was murdered, and therefore Alyosha shares a small portion of the collective responsibility for Fyodor's death. This shared blame confirms Zossima's contention that every person is responsible for every other person, even saintly men like Alyosha.

Fyodor is Guilty: In one sense, Fyodor is responsible for his own murder. He fuels the disintegration of values that causes his "gloomy death." He neglects and abandons his children, holds orgies in front of them, mocks them, abuses them, and never considers their welfare. The tragedy is not simply the matter of Fyodor's death, but the general moral collapse that renders the murder inevitable. The tragedy is that all of the Karamazov brothers are forced to feel some responsibility for the crime. The brothers make up a fragmented whole. Dmitri represents the physical, Ivan the intellectual, Alyosha the spiritual, and Smerdyakov the corrupted shadow of the three. Together, the four brothers share in the complete tragedy.

EPILOGUE

After the trial, Alyosha visits Katerina, who is now tending to the ill Ivan. She tells Alyosha that she regrets testifying against Dmitri. Ivan told her that a plan for Dmitri's escape from prison is already in the works. Before his illness, Ivan had begun bribing the appropriate government officials. The plan is to free Dmitri while he is in transit to Siberia and smuggle him to America. Katerina asks Alyosha to finish the job now that Ivan is sick. Alyosha agrees to do it, but asks that Katerina visit Dmitri soon before he leaves for Siberia. She says she will visit him later that day.

Alyosha then visits Dmitri, who has also fallen ill and is in a guarded wing of the town hospital. Dmitri faults himself for the crime. He hopes to find redemption through his own suffering but worries he will not be able to do it without Grushenka by his side. He prays that the prison officials will allow Grushenka to accompany him to Siberia. Alyosha then tells Dmitri about the escape plan, and Dmitri agrees to it. Dmitri feels pangs of remorse, though, and says he cannot leave Russia forever. He vows to return and live in disguise.

Katerina arrives. She and Dmitri join hands and forgive each other. Katerina says that their love is over, but their pain still exists because their past love was great. She admits that she never believed he was the murderer. Grushenka arrives unexpectedly, and Katerina shrieks. She asks for Grushenka's forgiveness, but Grushenka is too embittered to forgive her. Katerina leaves, accepting that Grushenka will never forgive her.

In the final chapter, Alyosha attends the funeral of young Ilusha. Afterward, Alyosha gathers Ilusha's friends and tells them to remember Ilusha fondly for the rest of their lives. He asks them to recognize the value of the love and friendship they felt from coming together in Ilusha's final days. The boys are touched by his words and cheer, "Hurrah for Karamazov!"

Fyodor Dostoevsky

Epilogue

In the End, Unity and Hope: The Epilogue wraps up many of the unresolved relationships in the novel. Katerina and Ivan are together, and she seems hopeful as she nurtures him back to health. Dmitri and Grushenka are prepared to leave Russia temporarily and start a new life in the newest place of all, America. They will suffer in exile from their homeland, but they welcome suffering, for they believe it will help them find redemption. Although young Ilusha dies, his death allows Alyosha to encourage the child's friends and urge them to remember Ilusha. The final chapters of the novel radiate hope and optimism.

> "In the end, the novel remains the remarkable culmination of Dostoevsky's dialectical and dialogical creativity, which moves without effort from one end of the human spectrum to the other, from the wonder of the spirit to the comedy of the body, and back again."
>
> **JOHN BAYLEY**

Love of Russia: Dmitri's plan to return to Russia reveals his deep love of his homeland, the kind of love that Dostoevsky felt for Russia. The desire to be unified with one's homeland is portrayed as the cause of fidelity to moral, religious, familial, and national authority. The idealization of fidelity to Russia, in particular, reflects Dostoevsky's Slavophile belief that Russian society, with its benevolent monarchy, was in many ways superior to Western European and American models of government and culture.

"Hurrah for Karamazov!": The triumphant final chapter of the epilogue is completely different from the novel's gloomy and ominous beginning. Alyosha is cheered by the children. He is successfully working to transmit Father Zossima's ethos of love to the next generation. The novel's final words, "Hurray for Karamazov," are heartfelt. Such a cheer would have seemed impossible at one point in the novel, but now the moral disorder of the Karamazov family is in the past, and a new harmony begins with the ascendance of Alyosha as the moral leader of the family. Tragedy is replaced with cheers of joy, and the novel ends on a note of great hope for the future.

Conclusions

The Brothers Karamazov is a tale of disorder, and disintegration in a family and in the minds of the family's members. In its tragic depiction of parricide, the novel shows the consequences of neglecting responsibility.

The parricide of Fyodor Karamazov is not just the narrative of one man's death. It serves as a metaphor for the moral collapse of the Karamazov family, the turning of Russia on its Tsar, and the disrespect of humanity for God. Dostoevsky suggests that only when a father shows careful devotion to his children does he become blameless. If he does not show devotion, his children have a right to ask, "Father, why should I love you?"

Each of the brothers Karamazov share some of the responsibility for Fyodor's murder. Smerdyakov was the actual murderer, but he acted on the darker impulses of Dmitri, the intellectual ideas of Ivan, and the absence of Alyosha. The shared guilt of the brothers reflects Father Zossima's belief that all people are responsible for one another.

SUGGESTIONS FOR FURTHER READING

Amoia, Alba. *Feodor Dostoevsky*. New York: Continuum, 1993.

Bakhtin, Mikhail. *Problems of Dostoevsky's Poetics*. Ann Arbor, Michigan: Ardis, 1973.

Breger, Louis. *Dostoevsky: The Author as Psychoanalyst*. New York: NYU Press, 1989.

Conradi, Peter. *Fyodor Dostoevsky*. New York: St. Martin's, 1988.

Dostoevsky, Fyodor. *The Brothers Karamazov*. Norton Critical Edition. Edited by Ralph E. Matlaw. New York: W.W. Norton & Co., 1976.

———. *Crime and Punishment*. Norton Critical Edition, third edition. Edited by George Gibian. Translated by Jessie Coulson. New York: W. W. Norton & Co., 1989.

———. *The Notebooks for* The Brothers Karamazov. Edited and translated by Edward Wasiolek. Chicago: University of Chicago Press, 1971.

———. *Notes from Underground*. Norton Critical Edition, Second Edition. Translated and edited by Michael R. Katz. New York: W.W. Norton & Co., 2001.

Farger, Donald. *Dostoevsky and Romantic Realism: A Study of Dostoevsky in Relation to Balzac, Dickens and Gogol*. Cambridge: Harvard University Press, 1965.

Frank, Joseph. *Dostoevsky: The Stir of Liberation, 1860–1865* and *Dostoevsky: The Miraculous Years, 1865–1871* (Parts 3 and 4 of 5-volume biography). Princeton: Princeton University Press, 1986.

———. "Nihilism and *Notes from Underground* ." *Sewanee Review* 69, no. 1 (Jan-Mar 1961), University of the South. Reprinted in *Fyodor Dostoevsky: Modern Critical Views*, edited by Harold Bloom. New York: Chelsea House, 1998.

Freud, Sigmund. "Dostoevsky and Parricide" from *Standard Edition of the Collected Psychological Works*. Edited by James Strachey. Translated by D.F. Tait, revised by James Strachey. London: Hogarth, 1961.

Fyodor Dostoevsky

Gide, André. *Dostoevsky*. New York: New Directions, 1961.

Girard, René. *Resurrection from the Underground: Fyodor Dostoevsky*, reprinted edition. Edited and translated by James G. Williams. New York: Crossroads, 1997.

Hingley, Ronald. *Dostoevsky: His Life and Work*. New York: Scribner's, 1978.

Jones, John. *Dostoevsky*. New York: Oxford University Press, 1985.

Jones, Malcolm V. *Dostoevsky: The Novel of Discord.* London: Paul Elek, 1976.

Kaufmann, Walter. *Existentialism from Dostoevsky to Sartre*. New York: Meridian, 1956.

Lawrence, D.H. "Preface to 'The Grand Inquisitor'" from *Selected Literary Criticisms*. Edited by Anthony Beal. New York: Viking, 1961.

Leatherbarrow, W.J. *Fyodor Dostoevsky: The Brothers Karamazov*. Cambridge: University of Cambridge Press, 1992.

Shestov, Lev. *Dostoevsky, Tolstoy, and Nietzsche*. Translated by Bernard Martin and Spencer Roberts. Athens: Ohio University Press, 1969.

Yarmolinksy, Avrahm. *Dostoevsky: Works and Days*. New York: Funk & Wagnalls, 1971.

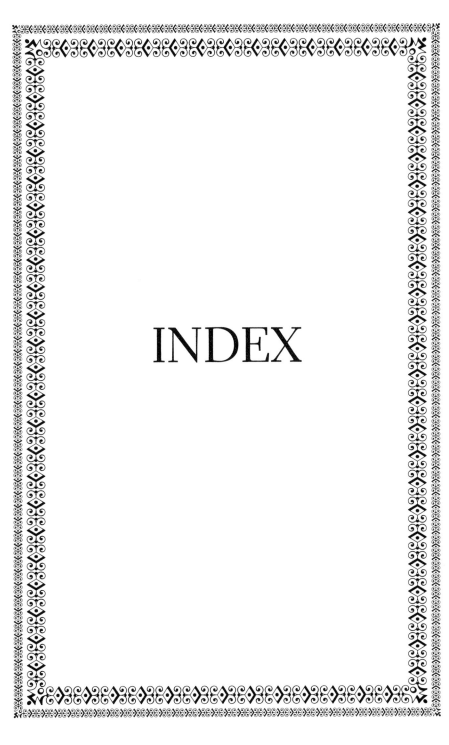

INDEX

Index